IBERIAN AND LATIN AMERICAN STUDIES

The Mexican Transition

IBERIAN AND LATIN AMERICAN STUDIES

The Mexican Transition

Politics, Culture, and Democracy in the Twenty-first Century

ROGER BARTRA

UNIVERSITY OF WALES PRESS
CARDIFF

© Roger Bartra, 2013

www.uwp.co.uk

British Library CIP
A catalogue record for this book is available from the British Library.

ISBN 978–0–7083–2553–7
e-ISBN 978–0–7083–2554–4

Translation by Gusti Gould

Typeset by Marie Doherty
Printed by the MPG Group, Bodmin, Cornwall

Contents

Series Editors' Foreword

Over recent decades the traditional 'languages and literatures' model in Spanish departments in universities in the United Kingdom has been superseded by a contextual, interdisciplinary and 'area studies' approach to the study of the culture, history, society and politics of the Hispanic and Lusophone worlds – categories that extend far beyond the confines of the Iberian Peninsula, not only in Latin America but also to Spanish-speaking and Lusophone Africa.

In response to these dynamic trends in research priorities and curriculum development, this series is designed to present both disciplinary and interdisciplinary research within the general field of Iberian and Latin American Studies, particularly studies that explore all aspects of **Cultural Production** (inter alia literature, film, music, dance, sport) in Spanish, Portuguese, Basque, Catalan, Galician and indigenous languages of Latin America. The series also aims to publish research in the **History and Politics** of the Hispanic and Lusophone worlds, at the level of both the region and the nation-state, as well as on **Cultural Studies** that explore the shifting terrains of gender, sexual, racial and postcolonial identities in those same regions.

Prologue

This book is a collection of essays on the Mexican transition to democracy that offers reflections on different aspects of civic culture, the political process, electoral struggles, and critical junctures. They were written at different points in time and even though they have been corrected and adapted, they have retained the tension and fervour with which they were originally created. They provide the reader with a vision of what goes on behind those horrifying images that depict Mexico as a country plagued by narcotrafficking groups and subjected to unbridled homicidal violence. These images hide the complex political reality of the country and the accidents and shocks, which democracy has suffered.

The transition was on the brink of disaster during the 2006 electoral process. Mexican politicians became entangled in an electoral war so rough and surly that it deeply wounded the country's citizens. However, nearly one year after the great confrontation, Mexican society was tranquil, and it seemed unbelievable to many that the roaring motors of rancour had been turned off and barely hummed with indifference. What was the soothing balm that attenuated the offences and resentment? What was it that forced the politicians to abandon their aggressive attitudes and dangerous provocations?

The phantoms the politicians had invoked were suppressed by the unsuspected civility of a large part of Mexican society. Civil society managed to subdue the effect of political society's agitated tremors. No matter how much some shouted their heads off, warning that Mexico was on the verge of collapse, divided between two irreconcilable factions, the end result was that, in some strange way, the political class understood that the time had come to stop the confrontations. It was evident that the wells of society were not flooded with harmful humours – civil society was not a treacherous minefield but rather a serene space. I cannot say what kind of communicating vessels carried this serenity to the political elite, but without a doubt they worked with amazing speed. Yellow bile did not spill out over society nor did the blue skies fall down upon everyone's head.

I would like to believe that broad sectors of society demanded that politicians act rationally and let themselves be guided by ideas rather than accumulated hatred. I would like to think that a civil society totally fed up with the aggressiveness of the electoral campaign cried out: 'Politicians, sirs! Give us a break! Take a break! Think hard and read more!' Television commentators and the press quieted down. When the polls revealed that public opinion did not endorse the threatening outbursts of the losing candidate or approve of President Fox's interference, calm began to settle over the scene. López Obrador's attempts to create an ungovernable situation were met with evident disgust. By the same token, the High Electoral Court's reprimands addressed to the executive office were well received.

The explosion of populist kitsch began to sicken leftists. Right-wingers were weary of a charlatan president driving along accident-strewn roads with his lights off. Society ran out of patience with the intellectuals in the Zócalo, who ridiculously handed out moral certificates of civilizing merit and burned their hearts on the pyramid of frustrated pride. Irritation grew with the threats of voracious and meddling businessmen. Disdain was spreading for an insulting Right, which although frightened, marred, and opaque, hid behind the good sense of the surprise candidate who won the presidency. Society had had enough of televised broadcasts fishing in dirty waters contaminated by the impertinence of their broadcasters. Obtuse, marginal leftists – but hardened and ready for a fight – were the motivation for writers who incessantly bombarded us with lessons in incongruence. So, was it civil society's general disgust with these excesses that put a stop to the political debacle? Not only that: strong doses of fear and apathy had to be added in order to gauge the strange ground we were treading. In any event, society protected the initial transition to democracy, and after enduring enormous tension allowed the political pulleys to start working again, although not without difficulties.

I suspected at the time I was being too optimistic and so did not hesitate to say that this apparent calm after the post-electoral storm could be broken at any moment. For that very reason, I felt it was urgent to stimulate debate of ideas and discussion of political principles. A basic problem is that many Mexican politicians are unwilling to foster discussion. They are too drenched in opportunism – trapped in cheap pragmatism.

We cannot ignore the fact that the criticism and debate of ideas are carried out in the fragmented world of an intellectualism in transition which has yet to totally abandon the old habits acquired from its entry into the former political regime. Unfortunately old-style intellectuals still exist who are involved both with political causes and the powers that be but shout from the rooftops that they are free and independent critics. It is an attitude inherited from the long era of the institutional dictatorship of revolutionary nationalism. This historical legacy explains how an intellectual allows him or herself to be used as a powerful presidential candidate's propaganda instrument and at the same time proclaims that this option is a product of his or her position as an independent. In the era of the 'perfect dictatorship' many intellectuals gave their support to the government, but they felt that by exercising free will in solidarity with those in power, they earned the right to criticize government policy now and then, at critical moments. The strength of an authoritarian power that proved very difficult to defeat was founded precisely on this complex ambivalence. The majority of intellectuals close to the old authoritarian government did not think they formed an organic part of a political party.

We live under the reign of images and rituals, rather than of ideas and concepts. Flooded with short-lived symbols that perish as soon as each phrase of a speech or icon on the screen vanishes, intellectuals are living through the transition to democracy with great difficulty. The essays in this book are inserted into the gaps in this fractured terrain. One of the essays, 'Mud, mire, and democracy', was published shortly after the elections and, to my surprise, contributed to reflection and discussion in the most unusual areas of both Left and Right. But it also caused animosity and aversion. I now surround this essay with other texts in an attempt to connect my ideas with new and old controversies that developed in leftist territories. They are based on the rich seam of ideas – at times buried and forgotten – that have illustrated the struggles of the Left in Mexico. They were not shouts launched into the void, but rather part of a group of often disconcerting voices that has encouraged the Left. The aggressive populist outcry, which became almost deafening, led to the belief that the vision of the Left was irretrievably clouded by thick cataracts of sectarianism and *caudillismo*. But in Mexico there are other Lefts: democratic, open, flexible, critical, and tolerant, removed from the militant networks of the political parties, and above all widely spread throughout society.

The difficult 2006 post-electoral juncture accentuated the differences between conservative populism and the democratic Left. Populism tends to emphasize the importance of movements over political parties, reinforcing the idea that the principal strength of change is found in popular mobilization. It praises the direct relationship between political leaders and their social bases through acts of protest and stresses the fluidity of a joining of forces concentrated on precise objectives as opposed to the rigidity of party bureaucracy, concluding that only movements of social resistance are able to modify structures. Of course, these ideas can also be illustrative of movements of the Right (fascism being the most tragic example). The democratic Left generally lauds the function of political parties, recognizing it as an essential link in the democratic constitutional system. It emphasizes the importance of accedence to authority over acts of protest and recognizes the necessity of establishing mechanisms of representation through electoral processes and promotes the strengthening of parliamentary institutions.

The most prosaic response to these dilemmas usually emphasizes the need to combine the work of institutions of democratic representation with the stimulus of popular movements that take to the streets. This is a mistake and a banal way of escaping the real problem. It is one thing to accept that every society generates popular movements, to a greater or lesser degree, but to adopt a permanent policy of stimulus and convocation of mass protests is very different. A democratic Left must be receptive to social movements, but it cannot constantly use them to achieve through pressure what it could not achieve through voting, conviction or alliance. Looked at from the opposite perspective, it can be asserted that resistance movements are central, that they should be receptive and know how to take advantage of representative democratic institutions in order to strengthen themselves. This point of view is derived from old leftist Leninism. It has only been able to function in its pacifist versions (Gandhi) in cases of non-democratic political systems closed to change (dictatorships, colonial regimes). Of course, everything depends on how the situation is looked at. From the viewpoint of the conservative Left, the hegemonic Right heading a government tinted with quasi-fascist hues has entered into a structural crisis and the moment for a change in regime has arrived. The democratic Left does not see a systemic crisis and recognizes electoral processes of representation and therefore sees the need to adopt a reformist policy.

The Mexican Left is presently encountering these complicated dilemmas. On the one hand, López Obrador heads a movement that obviously has weakened the principal party of the Left. On the other hand, the democratic wing of his party is beginning to oppose this movement and realizes that adopting a policy of mobilizing protest has weakened the party's electoral possibilities. But if the democratic Left gives in again to the pressures of conservative populism, the party of the left – the PRD – can expect a period of hard times to come. A parting of the ways with the populist *cacique* is difficult though necessary, and the process may well leave scars. However, if the authoritarian *cacique* continues to be the leader and symbol of the PRD, the democratic Left across civil society will abandon partisan bureaucracy and its leader will gradually, albeit very slowly, disappear.

* * *

If there is one thing that characterizes the Mexican transition to democracy it is its exasperating, albeit smooth, slowness. Twelve years after the Partido Revolucionario Institucional (Institutional Revolutionary Party, PRI) lost the presidential election the country is still faced with the solid presence of an enormous territorial space dominated by governors from the old authoritarian party who control their domains in the customary style of the country's PRI presidents. The transition has been hindered due to the fact that even though the Jurassic Park of the old regime was closed down in 2000, the dinosaurs that prospered there were now on the loose, with no president to control them. At present, they boldly fight to manipulate the party, gain influence, and eventually win the presidency in 2012.

The July 2010 elections showed that the transition has not come to a halt but they revealed the slowness of the process. The PRI was defeated in only three of the twelve governorships in which elections were being held. Of course, these defeats were enormously significant because they saw the collapse of the most enduring, corrupt, and authoritarian forms of government in Oaxaca and Puebla. The final balance was not positive for the PRI: it ceased to govern almost eight million citizens.

The elections were preceded by ominous signals; the most drastic was the assassination of the PRI candidate for governor in Tamaulipas, immediately followed by the chilling news that an alleged gunman from a drug-trafficking group was among the bodyguards of that state's acting PRI governor. The presence of organized crime in the top spheres of politics and its interference in the electoral process was not a good sign. Added to these unsavoury omens was the widespread conviction that we were at the gates of a total restoration of power by the PRI. The leaders of this party were convinced they would win all twelve governorships.

The big surprise of these elections was that the threatening presages were not fulfilled and that the elections were peaceful, dominated by encouraging symbolic signals: transition had not come to a standstill. The eroding of the remains of the old regime was still an ongoing process. This erosion continued to be propelled by the internal putrefaction of the PRI together with advances in the educational level, modernization, and urbanization of the most backward zones of the country. This enabled the victory of the alliances between the Partido Acción Nacional (National Action Party, PAN) and the Partido de la Revolución Democrática (Democratic Revolution Party, PRD) in Oaxaca, Puebla, and Sinaloa and the considerable advances made in Durango and Hidalgo.

But the striking novelty crystallized into an event that has become a symbol of these elections: Rights and Lefts joined together to defeat the corrupt and authoritarian power of the PRI. No matter how emphatically they claimed to be the primary political force of the country, the leaders of the PRI were not able to hide the fact that the restoration of the former regime had been held back by the coalition of the most advanced, modern, and democratic forces of the Right and the Left. This is the crux of the political drama that played out during the 2010 elections.

The alliances that have caused the PRI to lose its hold on these positions are not merely an effect of opportunism and pragmatism of marginalized politicians. Nor are they the unnatural acts the PRI has insistently been condemning. But my intention here is not to implement the alchemy of transforming political incivility into democratic purity. The candidates that get into government thanks to these alliances are individuals who are deeply steeped in the local mire of the political culture of the PRI, with all its characteristic sordidness. And, nevertheless, they are an expression of a trend of thought that has been expressed in different ways and different spaces for years. This trend supports the possibility and the need that the most liberal sectors of the Right and the most social-democratic groups of the Left come closer together and form alliances to modernize the country and block the restorative and regressive tendencies of the most backward ideologies of the PRI. I have diligently defended this proposal and explained its political bases, its possible effects, and its theoretical assumptions. And I have not been alone in this task, despite the fact that both the conservative Left and the reactionary Right have condemned pro-alliance ideas. In order to understand just how difficult it is to defend these ideas, it suffices to recall the tremendous forces that oppose alliances. Examples are the aborted pact between the Secretary of State, Fernando Gómez Mont of the PAN, and the governor of the State of Mexico, Enrique Peña Nieto of the PRI, and the frequent tantrums of Andrés Manuel López Obrador every time the PRD reintroduces the topic of coalition. In the first case, deals were made within the PAN to block the alliance with the PRD in the 2011 elections in the State of Mexico, and in the second case, unsuccessful attempts were made to undo the PAN–PRD coalitions in Hidalgo, Oaxaca, Puebla, and Sinaloa. Because of that boycott, Durango and Veracruz were not added to the list of States in which the PRI, after eighty years, was defeated. And in the end, López Obrador managed to block the PAN–PRD alliance in the State of Mexico which enabled the PRI to win the 2011 elections for governor by a landslide: this paved the way for Peña Nieto, the outgoing PRI governor, to become the most probable winner in the 2012 presidential election.

The 2010 elections opened a slit through which society could catch a glimpse, albeit a bit blurry, of the political machine that moves the elites and the obstacles that paralyse it. Added to the encouraging signals that display a very slow erosion of what is left of the old regime, are the disquieting signs that reveal a timid political class with very little capacity to intelligently and bravely confront the existing challenges. The success of the opposition to the PRI has prompted certain civilizing and democratizing effects, but the shadow of a disastrous series of situations makes one fear that the fruits of political alternation and coalitions could have bitter results. The putrefaction of the governments of Patricio Patrón Laviada in Yucatán, Sergio Estrada Cajigal in Morelos, Alfonso Sánchez Anaya in Tlaxcala, Ricardo Monreal in Zacatecas, and Luís Armando Reynoso in Aguascalientes are some of the most alarming cases that come to mind. All this leads to the suspicion that today the PRI is more a contagious disease than a political-ideological current. It is also a habit, a set of customs and guile that stems from a decadent and very tainted revolutionary nationalism. Alternation and coalitions are in no way immune to these ills. These are the shadows that hover over the new governments of Oaxaca, Puebla, and Sinaloa.

The 2010 elections marked the beginning of a difficult and dangerous era. The legitimacy Felipe Calderón had attained thanks to the war on drug trafficking has been used up. Mexican society's perception of this war was that it was not being won: on the contrary, the dominating image was of a country submerged in barbarous violence. This perception was a terrible exaggeration, largely a product of mass media sensationalism. The government became trapped: it would be dangerous and ill-advised to retreat and stop the war on organized crime, but it did not seem possible that any substantial progress would be made which might change the general opinion that the country was caught up in a veritable nightmare. Moreover, a new civil and democratic legitimacy did not take root and extend as it was expected to do, partially due to the fact that the political elite was incapable of working together to carry out important reforms. The 2010 elections killed and buried the possibility of approving a short-term reform of political institutions.

After the 2010 elections it became even more obvious that alliances were at the core of political tensions. Even before, there were those who firmly believed that the only alternative was a great alliance of the PAN with the PRI and they did not consider such a coalition to be unnatural. This path required the pact with Peña Nieto that I mentioned before, which stopped a coalition of Lefts and Rights in the State of Mexico in 2011 in exchange for PRI support of Felipe Calderón's tax policy. With this agreement a genuine restoration could be moved forward: a political reform would eliminate the legislative overrepresentation (of 8 per cent) that favours the plurality of political currents approved in 1996, and lock in governability in order to give an absolute majority of representatives to the winning party that obtained a relative majority of 35 per cent in the elections. Of course, the proposal for a second round of voting would have to be eliminated. Even after winning the first round, the PRI would certainly lose the second, as a result of the influx of the useful anti-PRI vote. The proposed restoration would be a return to the situation that existed before 1997, the year when the PRI lost the absolute majority in Mexico's equivalent of the House of Representatives. Governor Enrique Peña Nieto expressed it very clearly: 'The democratic State needs majorities in order to be efficient'.[1] There is nothing further from the truth, as pointed out by Jesús Silva-Herzog Márquez, when arguing that, for example, the extreme fragmentation of the Brazilian Congress, which for years has kept the governing party in the minority, did not prevent Fernando Henrique Cardoso and Luiz Inácio Lula da Silva from having been able to approve important reforms.[2] In addition, this example prompts us to bitterly reflect on the low level of the Mexican political class in which no one even vaguely resembles a Cardoso or a Lula. Perhaps many people had imagined López Obrador to be a great statesman, but that illusion quickly vanished. In Mexico we have political operators who are sometimes very good; but we do not have statesmen. There is an adept *operocracy* but there are no great politicians.

The alliance of the PAN with the PRI failed and consequently the Secretary of State, who had pushed it forward, had to resign when it became obvious that coalitions with the PRD produced good results. This situation clearly had disturbing consequences. A portion of the business class, which had already assumed the return to power of the PRI was a sure thing, showed its discontent and alarm. Claudio X. González Guajardo, a prominent businessman, president of the Fundación Televisa and promoter of philanthropic works in education, gave the first warning signal. In an article of his, he criticized Felipe Calderón's 'obsession' to keep the PRI out of the mainstream of power; he accused Calderón of having stopped governing for all Mexicans and reducing himself to being the leader of a political party.[3] This entrepreneur warned that in a situation such as this the PRI would stop collaborating on the reform agenda and he was concerned about the fate of public administration in the final years of the PAN government. What he did not say was that the PRI had actually never agreed to promote reforms that would confer prestige and popularity on Calderón's government; it always stingily haggled over funding and contrived to erode the government's precarious legitimacy.

* * *

This book would not exist without the work of Gusti Gould, who not only translated these essays but also had the idea of bringing them together so they could be available to an English-speaking audience; she was the driving force behind the form taken by the present edition. I thank her very warmly for her collaboration and support. The analysis I offer in this book is based on the study of political culture and takes a special interest in the dilemmas of the Left. The interpretations and analyses are meant as a call for discussion of ideas, and they seek to support democratic options in the face of populist authoritarianism. I touch on sensitive subjects such as the electoral behaviour of the Left, and the definition of the Right. I examine the nationalism crisis, the indigenist tradition, official art, and the labyrinth Octavio Paz bequeathed to us. The principal thread throughout the essays leads to reflection on the transition to democracy and to the proposition that, fortunately, the Mexican dictatorship was not perfect. The first part of the book focuses on political transition itself and the situation of the different currents and political parties. It includes an examination of the populist phenomenon in Latin America and ends with a reflection on the possible return of the old authoritarian party. The second part contains my interpretations of how intellectuals and scholars are inserted into society and is followed by an in-depth analysis of the exemplary case of the great writer Octavio Paz. From there I analyse two fundamental cultural phenomena in Mexican life: the indigenous problem and the student movement of 1968. And after studying those processes I jump to a complementary but significant theme: the counter-culture. I add a reflection about street life and then end the book with some general conclusions about the political future.

February 2012

Notes

1   *El Universal*, 16 March 2010.
2   'El artilugio mayoritario'.
3   'De Presidente de México a presidente del PAN'.

Part I

The Political Transition

Chapter 1

The Dictatorship
was not Perfect

1. Transition[1]

Around midday on Sunday, 2 July 2000, while I was still undecided about going out and voting, I heard the rumour that a survey carried out by the Institutional Revolutionary Party (PRI) was showing Vicente Fox – the opposition candidate – to be ahead in the votes. It seemed impossible that we could free ourselves of the ruling party in Mexico, after more than seven decades of authoritarianism. 'This must be some last ditch manoeuvre by the government's army of vote hunters,' I thought. Shortly thereafter, I was interviewed on the radio, where I stated that I had not yet decided how I was going to vote and was still thinking it over, but that I would soon go to the ballot boxes. A well-known journalist, Miguel Ángel Granados Chapa, who was also on the programme, asked me with some surprise why it was taking me so long to decide. I answered: 'It's a way of criticizing the politicians who have not done their job well – an ironic punishment for the political parties. The high percentage of undecided voters creates a healthy democratic uncertainty.' We now know that the majority of us undecided voters cast our ballots against the PRI as a push for change. That was why Vicente Fox won the election.

The authoritarian system had stopped functioning adequately many years before. It was evident that the political crisis had begun to corrode the government since 1988, but in 1994 the authoritarian power found itself enormously weakened, fatally wounded. However, so much had been said about the extraordinary vitality of the institutionalized revolutionary regime, and the strength of the 'perfect dictatorship' – Mario Vargas Llosa's curious expression – had been emphasized so much, that we ended up immersed in bitter scepticism.

Many of us were convinced the PRI would win the elections again, albeit by a narrow margin, and that transition would sooner or later lead to a new political crisis. I was afraid – and fortunately I was wrong – that the transition to democracy would come to an end due to the fragmentation of a system no longer capable of governing. That seemed to be our tragic destiny: to be governed by a completely out-dated, inefficient, and useless system, which despite its abject per-fection at one time, would founder, dragging us towards dangerous situations. We would have to wait until some factions of leadership openly accepted the need to negotiate the transition, as had been the case with the post-Franco and post-Communist sectors that emerged in Spain and Russia.

But the dictatorship was *not* perfect, and it came tumbling down through a surprisingly simple process: it only took the peaceful voting of citizens in clean and democratic elections. What had happened? Powerful forces within the government, encouraged by President Ernesto Zedillo, had neutralized fraud in a considerable part of the semi-public and state machinery. The growth of new democratic pro-cesses within the government was not obvious; it was hidden behind the grey and opaque mask of supposed weakness on the part of the executive power. Few recognized the evidence: the weakening of pres-idential power advanced democracy and generated great confusion in the most authoritarian traditional circles (the 'dinosaurs'). One of the representatives of authoritarian restoration, Manuel Bartlett, famous for having orchestrated the great electoral fraud of 1988, realized this too late: 'The president has lost his capacity to lead; he has ceased to be the moral leader of the PRI', he declared on 4 July. Actually, the presidency had abandoned that 'capacity to lead' quite some time before, leading the PRI to its ruin. In order to steer clear of dangerous interference by the PRI, President Zedillo quickly accepted Vicente Fox's triumph.

The Mexican authoritarian system collapsed in an unexpected way. The extraordinary event amazed many people around the globe. They contemplated the smooth and peaceful beginning of the Mexican transition to democracy with astonishment. Within the coun-try, numerous analysts and intellectuals were stunned and they did not know whether to praise or censure the electoral results. Not many realized that the twentieth century had come to an end in Mexico and that we now inhabited a different country, an unfamiliar territory full of unexpected alternatives. The progressive intellectuals believed they saw a strange conservative victory led by an incongruent charlatan that would continue the *cristero* tradition and converge with the neo-liberal politics of Carlos Salinas de Gortari inspired by Ronald Reagan and Margaret Thatcher. A senior PRI historian, Vicente Fuentes Díaz, criticized President Zedillo with rage: 'Let us not forget that sixty years ago General Cárdenas prevented the Right, led by Almazán, from taking over the government.' Most certainly, patriotic fraud in the name of the institutionalized revolution successfully took place for the first time in the 1940 election. Lázaro Cárdenas, himself, had justified the authoritarian power: 'The conservatives in Mexico,' he wrote in December of 1935 when confronting Calles, 'enemies of the social programmes of the Revolution, want the type of democracy that is practiced in the capitalist states to be in our government policy; that is, freedom for their interests and imposition of their criteria'.[2] General Cárdenas promptly applied this doctrine in 1940. In 2000 many experienced the defeat of the PRI as if it were the triumphant return of the ghost of Juan Andreu Almazán, perhaps the real winner of the 1940 elections, despite his fifteen thousand recognized ballots (as opposed to two and a half million for Manuel Ávila Camacho). The Democratic Revolution Party (PRD) candidate, Cuauhtémoc Cárdenas, possibly saw this spectre the night of 2 July, and for that reason refused to congratulate Vicente Fox; he justified his action saying that 'what is happening is a tragedy for the country'.

The supposed tragedy lay in the fact that Mexican society, besides having been the object of marketing manipulations, had suffered a displacement toward conservatism. This idea is incorrect. Vicente Fox and his group were a political expression of the Centre-Right, with strong modern pragmatic overtones. The mass of votes he received reflected an even wider range, since it included an enormous sector of the population that, in an act of simple good sense, opted to end the 'perfect dictatorship'. The strictly conservative ingredients were left marginalized as much by the overwhelming pragmatism of the 'friends of Fox', the independent group that supported him, as by a society fed up with corruption and fraud. However, it seems that some hardcore reactionary and conservative sectors – lodged in both the National Action Party (PAN) as well as in the Church or in business corporations – interpreted the events in the same way as the hard-core Left or the backward PRI: they believed Vicente Fox's victory was an invitation for the conservatives to take over the State machine.

For the Fox administration to be able to maintain an oscillating balance between the Centre and the Right during his entire six-year term depended on many very complicated factors. Foremost among them were the critical processes both the PRI and the PRD were going through. Economic and financial interests that had traditionally been represented by the PRI, were predictably shifted in an opportune manner to support the new administration. A section of technocracy did the same. The PRI remained propped up by the right wing of the unions, the most backward *campesino* organizations, the corrupt remains of a ramified reactionary bureaucracy and restoration groups promoted by certain regional influences. Some sectors of the PRI tried to metamorphose their political organization into a modern party in order to escape the restoration temptations that would lead it to suicide, but they were not able to do so entirely. During the first months of his government, President Fox lightened the pressure on the PRI when he became fearful of the following danger: if the members of the PRI were unable to recycle their party, instead of depositing its dead body into history's garbage dump in a civilized manner, they would leave a putrefying cadaver in the middle of society, causing alarming contamination and much provocation. The inveterate authoritarian party took advantage of that respite to recover its position in the 2003 elections.

The PRD, whose foundation was closely linked to the hopes of ending the authoritarian regime, experienced the transition to democracy as if it were attending its own funeral. In a certain way this is true: the mixture of hard-core positions, sectaries, blustering patriots and populists predominant in the leaders of Cuauhtémoc Cárdenas's campaign, failed completely. The PRD and its confusing allies unsuccessfully presented the voters with a slightly leftist version of the old revolutionary nationalism, the withered culture that had typified the official party for decades. But the former official party, in its attempts to renovate itself, now threatens to invade the left-of-centre territory that the PRD occupies in order to recover its old dominions. The alternative the Left has always had – the social democratic direction – continued to be attractive, albeit somewhat weakened. The PRD should have pursued that option in order to transform itself into a modern and dynamic party, but it could not put a stop to its permanent state of internal agitation because it was not able to abandon its habit of gulping down often indigestible, outdated ideas and backward social movements.

During the latter years of the twentieth century, the country was governed by a corrupt and terribly authoritarian right wing under a nationalist, revolutionary, and Carranza-influenced guise. At the beginning of the twenty-first century, a democratic and pragmatic

Right is governing. Its inclination is towards the centre of the political spectrum. It is full of unknowns, itself unaware of which profile it is acquiring. In this essay I will attempt to clarify some of these unknowns and look for guidelines for interpreting the strange transition process. I have wanted to put a personal mark on these pages, at the risk of being excessively subjective, because discovering the keys to the Mexican political system has been an obsession of mine throughout my intellectual life, and the desire for the authoritarian system to come to an end has been a permanent force motivating my reflections for more than forty years.

2. Conspiracy

In these times of disenchantment, when there is little faith in scientific and philosophical paradigms, any attempt to discover rules and tendencies in social and political structures may seem like an old-fashioned romantic scheme. Nevertheless, I dare to defend the idea that the social sciences are not irrevocably buried in sterility: I believe that it is possible to find profound processes, explain them, and to some extent, predict certain situations. To defend this idea, I will paradoxically utilize an image which does not come from scientific method, but rather from the universe of political adventure and literary intrigue: conspiracy. Also paradoxically, I will call on the vicissitudes of some personal experiences, which directly or indirectly, have thrust me into the conspirative currents of political and social life.

Many years ago, in 1973, I took part in a bitter debate with Fernando Henrique Cardoso, at that time the most celebrated sociologist in Latin America and later president of Brazil. Disillusioned by his own 'dependency theory', Cardoso explained that the horrors of backwardness, dictatorship, and authoritarianism in Brazil and Mexico could be seen in the end as a 'bourgeois revolution of dependent countries': a social opening that – being false and controlled from above – was nevertheless marked by a guided dynamism. Cardoso presented his cautious optimism in a seminar on social classes and political crisis in Latin America, held in the city of Oaxaca in June 1973.[3] At that time Brazil was still suffering the effects of the 1964 military coup and Mexico was experiencing a timid opening of the authoritarian political system. In my critique of Cardoso, I explained that where he saw a 'bourgeois revolution' I found the embryo of a political crisis. My research in Mexico had convinced me that the mediation systems that the Mexican political system based its legitimacy on were no longer functioning well. 'All this makes me think – was my conclusion – that the coming years will bear witness to the end of the famous "Mexican system", in the way it has been functioning since 1940, and with this I am not predicting imminent social revolution or the next *coup d'état.*'[4] Although my 'prophecy' of the end of the Mexican system did come about, I must admit my critical analysis was tinged with conspirative intentions, exposed by the repeated use of references to class struggle, bourgeois hegemony, and means of production, expressions in which Cardoso saw an assertion of the 'scholastic Marxist formalism' which the Oaxacan seminar was coated with. I was convinced that the 'popular forces' would in some way take advantage of the crisis to strengthen themselves and then, some day, encourage a revolution which would open the doors to socialism. But it was a forced and ritual optimism that all radical activists of the Marxist Left had to manifest at that time. In reality, my studies of rural society had filled me with pessimism, when they led me to the realization that the Mexican system had a solid base in very complex political mediation mechanisms. The government of the 'institutionalized revolution' sustained its legitimacy in a strange gestation of non-capitalistic organizational forms: a series of reforms and functional changes stimulated the expansion of rural and urban 'third forces' that formed the solid base of the authoritarian regime. As I had previously discussed in an even more pessimistic text, under certain conditions a 'modern despotic power' could arise (the so-called 'perfect dictatorship') that was neither a fascist regime nor an exceptionally repressive power, but rather a stable government based on a non-democratic mediating system capable of protecting the economic process from the dangerous jolts of a society still harbouring contradictions of a not specifically capitalist nature.[5] Under these conditions, both capitalism and socialism are rarely explored as alternatives; in contrast, it is common to observe a true 'putrefaction of society', to use Lenin's stale metaphor, which shows a privatization of the State and a nationalization of society: the State depoliticizes itself, turning into a technocratic shell and civil society becomes militarized, exerting repression against itself.[6] I thought I had discovered certain keys to understanding the ways in which power was legitimized in advanced, wealthy, and supposedly 'one-dimensional' societies – according to the deceptive expression of Marcuse – in the modern despotic power such as it functioned in Mexico. A new post-Hegelian political situation abolished the myths of the political State and civil society and marked the beginning of a displacement process of social conflicts. The new mythology – and this is where the idea of conspiracy comes in – depicted a comfortable nationalized and bureaucratized society, barely perturbed by the distant plots of guerrillas, hippies, the insane, communists or religious sects.[7]

Undoubtedly, since 1968, the Mexican system had begun a slow and exasperating process of putrefaction: a slow transition that led to at least three very tense critical moments in 1982, 1988, and 1994. I am still amazed that the leftist culture of the 1960s and 1970s, despite the overwhelming influence of dogmatism, managed to cultivate from within itself the critical, flexible, and imaginative visions that allowed it to confront the difficult period beginning in 1982. This was achieved thanks to the fact that the flourishing of Marxism had been accompanied by new movements inspired by the sexual revolution, rock, psychedelic trips, feminism, the Prague Spring, student revolt, existentialism, and the new psychiatry. After long years of scrutinizing political mediation structures, especially in agrarian zones, it seemed to me they were crossed with or permeated by the same movements that had left their mark on the sixties. Not only Bonapartist *campesinos* and populist *caciques* were in the legitimizing structures; observing their functioning in both Latin America and Europe, I corroborated the fact that they included a wide variety of marginal fauna in the shape of indigenous peoples, terrorists, ailing persons, criminals, and other outcasts, who almost always conducted a war more illusory than real against the silent majority of respectable citizens of the status quo. The result of these observations about the confrontation between normality and otherness was published in 1981 in my book *Las redes imaginarias del poder politico.*[8]

The notion of *imaginary network* continues, broadens, and modifies the concept of *mediation structure.* I give great importance to these concepts since, in my opinion, they allow the precise locating of a social environment that reveals the conditions in which political apparatuses are reproduced and legitimized. The peculiarities of these mediating processes – and the degree of efficiency with which they function – are like a political barometer displaying the pressures to which the political system is subjected. In post-revolutionary rural Mexico a complex mediation structure developed, made up essentially of two parts:

1. A functionally reformed *campesino* economy, which thanks to agrarian distributions extended itself as a way of controlling the runaway growth of modern capitalism in the farmlands.

2. A series of populist and supposed revolutionary institutions, organizations, and territories owned by the *caciques* controlled the crudest and most direct expressions of exercise of political power.

Within this mediation structure, signs of hardening could be observed: the *cacique*-operated and populist institutions were gradually invaded by economic and financial interests that began transforming them into more and more authoritarian, repressive, and corrupt organizations. At the same time, the *campesino* economy was being strangled by modernization. These interpretations were the cause of many debates because they underlined awkward realities. They uncovered the fact that the *campesinos* as a social group, far from being a source of advancement and progress, had been converted into a key factor of obstruction and authoritarianism. This idea irritated many specialists immersed in populist conceptions of different political persuasions, from Maoist orthodoxy to revolutionary nationalism.

My conclusion, in the study published in 1974, was that agrarian mediation structures were largely responsible for the famous stability of the political system. However, by narrowing its internal dialectic strategy day by day, 'the end of the current Mexican political system' was foreseeable, as I had written.[9]

I wish to point out one important aspect: mediation structures are a legitimizing political sphere that functions independently from democratic formality, although these structures have a solid and stable 'popular' base formed by a comprehensive but marginal social segment. If the mechanisms and mediation processes break down, it seriously affects the legitimacy of the entire system.

However, the idea of a mediation structure in crisis had some important limitations, one of which was that it did not reflect the importance of the imaginary and symbolic cultural forms of political legitimization. It was therefore necessary to broaden the mediation perspective in order to take into account the whole of imaginary networks of political power. Not only do we find an increasingly illusory *campesino* created by populist nationalism, but also diverse actors, actually an entire theatre company, staging a largely imaginary war. The imaginary actors are the so-called 'marginal individuals', a symbolic otherness very vaguely and distantly corresponding to real social groups, which more than marginalized, are persons who live materially crushed under the weight of misery and repression.

I wish to mention here another discussion related to these ideas, which turned out to be very stimulating. Just as the presence of *campesino* actors in an imaginary theatre has caused worries and criticism, the fact that the mediating culture places indigenous peoples or sexual minorities on the same stage as terrorists and criminals has also resulted in awkwardness. At a round table discussion in 1980, I was able to understand new aspects of the problem, thanks to the intelligent observations of Luis Villoro.[10] In the same discussion, Carlos Monsiváis also objected to the assimilation of harmful (criminals, terrorists) and harmless (indigenous peoples, homosexuals) 'marginals'. In contrast, Octavio Paz liked my distinction between true marginals and 'marginality created by power'.[11]

The discussion with Monsiváis, Paz, and Villoro prompted me to look for the form in which the imaginary networks of political power were manifested at the end of the twentieth century in Mexico. I was convinced that by examining the manner in which these networks were constructed, it would be possible to show the limits of the political system. But I must confess I was not motivated by a purely scientific interest: there was also a conspiratorial intention, to continue with the same imagery, encouraged by a political commitment to democratic struggles. The essays that ended up together in the book of the symptomatic title *La democracia ausente* (*Absent Democracy*) were a product of this political impulse.[12] But here I want to emphasize the process that motivated the conceptual mutation of the (mediation) *structures* into (imaginary) *networks*, in order to finally end up in a *cage*. Structures, networks, cages: related concepts whose sequence metaphorically expresses the big problem: how to understand authoritarian *order*, ideological *traps* or political *prisons* – how to first understand and then escape from the structures, networks or cages. My answer was crystallized in the research results I published in the book *The Cage of Melancholy*, published in 1987 in the original Spanish version.[13] The diagnosis was not optimistic: the mediating networks tightly linked to national identity were damaged and therefore the system was condemned to perish. Thirteen years later, I had the deceptive but pleasant illusion that my small conspiratorial contribution had joined forces with a comprehensive chorus to bring about the downfall of the authoritarian system.

3. Legitimation

With this journey through my research on political structures I have wanted to present the problem of the future of democracy in Mexico, as well as document my confidence that anthropological and socio-logical reflection is not a sterile exercise when it attempts to reveal the future of political processes. I have limited myself to a very brief out-line. Those interested in the details of my excursion should consult the works I have cited. I now wish to pose the following question: is it possible to predict the form that legitimizing mediations will adopt under the new democratic conditions that opened in 2000?

I would like to begin by taking a step backwards. As would have appealed to Niklas Luhmann, let us try to imagine that the new and democratic Mexican political system that emerged in 2000 could function and reproduce itself without deriving its legitimacy from the surrounding society, except for the functioning of its own elec-toral mechanisms, and could strengthen its cohesion without turn-ing to external normative structures. We would be dealing with an auto-legitimized, autonomous system based on the rationality and formality of the administration and on its capacity to generate the political conditions of well-being. Under these suppositions, the pol-itical system would no longer require mediations or consequently, extra-systemic sources of legitimacy. To continue in the metaphoric ambience of open system thermodynamics, we would have such a structured governmental activity that it would be able to not only dominate, but also reduce the complexity of the surrounding social environment insofar as the complexity of political action increased. In other words: chaotic uniformity – entropy – in society and systemic order in the government.

This is, without a doubt, the dream of many administrators and technocrats, who would like to have enough management freedom to try, from a base of quality and rationality, to have political manage-ment run on its own without the need to revert to ideological struc-tures or social mediations. In this dream, if there were to be a deficit of rationality and efficiency, the system itself would be able to heal the wounds administratively.

This systemic utopia allows us to rapidly determine several strategic points. To begin with, governmental management would have to oper-ate from a new cultural base substituting the revolutionary nation-alism of the PRI. A managerial culture has been referred to, whose symbolic structure must have the capacity to articulate the identity of the political system. On a worldwide scale, there is without a doubt an accumulation of many experiences that feed government culture and it is further enriched by the transference of habits and practices coming from the business world. Rather than going into technical details I prefer to ask the question of whether a managerial culture is enough to confer legitimacy on a democratic political system. I do not think so, not even in the dubious case that such a culture were to bring economic well-being to the vast layers of the most dispossessed population. Economy, alone, does not produce legitimacy.

Hegemony of managerial culture presupposes that the Mexican political system, from the time of the 2000 elections in which the PRI lost, would no longer require external sources of legitimacy: the very efficiency of the government apparatuses should be a sufficient enough base to guarantee its continuity. But as we all know, governmental apparatuses in Mexico are very far from this managerial efficiency and are too contaminated by corrupt, paternalistic or corporative forms of management to be able to function when sustained solely by a new marketing and managerial culture. It is strange that it was the leftist opposition that was the first to convey the image of a group of politicians, headed by Vicente Fox, as having won the 2000 elections thanks to their marketing and managerial expertise in the running of the political advertising campaign, and that in this way had managed to deceive millions of voters – that the new government had tried to transfer its managerial skill to public administration.

This is a simplistic explanation that does not recognize that the defeat of the PRI is one element in a complex process of democratic transition. I recognize two transition cycles: the short and the long.[14] The short cycle began with the 1988 political crisis, extended to the great tensions of 1994, and ended with the 2000 elections. The political transition to a democratic system was produced during this period. But the transition's profound causes, that imply a great cultural crisis, were inserted into a long cycle that began in 1968 and has not finished yet. This long cycle takes into account the crisis of the nationalist political mediations and the slow growth of a new political culture. It is precisely in this far-reaching cycle where we can find the signs of the new forms of legitimacy. Some indications can be recognized in the changes and adjustments that the system in crisis itself helped bring about. For example, when faced with the nationalism crisis the PRI government opted to promote the Free Trade Agreement and globalization, and then, when faced with credibility problems, it pushed a political reform installing an autonomous and trustworthy electoral mechanism. With these measures the PRI government accelerated its own demise, even though its objective was just the opposite: to prolong its stay in power. The opposition of the Left interpreted these situations very poorly: it believed it was necessary to return to the original revolutionary nationalism (that of Cárdenas, even of Zapata) and developed a populist attitude of distrust towards electoral democracy. The modernizing sector of the PRI also made an incorrect evaluation: it believed the technocratic sectors of government, immersed in a new efficiency-centred and managerial culture, had achieved sufficient legitimacy to win the 2000 elections. They were wrong and their candidate lost the fight. This development was also a warning sign to the new governing Foxists: their business abilities, their technocratic willingness and their managerial inspiration – undoubtedly useful in the daily tasks of the administration – would not be enough to guarantee new legitimacy. The new democratic regime would need to establish itself in the same far-reaching processes that were involved in the fall of the authoritarian system. What we know is that the government of Vicente Fox was incapable of promoting this profound process of change and it settled for a skilful and decorous management of democracy. The opposition contributed decisively to this standstill. Both the PRI and the PRD blocked every important reform in a legislative branch where the governing party was the minority. The recent history of other Latin American countries (Argentina, Bolivia, Ecuador, Peru, Venezuela) shows us we are not out of harm's way. This is why history will thank the Fox government for having been converted into an efficient funeral home in charge of burying the authoritarian system, but it will not be looked upon as the great reformer that opened the doors of a new political civility and an advanced political culture. Some sectors within the Fox administration were set against the profound course of transition and this contributed to further slowing down an already slow cycle. In any case, I do not think it is possible – or even beneficial – to combine the mechanisms that can be used by a democratic government to maintain and to even broaden its popular support, with the gestation processes of a new civic culture. But a conflict between the government and the new emergent civic culture would be dramatic and disastrous.

Regardless of the new government's advertising wherewithal, the governing group understood that a reform of the Mexican State was necessary. But it was not able to induce it. Both globalization and the democratic electoral reform (and their consequences, NAFTA, and the defeat of the PRI) have shown that Mexico is advancing along a road leading towards decentralization, federalization, and parliamentarization. This process presents us with a problem: current political tendencies have challenged preconceptions. The boundaries and central ideas that defined and classified state activity have been broken or altered.[15] One of their most spectacular manifestations can be seen in the fact that the functions of the three branches of government (executive, legislative, and judicial) have found themselves widely disrupted and overtaken by a fourth power that does not respect boundaries: the *legitimizing power* that guarantees governability.

An efficient executive branch, a representative parliament, and impartial vigilance, on their own, do not legitimize state power. It is legitimized principally by cultural, educational, moral, and informative processes which constitute networks of communicating vessels that pay no attention to traditional limits; not to those which divide the three powers, not to those of a territorial nature (be they electoral, state, national, etc.) nor to those that separate hierarchal orders. These networks tend to establish new and diverse and relatively autonomous forms of citizen power.

These are extraterritorial, metademocratic, transnational, global or even post-national networks. At first glance, these cultural networks cover an extremely heterogeneous group: mass communication media (press, radio, television, the internet); schools and universities; ethnic, religious, and sexual groups; publishing houses and hospitals; non-governmental organizations, churches, sects, and marginal groups of diverse vocations (from paranormal activities to paramilitary actions, from vegetarian pacifists to dogmatic terrorists).

It is a new power space penetrated more by cultural and symbolic flows than by the exchange of material goods: a legitimate and legitimacy-generating space, but barely or poorly legislated, propelled by an emerging economy that is based more on the production and circulation of ideas rather than objects, more on *software* than *hardware*.

In the context of the division of power, decentralization, federalization, and parliamentarization of the Mexican State leave unresolved important problems of both a general and national character that are tightly bound to governability. Therefore, within the constitutional sphere, legislation is required for the existence of highly autonomous management areas in regard to the three branches of government, and also with respect to their relation to municipal, state, and federal spaces.

Councils, commissions or agencies could be established within these autonomous management areas that would be in charge of running, on a national scale, sectors such as: culture, higher education, indigenous autonomies, churches, communication means, electoral processes, and even certain tax collecting institutions. Their formation implies the moving of certain institutions of state power closer to civil society: it is in a way, a 'statizing' of civil society, but also a 'civilizing' of state management.

Howsoever these reforms in the state apparatuses occur, they will continually accumulate throughout a process of changes that will gradually insert Mexico into a global network of democratic countries equipped with expanding economies. I have established a link between, on the one hand, regulated development of autonomous areas and, on the other, Mexico's fulsome entry into the so-called globalization – that neo-capitalist economy propelled by a great technical revolution – which is spreading on a worldwide scale from both the north of America and the European Union. I am well aware that the entry of backward countries with authoritarian bad habits into this process is extremely difficult. But it is not impossible. The experience of countries such as Spain, Greece or Portugal can shed light on the difficulties in and the advantages of this entrance into neo-capitalistic globality. If we add the experiences of some Asian countries (such as South Korea or Indonesia) to this observation, our optimism will doubtlessly dampen. But even so, given the geopolitical coordinates defining Mexico, I see no better option. Besides, it seems to me that we are dealing with a predictable process that forms part of the long transition cycle I have already referred to. In relation to the most advanced economic sectors, there should be a high price, in both money and reforms, for the accumulation and circulation of wealth in order to contribute to the extension of well-being. But this is a topic I shall leave for another time.

The expansion of areas of democratic and autonomous management tends to be linked to another phenomenon: the gradual surfacing of a post-national condition. The erosion of nationalism and its crisis as a legitimizing mechanism are not an invitation to project a new nationalism as a replacement: rather it is a sign that we are beginning an era in which governability mechanisms are not found in the ideological exaltation of national values. It is understandable that this situation has alarmed the democratic Left: in a certain way we are witnessing the collapse of old progressive paradigms and the emergence of renewed threats. But the Left has confronted the new processes with a narrow-minded and conservative attitude: it only sees the threats of privatization and dependency with respect to global networks, but it does not comprehend the importance of projecting other aspects of the process, such as the expanding of democratic autonomies and the fight against corruption (in business, in bureaucracy, or that linked to drug dealing and organized crime).

The old Left still has conservative reactions to these changes and adopts the so-called 'globaphobic' attitudes, instead of critically analysing the process to discover those facets whose projection could promote a general rise in living standards and quality of life. We are facing a complex and dramatic situation: it has been shown that capitalistic development does not necessarily cause – as had been believed and still is believed by some – a population's material pauperization, but it does open new spaces which contribute to a society's cultural and spiritual impoverishment.

This is a prickly and complicated problem. Cultural impoverishment is not, as was thought in the 1960s, a world-wide uniforming effect to adapt the population to a single market, in accordance with models created by highly industrialized consumer societies. The big threats do not come from the global circulation of ideas, values, and cultural symbols, but rather from another process accompanying globalization like its shadow: the strengthening of local powers which, in many cases, recover provincial cultural traditions soaked in religious customs, ethnic fanaticisms, and the interests of political bosses or companies. I am not referring only to regional powers that come into being thanks to decentralization or federalization, but also to those forces that take advantage of deregulation and autonomy of what I have called the fourth power (or cultural powers, especially in the media, education, and religious institutions). They do not promote the globalizing symbols of neoliberalism and the world market but rather a strange mixture of stale conservative values with the vulgar aggression of the *nouveau riche*. This combination of globalization and provinciality is presented to us in many declarations by Church leaders as well as on numerous radio and television programmes. An extreme but revealing example is that of the drug trafficking culture, a combination of provincial Catholicism with cruel and unrestrained appetites for wealth – of rustic crassness with transnational business. Another example: when certain provincial customs are transformed into legally sanctioned rules in municipalities or states, there is the risk of establishing fundamentalist, sexist, discriminatory, religious, corporative or authoritarian forms of government; the example of Guanajuato in 2000 was stunning: a small state created a dramatic confrontation on a national scale when it transformed the customs and traditions of the taboo subject of abortion, based on religious beliefs, into legal proclamations. Local problems were converted into national ones, and the governor had to veto the legal directives voted on by Guanajuato's congressional representatives.

4. Extra-systemic marginality

I have emphasized cultural problems not only because as an anthropologist I am obliged to do so, but also because I am convinced that
the future of democracy in Mexico is closely linked to the ways in
which political culture will disseminate new legitimacies. I have also
pointed out reforms that could regulate the new cultural processes.
But, continuing my interpretation, I would like to pose another question: what cultural processes will really be implemented in the coming
years? Since I was never so optimistic as to believe that Fox's new government would decisively promote a broad reform process, or to think
that there were not powerful forces in Mexican society that would try
to block changes even before they could be formally proposed, it was
obvious to suppose we would face political turbulence. I had hoped
that same turbulence could provide stabilizing elements that would
end up strengthening the cohesion of democratic forces and increase
the efficiency of the democratic system. Symptomatically, they are
extra-systemic elements generated by the tension the old structures
and former ideologies find themselves subjected to, as well as by the
tendency to savagely accumulate capital. These extra-systemic elements form what could be called a hyperactive marginality strip, made
up of segments of the fragmenting PRI, virtual and real guerrillas,
organized crime and drug trafficking cartels, urban and suburban
protest movements, and diverse paramilitary or terrorist groups.
This is not an unknown phenomenon; actually since 1994, with the
Zapatista uprising and the dramatic political assassinations, Mexican
society began to experience the typical processes of cohesion and con-
traction that – if they do not go beyond critical thresholds – provide a
certain legitimacy to governmental activity.

I believe one can observe a slight fragility in this peculiar theatrical dialectic between hyperactive marginality and the corresponding
cohesion of forces that aim to stabilize democratic normativity with
respect to the new government. It is true that this process implies the
legalization (or, at least, the legitimization) of a great variety of political, ethnic, social or religious expressions, which is an enriching phenomenon. However, it also elevates customs associated with violence,
corruption, and illegal forms of protest, and they should be prevented
from spreading. These customs are like drugs: their use can lead to
addiction. They only strengthen the stability of forms of united consensus that are reached more out of fear than civic conviction. At
the same time they hold back the consolidation of a democratic and

republican system of modern political parties, a system without which it is almost impossible to conceive of a new democratic legitimacy whose diversity opens the doors of social imagination and political creativity.

I would like to pause to examine the situation generated by the largely imaginary confrontation of the state with the Zapatistas. It seems to me to be a very revealing display of the cultural processes that are part of transition and a symptomatic example of the functions of hyperactive political marginality. Other examples might be the aggressive opponents of the construction of Mexico City's airport in Atenco or the agitated teachers of the CNTE who frequently invade the streets of the capital. The march of the Zapatista National Liberation Army (EZLN) through the country was the first act of great political theatre. At the beginning of 2001 the EZLN command decided to abandon the 'white night of oblivion'[16] in order to march towards Mexico City and begin what seemed to be a long journey to the heart of the republic. The journey was not as long, politically speaking, as had been expected, because it met with a completely new situation: with the defeat of the PRI in the 2000 elections, Mexican politics had changed substantially. The democratic ocean that swept across the EZLN march turned out to be much more difficult to oppose than the old authoritarianism of the PRI: the rebels were received with empathy by Vicente Fox's new government, by the Catholic Church, leftist groups, television and press, local governments, Congress, the police, and even by some business groups. The new president of the republic had sent the Zapatista-endorsed Cocopa proposal to the Senate and Mexican society prepared itself for a complex and democratic discussion of indigenous law. Few seriously thought that the 1996 Cocopa initiative on indigenous culture and rights could be a threat to national sovereignty or promote the fragmentation of the country. The principal pressure groups and the different interest conglomerates – all leaning to the Right – certainly had nothing to lose with the approval of modifications to the constitution inspired in the San Andrés Agreements. Do bankers care if indigenous people apply their own normative systems in the regulation of internal conflicts in indigenous zones? Can the collective enjoyment of natural resources in the habitat of indigenous people affect industry? Is the former ruling party's (PRI) vast hegemony in rural zones to be threatened if some indigenous municipalities opt for traditional political practices? Are the big companies that exploit natural resources disturbed by the payment of royalties to local indigenous governments instead of to state institutions or *ejidos*? Is the Catholic Church affected by the preservation of indigenous languages? Do merchants have any interest in opposing changes in electoral district demarcation? Are the big unions threatened by the formation of associations of indigenous communities? By any chance, do the large radio and television monopolies see a danger of real competition if indigenous towns operate their own systems of communication? Will judicial or military bureaucracy break down if indigenous prisoners are brought closer to their communities? All these questions can be answered with an emphatic no.

The Cocopa initiative's inoffensiveness is so obvious that the very president of the republic – who is not a leftist – decisively supported it and sent it to the Senate for approval, and his predecessor, Ernesto Zedillo, had accepted the San Andrés Agreements. Reforms of a similar spirit have been introduced in Oaxacan legislation, with the support of the PRI. Besides, the proposals are guarded by an international organization – not exactly subversive – dedicated to protecting the rights and standard of living of the workers, by which I mean Agreement 169 of the ILO (International Labour Organization), which implicitly brings indigenous or tribal identities into its organization as protected labour.

However, it was evident that the original proposal, inspired in the San Andrés Agreements, would not be approved without important modifications. Empathy for the Zapatista rebels did not translate into uncritical and mass support of the Cocopa proposal, because it harbours a strange but fascinating contradiction: the San Andrés Agreements appear in symbolic imagery as the expression of the people's most advanced and rebellious impulses, while on the legislative engineering plane they are proposals which at the very most just inconvenience the most backward economic interests of some excluded sectors of parasitic merchants, companies dedicated to the savage exploitation of natural resources, and other similar groups. Who can they affect? First of all, without a doubt, they would affect the indigenous peoples themselves, and secondly, the democratic system of political parties. The legal proposal contains aspects that can perturb representation mechanisms and thus, indeed, disturb democratic political parties. And here lay the heart of the matter: under the newly existing democratic conditions it was very unlikely that the parties represented in congress would approve the most conservative and even reactionary aspects of the Cocopa proposal, despite the aura of showy progressive imagery surrounding the San Andrés Agreements.

In these agreements, indigenous government forms are tied to populations that conserve their ancient institutions, which define their political practice according to *tradition*, which enjoy (or want to enjoy) their surrounding habitat in their *traditionally* collective way and exercise forms of justice based on *custom*. The conservative, traditionalist, and custom-oriented spirit is evident, although it is weakened by additions that symptomatically place conditions on the necessary respect for individual guarantees, human rights, constitutional precepts, and, most especially, the dignity of women.

The dangers of this conservatism for the indigenous population itself are apparent: exclusion from political parties and new institutions containing the seeds of change, confusion about political and Catholic ecclesiastical functions, exclusion of youth, women, and dissidents from the daily practice of a direct democracy carried out in assemblies, transformation of collective enjoyment of natural resources into corporative usufruct of rents and royalties charged to private companies, and other threats too numerous to list here. The conservative aspects of the Cocopa initiative are not imaginary inferences: anyone could confirm their existence in the Zapatista interventions themselves before the Congress of the Union on 28 March 2001, which were broadcast live on television. There they defended an unsettling 'legal pluralism' that had to accept normative systems already existing in the communities (as Adelfo Regino said) within the scope of the Constitution; that legitimized those customs and traditions that were considered 'good', such as, in the words of the Indigenous National Congress delegate, María de Jesús Patricio, recognizing that the husband takes 'the participation of the woman' (who stays at home) to the community assembly, accepting that 'there is no vote' in these assemblies but rather unanimous agreements put into effect by the 'true word' of the elders, or recognizing that more justice is done 'repairing the damage rather than punishing the guilty party' (a practice in which there is a great variety of traditional punishments: from public exhibition of the presumed guilty party, so that he or she feels ashamed, to hanging or forced labour at the service of the persons affected). In the presence of the doubts floating in the political atmosphere, Commander Esther of the EZLN defended the Cocopa initiative, stating that it has been criticized for things that are really problems of the whole of society: the indigenous peoples now live on reservations separated from the rest of the Mexican people; the legal system of the country is backward and promotes racism and confrontation; it is the government that makes exceptions in politics by converting posts and positions into spaces of impunity and the corrupt accumulation of wealth. All this is true and needs to be fought against: it is precisely these 'customs and traditions' that need to be changed, even though they are presented in the folkloric form of supposedly indigenous 'normative systems'. Their presence in the whole of Mexican society is one more indication that these are not values inherited from the ancients, but rather a disastrous contamination of authoritarian colonial traditions that have been accumulating over centuries. This should not hide the extraordinary and welcome fact that, with its presence at the Congress of the Union and its discourse delivered to representatives and senators, the EZLN seemed to formally accept the beginning of talks with the executive and legislative powers. With the collapse of the authoritarian system, the EZLN found itself faced with the need to make a significant change in strategy, in order to lead its march toward the democratic heart of republican civil society.

But that did not happen. The EZLN command, in an absurd gesture, preferred to head back to the highlands of Chiapas and remove itself from the discussion. And Congress approved an indigenous law in which the most conservative aspects of the San Andrés Agreements are avoided and which introduces an uncomfortable federalist principle: each state will define the autonomous forms of the indigenous groups. The legislators decided not to bind the exercise of autonomy of indigenous peoples to a territorial environment, and thus refrained from establishing a Mexican version of the Indian reservations in the United States. With this they kept clear of one of the most conservative dimensions of the San Andrés Agreements, but they provoked the indignation of the EZLN.[17]

In this way, the Zapatista guerrillas were like a barrel that floats in the sea because it is empty. To understand this we must turn to the whaling metaphors that Jonathan Swift used ironically when referring to Hobbes's *Leviathan*: '. . . that seamen have a custom when they meet a Whale, to fling him out an empty Tub by way of amusement, to divert him from laying violent hands upon the ship.'[18] Swift explains that the whale has been interpreted as Hobbes's Leviathan, an immense animal that shakes up and plays dangerously with different political and religious alternatives; the ship would be the Republic, a civil society threatened by lashings of the state's tail. To avoid damage to the republic, the spectacle of battle must be presented: the governmental whale busy fighting in a mock battle – an empty threat – to bring about the tranquillity and legitimacy of the Republic. Thus the barrel is like those political proposals which are 'hollow, and dry, and empty, and noisy, and wooden, and given to rotation'.

By this I mean that the fall of the authoritarian political system has opened the door to a reorganization of legitimization and cohesion processes: now the Zapatista guerrillas of Chiapas – together with the rest of the armed groups – represent in political imagery the dangerous liminal actors, whose presence provokes 'normal' society to stick together around the democratic *Establishment*. This is the spectacle I have called the 'Jezebel syndrome', a postmodern expression of imaginary networks of political power. With the new millennium, this syndrome begins as a Mexican version of the tub game described by Swift: 'In order to prevent these Leviathans from tossing and sporting with the commonwealth, which of itself is too apt to *fluctuate*, they should be diverted from that game by *A Tale of a Tub*.'

5. Boredom and the final start

But democracy is not usually entertaining. Instead, it is boring and inspires tedium. If we exclude the spectacular circus of hyperactive marginality from the political system, democracy appears to be a grey mist penetrating all of society's pores. Some analysts seem surprised at the obvious fact that democracy has submerged Mexico into a sea of boredom and predictability.[19] From 1988 onwards we had become accustomed to every electoral moment seeming to be a decisive alternative that would finally open the door to democracy and civility. When that door *did* open we observed, in amazement, the immense waters of weariness in which a political class lacking both imagination and bravery was swimming. The best map for political navigation could be that oceanography of tedium, invoked by Eugeni d'Ors.

I wonder if we are not dealing with an inheritance from the old political culture. After all, the Mexican system functioned in a stable and predictable manner for nearly half a century, from 1940 to 1988. There were few surprises. One of the few was in 1968: a surprise that fatally wounded the system. But even the agony begun that year was slow and tedious, carried out by predictable politicians and technocrats. We seemed condemned to a Nietzschean nightmare – the eternal return to the same. Perhaps it should not be so surprising that the new democratic condition has found itself immersed in the grey and fastidious culture of the institutional revolutionary tradition. Perhaps our past brought us to such an exaggeratedly smooth transition, that it ended up turning out the already dying lights of the political parties. We must keep in mind that the political class was shaped from the mediocre mould of the PRI.

Of course, I am not saying that it is preferable to have a democratic life conditioned by shocks and risks that endanger tolerant civility. One only needs to look at Latin American countries such as Argentina or Venezuela in order to understand that there are rescuable values in the traditions founded by long years of domesticated revolution, and that they promoted a governability culture (and a cult) in Mexico. During the first years of transition many of us wondered where surprises might come from, which political spaces were the least predictable and what the sources of instability were. Of the three largest parties, the PRI has traditionally been a kind of Pandora's box, full of unexpected situations. In its strange debacle, in its crisis, it is capable of generating situations that contaminate the political habitat, that pervert transition, and that poison civic culture. The surprises that emanated from the old official party did not seem to be innovative or creative. The PRD, party of the populist Left, opened a space of unknowns, as it was difficult to predict the form in which it would recycle the ideological rubbish the PRI was throwing out. The PAN, the ruling party, could offer the surprise of growing into a modern centre-right party. We were also facing political jolts from a source that had traditionally been a kind of safety cushion. I am referring to the government of Washington, whose orientation, since the fateful 11 September, placed Mexico (and the world) in a difficult situation. From that moment it has no longer been easy to guess which direction the group that surrounds the president of the United States will move towards. But it is obvious that Mexican problems and those of Latin America in general are not a top priority.

How do we cope with this difficult juncture? What could the political response be to the strange effects that produced these black holes in Mexican politics? Two alternatives had been discussed: the introduction of a new political culture or repairs to the damaged political institutions. I believe this problem has its origin in the old dichotomy between the patient labour of humanistic educators and systems efficiency. It would seem that the apparatchiki capable of repairing the damage caused by democratic transition were more important than those responsible for providing the basis for a coming culture. Was it the hour of slick systemic politicians – avid readers of Niklas Luhmann – who believe in the potential efficiency of institutions to legitimize themselves with no need to recur to 'popular culture'? Had the example of politicians – avid readers of Jürgen Habermas – who invoke the ideas of the Enlightenment in order to consolidate a culture of modern civility grown stale?

As I mentioned before, the new Mexican democracy can no longer obtain its legitimacy and stability by resorting to translating popular cultures into national identity, and then using this identity to exemplify eminently Mexican institutions – unique and original artefacts emerging from the inner depths of the country. What could be the source of legitimacy and governability? It could be born from the so-called constitutional patriotism, to use Habermas's expression. To me, the essential part of this 'patriotism' is that it consolidates the autonomy of the spheres of political culture and guarantees its separation in relation to the three traditional powers (executive, legislative, and judicial). In other words: political-administrative functions are radically separated from cultural-legitimizing functions. In this new condition – which I have named *post-Mexican* – presidents, representatives, and judges do not need to compete with one another to demonstrate their pure and authentic Mexicanness, and neither do the political parties or scores of civil servants. The continuity of a particular democratic cultural 'style' would emerge from learning centres, the press, electoral institutions, television, radio, literary and artistic creation, Churches, and many other more or less autonomous organizations.

On the other hand, by emphasizing the necessity of institutional reform, it is logical that we pay close attention to the battered political parties, especially the most broken down of all: the PRI. Broken down, indeed, though not so much like a poorly functioning machine but rather in the sense of finding itself affected by a process of organic decay. Nevertheless, the PRI was far from being a dead beast, and it was sustained by an extraordinary will to live. The very same thing occurred with Peronism in Argentina. I am very fearful of PRI politicians, who, when possessed by systemic fury want to repair their institutional machine with a mixture of organs dug up from the political cemetery. The 2003 elections show that they did just that.

After 2000, the perspective of a powerful, disorganized, and, most importantly, corrupt party, capable of contaminating the entire political system, was alarming. Its dreamy spreaders of culture, illuminated by an outdated adherence to the ideas of Vasconcelos, could do nothing about this situation, and neither could its ideological plumbers, belated apprentices of the social democratic sorcerer, who wanted to fix the institutional imperfections of the old official party. Was the PRI condemned to be a powerful zombie, an unrelenting living corpse filling the political panorama with uncertainty? There were no clear answers, but many of us expected the machine repairpeople to provoke a healthy fragmentation in this party, which would encourage pluralism.

Mediation and legitimization mechanisms broke down, the transition process was weakened, we had to put up with leaders who were disoriented and manipulated by the alchemists of opinion polls. There was much immaturity or lack of experience. And very importantly, an administrative framework full of all kinds of traps that paralysed the most resolute reformist pursuits was maintained. However, it was precisely in the intermediary areas of power where it was possible – although risky – to carry out important reforms that did not require the approval of the legislative power (where the paralysis was predominant). In general, these reforms were not carried out, although important advances were made in getting rid of corruption and achieving transparency.

Pessimism spread: the reforms that were necessary required a favourable atmosphere that did not exist in the country. They required institutional engineering jobs that could only be effectively begun if a new democratic political culture were established. I am referring to the anthropological notion of culture, which has little to do with the literary ideas of enlightened teachers imparting lessons to a civil society eager to receive their knowledge. But short-term repair did not seem possible for the institutional organizations. A long institutional dictatorship had made us very suspicious of the glorification of institutionalism. I greatly value the *constitutional patriotism* of which Habermas speaks, which is the crystallization of political pride in having been able to peacefully and legally overcome authoritarianism. But I do not care for the jump from that to another very different thing: *institutional patriotism*. I believe excessive devotion to institutions is damaging to the constitutional health of a state. Of course, I believe institutions are indispensable for receiving and directing democratic energy in a transition process. Institutions give coherency and continuity to the practices that organize legitimate forms of social control. Besides, they are the necessary framework for satisfying social needs. But I reject worship of the state that is the result of exaggerated veneration of institutions – be they the family, Churches, schools or ministries.

I began this essay[20] with a comment about the presidential election day of 2000. I would like to end it also with a reference to 2 July 2006. Just as six years previously, when I had not yet gone out to vote,

I received information from surveys carried out at the voting booths. Unlike the previous presidential election, these results showed a technical tie between the PAN candidate, Felipe Calderón, and the PRD candidate, Andrés Manuel López Obrador. And unlike the 2000 elections, which had taken place in an atmosphere of peacefulness, now there was a predominance of tension, rancour, and extreme aggression. What had managed to poison the electoral confrontations to such a degree? Something symptomatic had occurred: infighting had weakened the PRI and the PRD candidate had been the favourite in opinion polls for many months, even before other parties had chosen their candidates. This change in electoral preferences could have been something completely normal had the political context not been full of surprises. The decadence of the PRI was predictable; the rise of the PRD candidate was a surprise that broke the boredom.

The history of this surprise began almost imperceptibly when the head of the Mexico City government began his presidential campaign in 2001. López Obrador's campaign, from the second most powerful government position in the country, altered traditional rhythms; in a curious see-saw of aggression and hypocrisy he managed to generate, little by little, an attractive spectacle. The frightened Right also used government institutions to influence the political campaign. A populist politician who had recognized the weakness of the democratic institutions had come into power. With great shrewdness, and willing to do whatever it took to reach the presidency of the republic, he provoked critical tensions that hurt the transition process. He was a leader who had been trained in the wild political school of the PRI in Tabasco: fiery, puritan, dubious, and turbulent. Then, as a member of the PRD, he had run for governor of Tabasco in 1994: he lost by a narrow margin in very suspect elections. His followers seized oil wells, set up a sit-in in downtown Villahermosa, and proclaimed victory for López Obrador. But the official triumph went to Roberto Madrazo, a backward and authoritarian leader who had been opposed to the political opening which took place during Ernesto Zedillo's presidency, and who, through all kinds of trickery, became the PRI presidential candidate in 2006. In 1994, López Obrador, in his protest, led a march to Mexico City accompanied by *campesinos* from the state of Tabasco who emptied out into the Zócalo, the city's main square, barrowloads of boxes piled high, it was said, with proof of electoral fraud in Tabasco. No one ever examined the contents of those boxes, which mysteriously disappeared. In 2006, López Obrador lost the presidential election by a very small margin, but this time in a democratic and transparent election. He repeated his protest, also in the Zócalo, and this time dumped barrowloads of mire over Mexican democracy.

2007

Chapter 2

Mud, mire, and democracy[1]

The candidate of the populist Left has dumped an avalanche of mud over the most transparent and authentic presidential election ever held in Mexico. He has not accepted his defeat, he has reported immense fraud, with no proof, and has rejected the decisions of the Electoral Tribunal. This is how the process of his metamorphosis has ended, and from being a political option, he has become a social nuisance. He has poisoned the electoral atmosphere and suddenly placed the Left in a marginal contentious position. With his aggressive populism he has helped the Right to stay in power. How can these extraordinary results be explained? The moment to reflect, to discuss, and to abandon Manichaean positions has arrived. Behind the scenes of the confrontation between two political opponents, Felipe Calderón and Andrés Manuel López Obrador, is an extremely complex texture encouraging us to explore the nuances of and unravel the least visible mechanisms of political struggle.

1. Conservative populism

Why did the Left lose? Since 1988 the Left had managed to place itself in the position of being the moral leader in the transition to democracy and, almost a decade later, of being the most important driving force in the establishment of trustworthy electoral processes operated by autonomous public institutions. However, from the beginning, tendencies that undermined the Democratic Revolution Party (PRD) were becoming visible. I am referring to the expansion of a conservative populism that was picking up the rubbish of old revolutionary nationalism left along the way by the Institutional Revolutionary Party (PRI). I call it 'populism' because its base is the relationship of the chief with 'his' people, outside the boundaries of democratic

institutions of representation, thanks to an informal mediation structure flowing with support-and-favour exchanges. It is the traditional
way in which *caciques* have operated, in the *ejidos* as well as the unions,
in rural areas as well as in the cities. I call it 'conservative' because
it aims to preserve or restore the ideas and power forms belonging
to our *former* 'regime', the revolutionary authoritarianism that dominated Mexico for seven decades.

The hegemony of conservative populism in the Left was one of
the causes contributing to the defeat of its presidential candidate in
2000, Cuauhtémoc Cárdenas. In those first clearly transparent and
democratic elections, the PRD and its confusing allies presented a
withered image of the old revolutionary nationalism compared with a
democratic, modern, and pragmatic Right led by Vicente Fox. But the
Left failed to grasp the situation and incorrectly attributed its defeat
to marketing manipulations by the extreme Right, business corporations, and conservative militant Catholicism.

López Obrador continued in the same vein during the 2006 campaign. Despite the fact that he was offering a lukewarm political programme, he developed a furious campaign against the middle class,
the rich, and President Fox. In the name of the poor, he adopted a
spectacular policy of confrontation that alienated him from the support of sectors that have crucial influence on society. The height of
contempt for the middle class was displayed in June 2004 when he
crudely discredited the hundreds of thousands of people who marched
in Mexico City demanding that the authorities provide public security.
Only under exceptional circumstances of great political deterioration
of the traditional parties (as occurred in Venezuela) can a populist
leader, aggressively confronting the middle sectors, obtain a majority
vote. López Obrador's incendiary speech against the easily frightened
middle class cost him millions of votes. That was compounded by his
repeatedly lashing out at the president, without realizing that for the
majority of Mexicans, Vicente Fox is the symbol of the transition to
democracy and represents the force that defeated the authoritarianism
of the former regime. In this electoral campaign the populist Left committed a terrible error of judgment: it denounced the government of
Fox as the repressive and *quasi-fascist* power that had led the country to
economic disaster. It proclaimed that the people could no longer toler-
ate such oppression provoked by a group of traitors to democracy who
conspired against the popular causes represented by López Obrador.

However, it was obvious that the majority of people did not perceive this 'catastrophe' in which the country was supposedly living.

Nor did the threat of conspiracy, of the secret ultramontane right-wing organization El Yunque, of corrupt businesspeople, and socio-economic bankruptcy, become a generalized 'perception'. These exaggerations created a ghost confronted by the populist Left in its electoral fencing, but its sword thrusts merely scratched the air in an empty space. This resulted in the disappearance of the four or five million votes by which López Obrador believed he led his opponent. According to the Federal Electoral Institute (IFE) data, Calderón won by nearly a quarter of a million votes.

2. The *cacique* and his pyramid

The above reflections should be clarified. The Left received a very large proportion of votes, it is the number two power in the congress and its candidate *almost* won the presidency. This means that, besides the abovementioned factors which undermined the volume of its votes, the Left received new support it had not had a few years before. Many find the explanation for this in the rise of the apostle – López Obrador – who seems to have escaped from the flowery pages of Latin American magic realism. The Mexican Deep South had finally given birth to a chief capable of leading the fight of the dispossessed and the oppressed.

Although the folkloric aura López Obrador generates seems at times to confirm the stereotype of the epic leader, I believe the PRD presidential candidate is a political phenomenon of a much more prosaic nature. I believe we are dealing with a populist urban *cacique* who weaved his web of strength thanks to a structure of social mediations copied from the model which has been the traditional base of the PRI. We are dealing with a dense clientele network of more or less informal organizations linked to popular neighbourhoods, to political groups connected to marginal sectors, to merchant groups, taxi drivers, mini-bus drivers, and street vendors. A framework which includes investment management, the distribution of economic aid to the elderly and the handicapped, the legalization of illegally occupied land, and support for construction or supply companies, unions, and small-time leaders of pressure groups. This aggregation constitutes a mediation pyramid moving through the delegations with the Mexico City governor at the top. From this post, which is the second most powerful political position in the country, López Obrador carried out a long electoral campaign for more than five years. No governor concentrates as much political power as the head of government of Mexico City does. López Obrador reached the height of power when he won the 2000 election, but he did so based on the widespread prestige of Cuauhtémoc Cárdenas and on the network of clientele mediations that Rosario Robles had both recycled and created. Everything was handed to him on a silver platter, and as soon as he sat down to feast, he politically eliminated his two predecessors.

This elimination produced a dramatic rupture and opened a crack through which a glimpse at the entrails of the mediation pyramid was possible, confirming the fact that the clientele networks which form the base of the urban *cacique*'s realm of power and authority are contaminated by corruption. Actually, corruption is the lubricant that allows the *cacique* machine to run efficiently. If the mediating axles are not greased, those in power at the top of the pyramid are left to their own fate and isolated from their popular base. This is nothing new, but such corruption was publicly exposed in a video shown on a television programme hosted by a professional clown, capturing the shady dealings of López Obrador's right-hand man and leader of the PRD faction in the Assembly of Representatives in Mexico City as he was receiving money from a businessperson, a very close friend of the previous Mexico City government head. Other videos from that epoch, early 2004, revealed the sinister action of the finance secretary of the López Obrador government entertaining himself by gambling in a Las Vegas casino, killing the free time left to him by hidden financial operations which presumably recycled money destined for his boss's campaign.

Besides the great mediation pyramid upon which the populist *caciquism* power is settled, there were two other phenomena – tied to each other – which increased the vote for the Left: the breaking down of the PRI and the deprivation of rights of López Obrador. In reference to the former, it must be noted that the PRD not only recycled a large part of the old PRI ideology but also a very significant number of its leaders who, in the presence of the decay and decadence of the ex-official party, were abandoning the sinking ship. The flow of former PRI members filling the ranks of the PRD grew in direct relation to the polls showing López Obrador to be the favourite in a practically one-man race. When Roberto Madrazo, after a bitter internal fight, was named the PRI presidential candidate, the unrest and discontent of large sectors of that party increased. Of course, the PAN also benefited from the breaking down of the PRI and principally was able to pick up the support of technocratic sectors and Zedillo followers.

The more backward sectors were sympathetic to the PRD, such as those of corrupt syndicalism or those represented by Senator Manuel Bartlett, the demiurge of the tremendous 1988 electoral fraud, who publicly expressed his preference for López Obrador.

The errors committed by the Fox administration were the other great source feeding López Obrador's popularity, principally the ill-fated trial concerning deprivation of rights. With a leader who was complaining every step of the way that there was a conspiracy against him, the worst thing that could have been done was to pursue him through the courts. And that was precisely what President Fox decided to do, to the discouragement of many and the heightened paranoia of others: initiate a judicial process against López Obrador for not having complied with a writ of habeas corpus in an injunction related to the opening of a street which was supposed to be the access to a private hospital. It exploded into a scandal due to the fact that the trial would have disqualified López Obrador from being a presidential candidate. He took full advantage of the proceedings, as if they were a gift from above, to powerfully project his conviction of the existence of a complot to eliminate him from the electoral contest. The PRI, which had boycotted various important reforms the government had proposed to the House of Representatives, enthusiastically supported this foolishness. The result was predictable: the president had to ignore the legal principles he had defended, ask for the resignation of his prosecuting attorney, stop the proceedings and contemplate in dismay how he had managed to extraordinarily amplify López Obrador's strength.

And so, the candidate of the Left was positioned in first place, according to the polls. But from that moment the factors that would gradually weaken his campaign began to operate. López Obrador missed the opportunity to change direction and establish himself as a social democratic statesman and instead stubbornly insisted on remaining a populist conservative.

3. Modern rights

Because of the considerations stated above and after having taken stock of the contradictory political tendencies, I was convinced, as soon as the electoral process began, that López Obrador would most probably lose the election. Towards the end of the race, when the poll results separated the two candidates by one per cent, my interpretation was confirmed. Furthermore I criticized the difficulties the conservative Left was having in accepting democracy and legality. Old 'revolutionary' habits scorning the electoral system and democratic legality had extended themselves and promoted a reaction against the transition process begun in 2000. But, no matter how extensive an antidemocratic reaction there was, I believed a modern civic rationality had now spread considerably among the electorate. To my consternation, as I became aware of the electoral results disclosed by the IFE and the vehement protests of the forces supporting López Obrador, I realized that irrationality was much more widespread than I had imagined.

Many tore their hair out and wailed that thanks to a mysterious fraud – nobody knows whether cybernetic or calligraphic – a conspiratorial gang of traitors to their country made up of corrupt neoliberals, unscrupulous businessmen, fundamentalist priests, reactionary heirs of synarchism and El Yunque, and mud-slinging fascistic manipulators had won the elections. I have already explained that this false perception is one of the causes that has disoriented the Left and is leading it towards failure. Of course, it is obvious that within and around the PAN examples of such hideous characters exist. Fortunately, they only make up marginal political segments.

But yes, there is a vast faction of the hard Right, frequently expressing itself through Manuel Espino, that usually responds to corporate interests – economic and ecclesiastical – and does not believe in the redistribution of wealth as a guarantee of equality and well-being. There is a Right which prefers to be inspired by the furious attitudes of Diego Fernández de Ceballos and in the prescriptions of Luis Pazos, a Right which thanks God rather than the country's citizens for electoral triumphs and which likes to dispel clouds of incense from the thuribles of the most rancid Catholicism.

This hard Right is strong within the PAN, but is apparently not represented by the winning candidate, Calderón. He expresses a modern, centrist, and pragmatic Right, with a pronounced democratic vocation, inspired by a lax and tolerant Catholic humanism. In fact, Calderón does not consider himself to be a right-wing politician, and now that he has won by such a narrow margin, he will have to demonstrate boldly and creatively that fact when rearticulating his political programme. The most obvious aspect, which he himself has pointed out, is the extraordinary emphasis that must be given to policies directed towards combating misery and poverty. But it seems to me that a transition towards new forms of government must also be contemplated. Calderón should direct his positions towards the Centre and the Left of the political spectrum to adopt the social democratic positions that his leftist opponent refused to consider. Will he be able to combine solidaristic, humanistic, and liberal traditions with the social democratic and reformist expressions of the modern Left? The right wing of his party will do everything it can to prevent that from happening.

Obviously, Calderón will be faced with a problem of legitimacy. It is not easy to replace the defunct revolutionary nationalism with a new political culture that can legitimize democratic governments belonging to the transition begun in 2000. A coalition government with a more solid and consistent base than that of the sordid manoeuvres of legislators who froze every possibility of political reform needs to be attempted. Not only a coalition government but also a plural government must be considered. Coalitions correspond to political alliances, especially in Congress. In turn, the plural aspect of government is what assures a democratic style of government and sends symbolic and cultural messages that contribute to stability.

I would like here to point out something that seems fundamental to me: a large mass of citizens voted for the Left not only because they supported a policy favouring the popular classes but also because they rejected the appetites and aspirations of the extreme Right, of ultramontane and conservative interests, of militant and fanatical Catholicism, and of all those anti-modern expressions rooted in anti-communist traditions typical of the Cold War. The majority of voters do not trust the presence of corporate interests, whether they come from the business world or the Catholic Church. Calderón needs to convert himself into a champion of secularism and tolerance. If he makes a change towards social democracy, it means going beyond supporting programmes to fight poverty. With that, he would remind everyone that he won the election not due to divine intervention but to the very earthly political will of the majority. What Vicente Fox called the 'red circle' must not be underestimated. The new government should not let itself be frightened in the presence of the demands of modernity (and postmodernity): the use of contraceptives, stem cell research, the acceptance of alternative lifestyles, the morning-after pill, and other expressions or needs of new ways of living. Calderón witnessed at first hand the political discredit that opposing the use of condoms had for his friend Castillo Peraza and knows the price he himself paid for giving conservative answers to the incisive questions of López Dóriga on his news programme in January 2006. Calderón immediately corrected the situation when he admitted that his answers did not reflect his true feelings on the subjects and he made a significant change of direction in his campaign. Much political ingeniousness will be needed to achieve the combination of the liberal tradition of the PAN and the social democratic ideas, which I believe the government will require. Will this be possible or is it one of those utopias that momentarily lets us escape from cruel reality?

4. The de-modernization of the Left

A significant section of the intellectual elite, which leans towards the Left, has lost its balance, independence, and serenity. The same thing has happened to many intellectuals as happened to the modern reformist and social democratic currents of the PRD and other parties: they were captivated by the populist mirage and have been integrated as an organic part of an 'alternative project of the nation' that seems to be pulled out of an old trunk of obsolete prescriptions from half a century ago. I wonder what it is that could fascinate the hundreds of artists and writers who supported López Obrador's 'alternative project', which under the sign of a stale interpretation of Juárez's ideas, offers a mixture of conservative (lower taxes), nationalist (curb the *maquiladoras*), and antiquated (base development on oil, electricity, and construction) economic measures. It is also a regression to a welfare system that treats the poor as if they were handicapped, sick or old. It is a project in which, pathetically, the only thing it affirms about Mexican culture is that it 'has survived all its historical misfortunes' and is our 'strength and badge of identity'. Some of these intellectuals, who now criticize Subcommander Marcos, will remember that yesterday they were as fascinated with *neozapatismo* as they are today with López Obrador and his populism.

Many intellectuals asked the Electoral Tribunal for a new recount of all the votes, explaining to the judges that they must not use 'legalist arguments', since an exact application of the law would not give legitimacy to the next government. I can imagine the astonishment of the judges upon hearing such a strange demand: it is like asking those in charge of counting the votes not to use arithmetic. The enormous irritation felt by many intellectuals at, among other things, the shameful boorishness of Vicente Fox in relation to the world of culture, is understandable. But they should not allow their indignation to rekindle that old nationalist rancour which, in the name of the Revolution, was determined at all costs to block the road to any alternative that was not its own. López Obrador, in reference to the words of Benito Juárez, has clearly stated: 'The triumph of the Right is morally impossible'. That is how he erects a superior moral rationale over the worldly and democratic vote count. In the shadow of this fundamentalism there were those who – before the final declaration of Calderón as president-elect on 5 August – dreamed of the strike of an avenging lightning bolt that would favour the arrival of an interim Bonapartist president.

The chance to have a modern and rational Left is slipping away. We are witnessing the disastrous process of demodernization of the Left. The driving force of this demodernization is solidly installed in Mexico City and it will not lose its strength anytime soon, since it is part of the powerful apparatus of the urban government. This is most certainly why many people demonstrated their intense dislike of populist demodernization by spoiling their votes or giving their support to a marginal option.

5. Irrational perceptions

In the days before the elections of 2 July it was very difficult to find any intellectual, journalist or commentator who was not convinced that López Obrador would win the presidential race. Within the political circle surrounding the populist candidate, everyone was absolutely certain of winning the elections and they had already begun to hand out pieces of the power pie. They were so sure of their victory that Manuel Camacho, one of their closest operators, extended his hand to the opposition, offering to form a broad coalition in a triumphant article published the day after the elections in the newspaper *El Universal*, written before the election results were known. Despite numerous indications pointing to the existence of a technical tie, a large part of the political class and the intellectual elite thought the Coalition for the Welfare of All would win the elections. I mention these slightly irrational previously-held beliefs because they have had a great influence on the reaction since the election: those close to López Obrador simply could not believe they had lost. Blindly convinced that their candidate was ahead by a 10 per cent margin, the only explanation for the results of the IFE vote count was that a gigantic fraud had been committed. The first thing López Obrador did, before anyone else, was to declare himself the winner by half a million votes, certainly the first number that popped into his head in that moment of stunned confusion (the 10 per cent he had always proclaimed was suddenly erased from his memory).

Moreover, the populist Left immediately began once more to denounce the lack of fairness during the electoral campaign: dirty propaganda which portrayed their candidate as 'a danger to Mexico', the use of federal government social programmes for proselytizing purposes, President Fox's interference in the race, and enormous publicity expenses. Undoubtedly these vices were present, but they were counterbalanced with similar acts by the parties united in support of López Obrador: statements and advertisements denouncing a conspiracy, use of welfare programmes for the elderly and handicapped, electoral activism from the Mexico City government, and mountains of money spent on political advertising. Business corporations publicly supported the PAN candidate and unions that used to be looked down upon as '*charros*' now supported the Left. But there were also unions, such as the teachers' union, that supported Calderón and business sectors that were sympathetic to López Obrador. All in all, it is difficult to determine which parties threw more rubbish out to the citizenry during many, too many, months. The parties carried out a campaign that they cannot be proud of and which convinced many of us that it is necessary to shorten the electoral period and block uncontrolled propaganda in the mass media and on the streets. One or two months of campaigning and advertising on radio and television limited to official times by the electoral authority would be enough. And consequently the amount of money the parties receive would be drastically reduced.

The irrational reactions began to look frenetically for secret and sophisticated algorithms that had fraudulently modified the IFE's electronic systems, and they imagined suspect tendencies during the counting process, erroneously assuming that there must have been a random information flow. They believed they had found the proof of fraud in the dramatic technical error of the IFE, which on the one hand separated some 2.6 million votes in spoilt ballots, and on the other hand, added the more than 11,000 voting centres from where those votes had come to the total percentage registered. When those votes were added, the percentage separating Calderón and López Obrador dropped nearly half a point. The parties knew about and had approved the separation of ballots containing inconsistencies, and so López Obrador acted in bad faith when he made the accusation that three million votes had disappeared or had been lost. Later, the same candidate admitted there had been no cybernetic fraud, but rather that the 'old school' trick of tampering with ballots and miscounting had been resorted to. The suspicion – linked to a culture having a long history in Mexico – remained rooted in a part of society, which before the final ruling of the Electoral Tribunal, was sympathetic to the proposal of a vote recount.

From the moment the IFE figures indicated an outcome, Calderón announced his intention to move towards the Centre and even towards the Left. In contrast, López Obrador once again made the mistake of radicalizing his speech, initiating civil resistance, and calling enormous demonstrations because of the supposed fraud. Calderón did what his opponent would have done if he had won: he offered a coalition government. López Obrador did what the PAN certainly would not have done: resort to acts of rebellion. At the same time, contradicting himself, he turned to judicial lawsuits to demand a new recount of all the votes and to punitively accuse the IFE advisors of being delinquents. In other words, on the one hand he called for a ritual and peaceful transgression of the law, resulting in the occupation of the Zócalo and the blocking of Paseo de La Reforma; and on the other hand he took legal recourse, principally in the Electoral Tribunal, to get a recount or annul the elections.

On Sunday, 30 July, in his speech at the third large demonstration – called an 'assembly' in order to simulate an act of direct democracy – López Obrador proposed that 'we stay here in permanent assembly . . . until the votes are counted'. He then submitted his proposal to a vote and the crowd shouted out its approval; continuing the simulation, he asked those who were in agreement to raise their hands (he also asked those who were in disagreement or who abstained to make it known: to which of course, no one put their hands up). Symptomatically, those who voted *yes* with their hands then voted *no* with their feet: when the speeches were over, the masses dispersed and the long corridor going from the Alameda to Chapultepec appeared desolate, with only a few activists setting up rickety tents along the avenue. Where did the millions of attendees who had agreed to stay go? Why did the masses not stay to celebrate a great popular street party? Why did the people not bend over backwards during the following days to participate in the anaemic permanent assembly that painfully extended itself along more than seven kilometres, provoking more irritation than enthusiasm? Perhaps the people had more sense than their leader.

The explanation of the failure is that López Obrador is the head of a *cacicazgo* in Mexico City, more than of a social movement. Although the protest reaction has the support of some marginal social movements, its strength comes principally from the *cacique* mediation pyramid I described above. *Cacicazgos* and social movements are not the same phenomenon. A theoretical discussion of concepts is not of interest here, but I would like to point out the difference that exists between fluid social processes (which give impulse to the mobilization of social sectors in the defence of their interests) and the most rigid structures made up of support-and-favour exchange channels between power and its social base. Movements usually demand changes in the systems and the *cacicazgos* are components of the system. Some are like rivers and others are like pyramids. The first can stagnate and the second can collapse.

López Obrador is trying to convert a *cacicazgo*, forged from the Mexico City government, into a long-lasting civil resistance movement. It is not an easy thing for him to achieve, but he will try to do it with the support of social groups from different parts of the country, even though their dispersion and weakness make it a very complicated task. In the short run he is building an active focal point of de-legitimization of the transition to democracy, which is aggressively confronting the government. He wanted to prolong his appropriation of public spaces in Mexico City in order to monopolize the official 15 September commemorations through a demonstration at the site where the Cry of Independence is celebrated, and the following day, in a 'democratic' convention, he had the ridiculous notion of appointing an alternative government in the shadow of his purifying fundamentalism. Will he be able to continue to control the support structures of the PRD, which until now have been marginalized? Will he manage to keep the head of the Mexico City government in a subordinate position? We do not know how long he will be able to keep the senators and representatives of his coalition subjected to his contentious and de-legitimizing campaign, before they manage to concentrate their minds on less destructive politics.

6. The rubble

The Electoral Tribunal did not consider the recount of all the votes justifiable but it did order the revision of nearly 12,000 ballot boxes contested by the Coalition for the Welfare of All. This meant a sample (9 per cent of the total) was taken in places where Calderón had more support. If the monstrous fraud denounced by López Obrador had occurred, signs of it would have been found. No such thing happened and the tendencies the IFE had originally reported were validated.

Calderón has been endorsed as president-elect. There have been no grounds for the tremendous scandal organized by López Obrador and the Left will sooner or later have to face the difficult task of repairing the damage caused by their populist *cacique*. How long will it take to begin to remove the obstructive rubble of the protest and the spectacular exhibition of his errors? It seems certain López Obrador will stubbornly refuse to vacate the pyramid of rancour from which he is determined to disturb the democratic institutions. How many scenes of humiliating resentment will we have to put up with, before the more sensible factions of the Left are able to restrain their *cacique*? I hope the most democratic leaders, the most sensible governors, the most intelligent allies, and the most critical intellectuals of the Left intervene. If they do not manage to change the course of this confrontation, they will come up against the solid wall of a legitimate government and a coalition that will represent the large majority of citizens, and the Left will continue to stubbornly kick like a bull in democracy's china cabinet.

2006

Chapter 3

Can the Right be modern?[1]

Mexican political life is going through turbulent times. After a few years of democracy, the 2006 presidential election abruptly cast the country into a sharp and dangerous confrontation between the Left and Right. Although many politicians reject this polarity, which they regard as outdated, a large number of citizens and analysts utilize these two concepts to understand and describe the Mexican political dynamic. While many politicians are pleased to be considered leftists, there are few who accept the right-wing label. However, it seems to me that Right and Left are terms that can be useful guides within the Mexican political geometry if they stop being utilized to depict and disqualify political opponents. I will use these substantial terms here to describe the situation Mexico is going through, which can be summarized as follows: the great difficulties facing us are largely due to internal tensions taking place in the political space of the Right as well as of the Left. I believe the contradictions within each pole profoundly affect the present political situation and impose a damaging confrontational dynamic that muddies our precarious and not yet consolidated democratic system. I have already analysed and written about the contradictions penetrating the terrain of the Left that have resulted in excessive aggressiveness, acute incoherence, and alarming retrocession. I have pointed out the presence of a disastrous paradox: social democratic currents of the modern Left find themselves bound to a populist movement of conservative and sometimes reactionary tones.[2] I now would like to critically examine some of the problems facing the Right and show how they frequently contaminate political life as a whole.

The Right in Mexico has suffered from a chronic problem: difficulty in reconciling conservative Catholic traditions with modern liberalism. The Right that was expressed through the PRI during the former authoritarian regime apparently resolved this tension by hypocritically hiding the problem and crushing the critical voices which attempted to express themselves outside the official system. In a way, this conflict is similar and parallel to that suffered by the Left, with its difficulty in reconciling authoritarian communist traditions with modern democracy.

The tensions between Catholic traditions and liberal pragmatism have had highly complex manifestations and vicissitudes, which I do not intend to review here.[3] These tensions are an inseparable part of the historic fabric that was turning the National Action Party (PAN) into the powerful political organization that governs the country today. However, I do want to determine whether an expression of the old contradictions exists at the present time. I believe these tensions are still being manifested. Their consequences in the development of the PAN and, especially, their effects on the condition of the entire political system should be carefully thought through.

Christian positions are based on the idea that modern democracy is not capable, on its own, of generating the legitimacy necessary to survive and reproduce itself, hence the need to look for a meta-democratic legitimacy coming from the 'human person', which from the conventional Christian perspective, is a spiritualized body or an embodied spirit. When speaking of such a human person it is usually implicitly accepted that non-human, or to put it another way, divine persons exist. Absolute moral precepts that are crystallized in the family, in civil society, and the national state are instilled in the human person. Only this person is capable of reacting morally in the presence of individualistic and hedonistic secularism, which supposedly corrodes institutions. Somehow, the subjectivity of the human person emerges in a cultural order that is expressed as a penetrating popular identity. So it is believed that government can only truly be legitimized if it is capable of being supported by this national ethos, at the base of which is the religious phenomenon of the Mexican Christian identity. The political consequences of these postulates are obvious: legitimacy cannot be generated within a democratic system and so an ethical foundation beyond institutions must be sought. Thus, Rodrigo Guerra has concluded that 'the nation's cultural sovereignty is above State political sovereignty'.[4] This is a religious version of the nationalist theories that for decades validated the legitimacy of the institutional revolutionary government because it was derived from the Mexican national identity. This identity was conceived as an extra-systemic entity that gave support to the authoritarian state.

It should be pointed out that for the last few years, in the political formulations of the PAN, notions such as these of the human person

– together with concomitant ideas of solidarity, subsidiarity, and the common good – have been weakening and receding, paving the way for new ideas.

In contrast to the old Catholic notions, there are those who consider that political action itself can legitimize parties and governments. The liberal influence here is obvious, although it has not been articulated in a coherent and systematic form within the PAN. And nevertheless this is the political expression that has given the party most of its political triumphs. Liberalism is a widespread but diffuse presence in the PAN and it is seen in the accumulation of pragmatism during electoral campaigns, municipal management or business administration. The beginnings of this liberal presence, according to some, can be traced back to the line of thought of Manuel Gómez Morín. It is easy to see the liberal influence in the preference for individual values of citizens with rights, who vote, struggle, and occupy positions in a system that is more and more democratic. Here the individual is personified in the representation and management mechanisms that develop within a state under the rule of law. Both the political system and the political parties have their own legitimating processes and it is not considered necessary to resort to external religious fundamental principles. What is important is the construction of an electoral apparatus, the stimulus towards a gradual gestation process of a modern Centre-Right party capable of assuming government tasks and of managing the development of industrial and financial capitalism. In the 1970s a variant of this form of political action, called participationist, and supported by reactionary business sectors, very harshly confronted abstentionist currents derived from social Catholic thought. But once the internal crisis had passed, the PAN took up its electoral actions again and based on the constitution that governs us – which is essentially liberal – pushed forward the transition to democracy. Alonso Lujambio has said that 'undoubtedly it is the actors who finally define the character of constitutional institutions. In this sense it is clear that the gradualism which the PAN promoted as a strategy for decades ended up marking a rhythm for political change in Mexico'.[5]

This political vision, which exalts individual freedom and has confidence in the markets, is clearly opposed to the concepts that, in the name of Catholic morality, reject enlightened modernity that is believed to be in crisis and attack the pragmatism that separates public life from religious faith, as pointed out by Carlos María Abascal.[6] It is a conflictive fact that Christian-oriented policy makers have come into power thanks to the work guided by the modern liberal pragmatism they scorn. This is a contradiction that deeply permeates the Right and has no easy solution.

By exalting the human person that must be embodied in the State through family and civil society, Christian visions are in fact allowing ecclesiastical powers to intrude upon political spheres.

Not only do these visions defend – and rightly so – every person's freedom to follow his or her religious beliefs, but they also introduce the doctrinal and material corpus of the Catholic Church, with all its corporate strength in Mexico and Latin America, into politics. Of course, we can think that when all is said and done politics is a grand theatre in which the characters represent forces that are not apparent. Let us not forget that the word *person* is derived from *mask* in Latin. And most certainly the person exalted by Catholic thought is the mask hiding the Church. Of course, the individuals defined by the liberal tradition are also theatre performers – actors on the capitalist market stage, in the great forum of this world's injustice and misery. The critical weight of Christian reflections that have denounced how inequality, exploitation, discrimination, and violence are hidden behind the liberal actors is in no way insignificant. These perceptions have led to the defence of the common good, an idea which on occasion has acquired an anti-capitalist tone and implies that corrective measures must be taken in order to attenuate the social ravages provoked by market economy. The idea of seeking the common good, so present in the ideology of the PAN, forms part of the social Christian doctrine of the Church and was brilliantly developed by the great Catholic philosopher, Jacques Maritain.

It is not difficult to understand my resistance – together with that of many Mexicans – in accepting the intrusion of the ecclesiastical corporation upon political spheres. Manuel Gómez Morín himself, who did not care for the Christian-Democratic option, which he saw as a denominational movement, once said that this tendency 'does not conform to the Mexican experience of profound anti-clericalism'.[7] I would add that these positions inject anti-modern conservative elements into the political programme, such as the promotion of the traditional family, respect for the so-called natural order, religious exaltation of national identity, and the definition of life according to ecclesiastic, not scientific, criteria. As a consequence, the legalization of abortion is rejected, birth control methods are viewed with aversion, stem cell research for healing purposes is maligned, hedonism is condemned, especially in its erotic expressions, and the spreading of cultural and scientific values coming from other countries is viewed with distrust.

I am certain that if these types of proposals had been a major and obvious strategy of the PAN's 2006 electoral campaign, Felipe

Calderón would not be the president of Mexico. A party having an authentic modern democratic vocation cannot fail to understand that the family is an institution that evolves, that we do not live in an irremovable 'natural order' but rather in an artificial social order created by man, that national identity is not an eternal essence, and that today's science defines life with a greater depth than any religion. Of course, politicians are free to hold whatever opinion to which they are inclined on these subjects. But a political party, if it wishes to insert itself into society as a modern institution, should not incorporate into its ideology archaic theses that can rarefy the democratic atmosphere in which we Mexicans are just now beginning to live.

From my socialist perspective I can only express my affinity for the enlightened liberalism impregnating many sectors of the PAN. I appreciate the pragmatic scepticism and exaltation of democratic values that have helped the PAN members win elections. But it is troubling to observe that conservative tendencies have considerably restrained the enthusiasm and creativity of modern currents. The dubious amalgam of unimaginative neoliberalism and stale Catholicism that at certain moments influenced Vicente Fox's behaviour – and that made him falter more than once during the final stretch of his government – was a factor which contaminated and degraded the political atmosphere. All of that clearly provoked a decline in sympathies towards the PAN, whose triumph in the 2006 elections was largely due to the tremendous errors committed by the candidate of the Left. The extremely close race, which has left us a cumbersome inheritance, is the product of the accumulation of errors committed by all sides. The presence of fundamentalists of the Left and the Right not only poisoned the atmosphere, but it also undermined the strengths of the contenders and vitiated their behaviour.

In Mexico, if we wish to elevate the quality of our democracy, both the Right and the Left need to become modernized. We need the Right to become liberalized and the Left to become democratized. A more liberal PAN and a more social democratic PRD would contribute to stabilizing the political system in an international context of inevitable globalization. That would contribute to developing democratic pride: a pride based on the confidence that democracy can be legitimized within the social system that nourishes it, without the necessity of adding dogmatic ideologies or religious doctrines. Democracy is not a formality to which a classist content must be added, nor is it a structure that needs absolute values in order to exist. In this democratic pride, a modern Right and Left could converge and they would undoubtedly be competing for a hypothetical political Centre. In this ideal situation – admittedly utopian – there would be a healing of political life that would begin to reduce the detestable role of the former authoritarian party – the PRI – which today, in order to survive, takes advantage of the backwardness and errors of the Right and Left.

But if the backward and barely modern expressions in both the PAN and the PRD persist, we could witness a type of resurrection of the old PRI, which would attempt to once again occupy the spaces it lost in the Right and, at the same time, to recycle populist attitudes that characterized it for many years. It would not be an easy operation, but the foreseeable descent of the Left's electoral weight could accentuate these restorative tendencies. And this restoration could also be facilitated if the modern liberal inclinations of the PAN continue to be held back by the weight of the conservative sectors. Worse still is that this restoration could be the destruction of the political parties themselves, since without them – even though we do not like them – democracy simply cannot exist. The aggressive sudden attack by television monopolies and by business groups against what they call 'particracy' is a very dangerous signal that a social Right, allergic to democracy, is sending today.

Much can be learned from the example of Chile. The right-wing Pinochet-supporting forces in that country have fortunately been contained by a concertation that has united social democrats with Christian democracy, a current that has moved towards the Centre of the political spectrum. It is a good example of just how much can be gained when opposing political forces become modernized and even succeed in forming an alliance in order to confront possible regressions.

The Mexican dictatorship that was not able to pass through the door of the twenty-first century – the last dictatorship to disappear in Latin America, if we make an exception of Cuba – certainly did not have the harshness or aggressiveness of the Pinochet regime. But the problems Chile has faced in transitioning to democracy are similar to those in Mexico. The comparison helps us understand the great importance of leaving behind the political dead weight that stopped Mexico's progress during the past century. Some of that dead weight stems from having wasted opportunities at different critical moments to form an alliance, coalition or Concertation between *panistas* and *cardenistas*, between the PAN and the PRD, in order to confront authoritarianism. Obviously no one is so naive – after the bitter 2006 elections – as to try to attain such an alliance within a short period of time. But, yes, we can aspire to overcome the resentment, the offence and the bitterness which have been the result of failed attempts to come to some kind of agreement that, had they taken form, would have facilitated a transition to a higher level of democracy. And, above all, they would have contributed to overcoming the monstrous social inequalities left to us by the former regime. The 2008 agreement for electoral reform is an encouraging sign that concertation can, for example, stop the voracious power of the monopolies (in this case of radio and television). The fact that the social democratic wing of the PRD agreed to negotiate the 2008 energy reform with the government of Felipe Calderón, even though that decision provoked the rage of the populist wing, is also a positive sign. However, the energy reform was poorly received by business sectors and by some intellectuals who felt it was a threat to the freedom of expression. The supervision of electoral propaganda by the IFE has been riddled with difficulty and missteps, and private television stations have engaged in all kinds of provocations to boycott the reform. Television's duopoly has become one of the most toxic sources of poison for democracy and one of the most notorious culprits of the fractures that weaken the political system, as was clearly displayed by the dirty war of spot announcements in February 2009.

Unfortunately, due to the sharp confrontations between parties, Mexican democracy is in a miry bog and reforms are advancing extremely slowly. The representatives and senators are stuck in a swamp-like condition that threatens to suffocate the proposals for change, and the members of congress's loss of prestige in the eyes of the citizenry is growing markedly. After having made important changes in their leadership, the parties of the Right and Left are at a critical juncture. The parties should, and each of its own accord, take advantage of this juncture to heal the political atmosphere and inject tolerance and reasonableness into their political behaviour. Since there are difficulties hindering the Lefts and Rights from reaching important agreements, the very least we can hope for is that they modernize their respective parties. The PAN has a greater responsibility to do so, since, thanks to the democratic struggle it promoted over a long period of time, it is now the party governing the nation. Many of us are wondering if it will be up to the challenge required by the critical times we are going through. The PAN, at its sixty-eight years of age, needs to have the maturity necessary for a transition that will help get us out of the political quagmire that threatens to paralyse the country.

2007

Chapter 4

The Left – in danger
of extinction?

On 2 July 2006, the political and intellectual elite associated with
López Obrador was absolutely certain that their presidential candidate would easily win the elections. The fact that he lost by very few
votes – less than a quarter of a million – generated great frustration
and even greater uncertainty. It was obvious that an ounce of reason
in the Left's electoral campaign would have been enough to win. If
the President had not been insulted, and called a *chachalaca* . . .[1] If the
spokespeople for the Left's coalition candidate had been less arrogant
. . . If there had been a more reasonable attitude in relation to the
middle class and entrepreneurs . . . If more of López Obrador's team
had been from the Left and fewer had been recycled PRI opportunists
. . . In short, if there had been a more intelligent and less aggressive
campaign, López Obrador would have become president.

López Obrador put together an incongruent mixture whose
fatal combination ended up exploding in his face. He presented a
programme that could scarcely be called leftist, but he presented it
with a very rough attitude. The combination of softness and hard-
ness – of tameness and stubbornness – was catastrophic. Soft ideas in
a hard head could not turn out well. And so the lead that the polls
had attributed to the Coalition for the Welfare of All for months was
squandered. The victory that had seemed to be within arm's reach
vanished.

I do not mean to say that the failure of the Left was its candidate's
fault. I believe these paradoxes belong to a much bigger problem.
For many years, especially after the collapse of the Socialist Bloc, a
slow process of substitution of ideas for feelings has been taking place.
Ideas have given way to passion. Since the traditional ideological corpus was steadily losing the capacity to show the Left the way, emotion

and fervour were increasingly turned to in an effort to prop up the
damaged structure of the progressive parties. To make up for ideological shortcomings, nationalist sentiments, phobias towards rich
countries, and love for the unjustly treated or the dispossessed were
appealed to. If Marxism, in all its different forms, was no longer useful as a way to understand the world, then emotions would be the
recourse to relieve frustration. This is neither unfamiliar nor uncom-
mon: the Right has frequently used religious sentiment to compen-
sate for its deficiencies and emptiness.

These processes are damaging because they are quickly used up and
they lead political forces into dangerous circumstances. There, hatred
for political opponents, seen as the enemy, originates. Politicians' dis-
tressed sobs for the horrendous situation of the poor and the miserable also appear. Both love for the charismatic leader and the lowest
political envy emerge with equal force. Tears hide the lack of ideas
and the angry fist substitutes lost radicalness. All this was concentrated
in López Obrador's electoral campaign, and it alienated the support
of very diverse currents of the Left, who alarmingly witnessed the
leader's opportunistic inclination. The new indispensible intellectuals
pointed the finger at those responsible for their candidate's failure.
López Obrador had lost because the radicals, the Cardenists and the
Social Democrats had not supported him. Elena Poniatowska was very
clear: referring to Subcommander Marcos, Cuauhtemoc Cárdenas,
and Patricia Mercado, she stated: 'If these three personalities had
joined in, if they had not backed out, there is no doubt López Obrador
would have won – but they acted as they did out of envy' (*La Jornada*,
10 September 2006). So, it had been sentiment – envy, and not ideas
– that diverted the few votes López Obrador needed to win. What
really happened was that the candidate of the Democratic Revolution
Party (PRD) was unable to get the support of three important trends
of the Left, largely because he had presented a completely insipid
political programme. In addition, he had preferred to ally himself
with a group of PRI opportunists (as in Chiapas) and ex-officials of
the former regime (especially ex-Salinistas). It is incredible that it has
been intellectuals, supposedly in charge of the creation of ideas and
reason, who have promoted the growing inclination towards feelings,
emotions, and passions. For example, a well-known member of the
PRD, Paco Ignacio Taibo II, made a declaration in an interview when
asked about Octavio Paz: 'I have no empathy with Octavio Paz: on the
contrary. I have absolute hatred. Paz seems to me to be one of this
country's biggest intellectual gangsters.'[2]

Anyone can see that expressions such as these reveal that something has been twisted in the currents of the Left. It has been twisted because instead of doing the most reasonable thing – revise ideas – when confronting a crisis, the Left that follows López Obrador has woven a sentimental blanket of loves and hates to justify its attitudes. And populism has been the best culture medium for nourishing these particular reactions by that part of the Left. Added to a loss of reason is an abandonment of a democratic political culture that implies both accepting electoral mechanisms of representation and exercising a tolerant and negotiating attitude. Perhaps one of the most obvious symptoms of this situation is the summoning to assemblies in the Zócalo by López Obrador, where the leader's decisions are approved by a show of hands. Democratic policies of modern parties are generally successful when there is a margin of mobility allowing pacts, coalitions, and agreements with other political forces to be made. Unfortunately the Mexican Right seems to have an equivalent of the so-called 'secret weapon' that right-wing parties in Israel have relied on: the systematic rejection on the part of the Arab elite. In the negotiation of each peace initiative that implies concessions by the Palestinians as well as by the Israelis (such as the Oslo Agreements), the Israeli Right counts on the intransigency of the governments of the Arab countries. In the same way, the Mexican Right has its 'secret weapon' in López Obrador's rejection of every negotiation or agreement. The PRD's deep-rooted resistance to all pacts or agreements with the Right has provided this 'secret weapon' for many years. Such an aversion to pacts forces the inevitable negotiations to be carried out clandestinely, with grave and scandalous consequences when they are discovered. The results of such openly opportunistic alliances like those in Chiapas, Hidalgo, and Tabasco, where the Left supported PRI candidates for governor and for the Senate (Juan Sabines, José Guardarrama, Arturo Núñez) have been disastrous.

I have insisted in vain, since 2000, on the necessity of the PRD's openly accepting pacts and coalitions with the democratic Right. By not doing so, the Left has been marginalized from the process of the transition to democracy and has indirectly contributed to halting the decline of the PRI, which has ended up presenting itself as an indispensable negotiating party for the procurement of reforms. Immersed in a stubborn sentimentalism, a large part of the Left tends to abandon one of its fundamental axes: equality. The Left has diluted the idea of *equality* to emphasize the importance of *difference*. Policy that changes the rules for specific groups, recognizable by possessing a different character or identity, is given preference over policy that eliminates misery and reduces poverty. Policy stops being oriented towards the distribution of wealth and instead emphasizes the creation of special rights for each social segment. Things are thought of more in terms of *equity* than *equality*, *equity* being the term most frequently used in reference to the multiculturalist – and relativist – inspired policies that practice 'positive discrimination' towards sectors in unfavourable conditions. 'Special rights' (such as the San Andrés Agreements) can be temporary recourses that undoubtedly need to be resorted to. But they should not substitute the much more costly actions that establish priorities for the distribution of wealth, directed towards eliminating the causes of inequality and discrimination, and, above all, directed towards the creation of wealth which, once obtained, can then be distributed. 'Positive discrimination' is a cheap circumstantial option that should not be allowed to erode the principles of justice based on equality and freedom.

But there are other truly unhealthy derivatives that come out of substituting *equality* for *difference*. 'Special rights' are also those that are informally acquired by corrupt clientele groups lending political support in exchange for benefits, such as pirate taxi drivers, street vendors, and squatters. These groups establish their 'difference' by the force of their acts and consequently demand and obtain 'special rights' that are unofficially (since they are illegal) granted to them. This is the *cacique* mechanism that operates in Mexico City and it is one of the most shameful authoritarian and populist traditions that the Left has inherited from the inveterate revolutionary nationalist party.

These populist inclinations were embellished with a curious *pauperology*, elaborated by López Obrador's intellectual advisors, that produced a series of incongruities and banalities that became the twenty points of the alternative project of the nation and the fifty commitments of the candidate. This *pauperology* proposed, for example, the construction of a bullet train for immigrants to connect Mexico City with the United States and a Disneyland for poor children on the Islas Marías. It proclaimed that the best foreign policy is domestic policy and that the future development of the country should be based on oil and electricity. López Obrador's programme was neither radical nor socialist. Nor was it social democratic. It was simply a foolish mixture of populism and liberalism, adorned with vague promises to the poor.

Liberalism in López Obrador's programme? I allow myself the (not very poetic) licence of mentioning the noose in the hanged man's house. In fact, liberalism has not been invited to the Mexican Left's banquet, and if it appears on occasion, it is as the empty seat left by the absence of radical Marxist – or socialist-style – proposals. However, in other countries, principally in Europe, liberalism is not only a venerable constituent ingredient of the Left: it is also an important component of modern social democracy. Social democracy – that great absentee in Mexican political history – is largely a fusion of socialism and liberalism.

The possibilities in Mexico of a social democratic alternative in the twentieth century were cancelled due to the fact that the official hegemonic party crushed the reformist tendencies in the workers' movement, attracted a large part of the intelligentsia to the service of national authoritarianism and rejected the socialist influences in the government apparatus. The result was authoritarian liberalism with irregular and changing doses of economic statism.

To think of socialist and liberal values coinciding today, at the beginning of the twenty-first century, could seem like an extemporaneous option, but perhaps it is not. The workers' movement is marginalized and has remained stagnant in an outdated expression of the old authoritarianism. Marxism and communist socialism are in the process of disappearing and do not seem to be fertile fields that could be worked by a renovated intellectual reformism. Capitalism turned out to be a system that was not condemned to death. On the contrary, it has been capable of major mutations. The proletariat, the supposed burier of capitalism, is a class lacking revolutionary inclinations. Its function in today's societies is similar to that of the peasants of the nineteenth century, whom Marx saw as a conservative class and as the support base for authoritarianism. The fact that Mexico is a backward and poor country does not place it outside the far-reaching tendencies of the postmodern era. On the contrary, besides experiencing the contradictions of the old capitalism, Latin American countries must cope with the latest forms acquired by the market economy: the tremendous effects of the scientific revolution and the shift in the creation of values towards activities that do not directly produce material goods.

Despite these extraordinary changes, it seems to me the confluence of social and liberal traditions remains fertile ground for new ideas. From the Left, this means accepting reform and giving up the hope of a revolutionary process. Not only does that mean renouncing violence, but also accepting that the proposed changes no longer need to be inserted in a quick structural shake-up of the system.

This is not about wishful thinking: it simply must be recognized that today there is no radically different model that can guide the construction of a completely new society. The model we know – socialism really exists – failed and was extinguished more than fifteen years ago. What President Hugo Chávez of Venezuela proposes is nothing more than a grotesque caricature.

The awkward question to be asked is the following: is it possible to have a socialist-oriented government that is capable of effectively and efficiently administrating the new forms of capitalist economy? Can a left-wing party govern the accumulation processes of the new capitalism better than or the same as the Right?

I would like to suggest a mental experiment to continue exploring this line of thought. The ideal social democratic government I am thinking of would have pushed a free trade agreement in 1988 with the United States and Canada similar to the one we have, but it would have directed the transition to democracy not only towards transparency but also towards equality. Did we lose this opportunity in 1988 when Cuauhtémoc Cárdenas could have been president instead of Salinas de Gortari? This theoretical contemplation leads to a real one: a democratic leftist government in 1988 would have placed Mexico in the fast track of an economic development driven by free trade, spurring on a representative democracy and a policy determined to use the resources of the United States to combat terrible inequality and widen the civil liberties space. Something similar took place in that same period in transitional Spain, under the socialist government of Felipe González. But in Mexico in 1988 neither the Left nor the PRI government was prepared for such an alternative. Twelve years had to pass before the transition to democracy arrived, but from the Right.

And since liberalism is not firmly rooted in the Mexican Right either, the transition has stuttered. The PAN is still trapped in the difficulties of reconciling modern liberalism with conservative Catholic traditions. Even though the two right-wing presidents – Vicente Fox and Felipe Calderón – have demonstrated centrist, pragmatic, and liberal inclinations, conservative Catholic currents exert enormous pressure, as was evident in the abortion legalization process in Mexico City in April 2007. The defence of the freedom of women to make decisions in relation to their own bodies is one of the most significant aspects in which, in many parts of the world, liberalism and the modern Left have coincided in a confrontation over the transfer of religious ideas about sin to the secular environs of modern civility, which is where punishable conduct is defined. Catholic conservatives do not defend life, but rather a concept of the soul that attempts to separate a woman's body from the pleasures and desires of this world. Therefore they are against the use of contraceptives and condoms. Let us not forget that Castillo Peraza's political career ended in 1997 when he lost the battle of the condom by condemning its use.

It is not a marginal problem. The expansion and consolidation of secular and lay spaces of modern civility is something of extraordinary importance, because it enables citizens to exercise the freedoms that can drive the country's development forward. This is connected to an idea I have defended for some time: industrial development and the production of wealth – indispensable bases for propelling equality – have a modern democratic culture as their principal driving force. Cultural transformations, not economic programmes, are what are capable of pulling countries out of backwardness.

In the face of these challenges, the Left must be capable of efficiently navigating the market economy ship and at the same time giving impetus to a lay, modern, and civic culture. If it does not attain this profile, I believe the Left will be threatened with extinction. Today, many doubt that the PRD is a left-wing party. Some are looking for new options within the party; others are doing so outside it.

The enormous difficulties for survival confronting the Left can be better understood when remembering that its two biggest expressions on a worldwide scale – communism and social democracy – have had a meagre and paltry presence in Mexico. Communism has almost completely disappeared in the world and only precariously subsists in Cuba and North Korea. Social democracy is firmly present in Europe and South America, but it has never taken root in our country. There were two other important, though relatively marginal, leftist expressions in the twentieth century: populism and the radical ultra-Left. Populism has had an important presence in Latin America: Getulio Vargas in Brazil, Lázaro Cárdenas in Mexico, the APRA of Haya de la Torre in Peru, and Argentinian Peronism (which was originally right-wing). In general, populisms have been slightly democratic conservative forms that have defended premodern privileges or conditions – peasant and indigenous peoples and others.

For its part, ultra-leftism is generally an extreme reaction against the capitalist system and globalization, and its different expressions (Maoism, Castroism, etc.) are usually authoritarian and dictatorial (Peru's Shining Path is the bloodiest example). The peculiar thing about Mexico is that while the two big leftist currents of the twentieth century do not have a very important presence today, its two marginal forms have a conspicuous position: Cardenist populism and neo-Zapatista leftism. It is obvious to me that both forms are a response to the conditions of backwardness and misery, and most probably will tend to recede and disappear to the degree in which the country is modernized (as has happened to the PRI). The problem is that modernization is slow precisely due to the fact that, among other things, conservative tendencies are strong in both the Left and the Right.

The Left could elude the threat of becoming an endangered species if it recovers the exercise of reason and ideas. It has to give up the habit of irrational tantrums and poisonous envies. The good sentiments of love for one's country and the poor are not a substitute for reflection, study, and knowledge. The recuperation of residual forms such as the revolutionary nationalist ideology of the PRI or a radicalization that looks back to the Marxist and Leninist past will not halt extinction either. Of course there is an enormous resistance to change in the old Left, and there are many who brandish the ideas of Slavoj Žižek, that Lacanian Stalinist who has come into fashion, to combat every postmodern mixture of socialism and market economy. This philosopher makes fun of those 'liberal communists' – referring to Bill Gates, George Soros, and the owners of enterprises such as Google and IBM – who maintain that today's capitalism has entered into a new stage. If the Left simply puts itself in the position of hating the new forms of capitalism, pretending they are a re-edition of the old savage capitalism, it will come to the same irrational conclusion as Žižek: 'Liberal communists are the enemy of the true progressive struggle of today'.[3] A good antidote to this conservative reaction can be the studies of sociologists such as Zygmunt Bauman, Ulrich Beck, or Richard Sennett, who pointedly analyse the particularities of the new capitalist society. Also, without a doubt, one must take into consideration what entrepreneurs such as Gates and Soros are doing today.

But this is not the place to explore the new phenomena that are changing the course of the capitalist system. I only wish to say that the conservative resistance in the name of revolution by a large part of the Left will contribute to the acceleration of its own extinction. The exaltation of the 'authentic revolutionary explosion of Leninism' that Žižek makes, inevitably leads him to the chilling assertion that the radical ambiguity of the communist ideology, 'even in its most "totalitarian", still reveals an emancipatory potential'.[4]

Those of us who, without being entrepreneurs, feel like those 'liberal communists' – defined by recycled Leninism as the principal enemy – cannot help but recall the secret telegram Lenin sent to Cheka during the great repressions following the October Revolution. As Paul Berman has reminded us,[5] that telegram gave the order: 'Execute more professors'.

Today, we professors observe with relief the extinction of such atrocious forms of politics, from which – of course – we see no emancipatory emanation.

2007

Chapter 5

The burdens of the Right

When I speak of the burdens of the Right in Mexico I am referring to the knot formed by three traditional threads: the fundamentalist Catholic tradition, traditions linked to the exaltation of national identity, and the traditional sector of the economy. Political currents of the Right find themselves facing the challenge of undoing these bonds in order to reach a modern condition. And this is where we come up against an initial problem: there are many who believe that the very definition of *right* is based on this knot of traditions and that if it is untied the possibility of defining that space will be lost. In this sense, the idea of a 'modern Right', free of these ties, would be absurd. Modernity itself would be in charge of dissolving the notion of the Right, which would evaporate before our eyes, leaving only faint traces of having passed through politics. However, there are modernizing elements that do provide a basis for the continuation of a space for the Right.

In this analysis, I will cite only four sources that keep the terrain of the political Right fertile: The expansion of the most sophisticated sectors of the economy, the influence of world centres of scientific, technological, and intellectual growth, the struggle of the big monopolies to direct public resource administration, and finally so-called globalization. We can recognize the influence of these modernization sources in the growth, albeit too slow, of a business-oriented civil society with civilized habits; in other words, a middle-class civility opposed to the corrupt traditions of the brutal and predatory capitalism that has wreaked havoc in the so-called Third World societies. An educated and cosmopolitan middle class is growing, also very slowly, which is eager to become immersed in the new scientific and intellectual tendencies and that pushes forward the application of new ideas and technology. At the same time, leaders watch apprehensively as their decision margins become narrower due to the powerful pressure large transnational monopolies exert in order to impose their conditions. And the expansion of a Western pragmatic liberalism that gradually abandons traditional cultural values – spurred on by globalization – can also be added. Rodrigo Guerra directly referred to this problem when he wrote: 'The "Right" is suffering its own modern-enlightened crisis. It is not unusual to find leaders of the "Right" who in the past possessed a strong ideological commitment and who today are decidedly dedicated to the study of self-help literature, "management" manuals, and novels converging happily in magic, esotericism and parallel worlds'.[1] It could be described as the sacrilegious mixture of Og Mandino and Harry Potter.

All this constitutes a powerful solvent for traditions tied to the heart of the old Right. But let us look a bit closer at the anatomy of this tying of traditions. Gabriel Zaid correctly stated that we should not ignore the fact that at one time 'Mexican Catholicism dreamt of modernity'; he was referring to three poets (Ramón López Velarde, Carlos Pellicer, and Manuel Ponce) who believed it was possible to be both Catholic and modern.[2] But the dream was forgotten and in 1989 Zaid accepted the fact that Catholic culture was done with, except for its popular expressions and some isolated vestiges. The result has been that all things modern are seen as a threat to Catholic culture which could end up, with luck, as a thin marginal fringe of modern culture or come to a final dissolution. Nevertheless, Zaid held out a slight hope of the possibility of the dawning of a postmodern Catholic culture.[3]

Certainly, with the electoral triumph of the PAN in 2000, there has been a perhaps postmodern impulse that has placed Catholicism at the centre of political culture. Today the Catholic politicians – not the poets – are once again dreaming of modernity, even though the abrupt postmodern ups and downs do not let them sleep in peace. But its forming a central part of political culture does not mean that a culture based on the Catholic faith has been reconstituted. Some believe that this can only happen through the solid hierarchies and teachings of the Church, supported by Catholic-oriented governments. This is precisely where we can recognize one of the burdens tied to the politicians and members of a political party such as the PAN, which gets part of its inspiration from the Catholic religion. As is to be expected, this dogmatic burden has a powerful influence on its vision of education, in which it demands that the teaching of morals to children and youths be ruled by religious precepts. Rafael Preciado Hernández, one of the most important leaders of the PAN, very clearly stated: 'A morality that is not founded on religious convictions, a positive-type "scientific" morality, such as a purely speculative or theoretic morality, is insufficient. Therefore solid religious and moral teaching is necessary.'[4] Of course, these ideas are usually tied closely to the condemnation of the legalization of abortion, the defence of the traditional family, rejection of new forms of family organization (based on same sex marriages) and the revulsion at the use of birth control and scientific stem cell research. These positions are fundamentalist because they defend the immutability of traditional doctrine.

In the absence of an active and creative Catholic intellectual culture, the Church seeks its legitimation in the popular tradition. As the Catholic priest, Rogelio Alcántara, has written, the Church 'believes that certain basic educational contents that must be taught in the country should flow out of our Mexican culture, as from a fountain'.[5] It is in the popular culture, deeply rooted in Catholicism, where Catholic politicians can find the support and justification for their moral positions. It is in the national identity where they can satisfy their thirst for legitimacy. The activities of many right-wing politicians were guided by the dream of an eventual reconstitution of the Catholic identity that had been submerged and crushed by the revolution. Salvador Abascal expressed this very well in May 1942, in his perturbing memoirs of participation in the synarchist movement: 'Just as when you're hungry all you can think of is food, international events are leading me to believe that Democracies are going to lose the war; that the United States will find itself prevented from intervening in Mexico as it had done from 1860 to 1865, and that triumphant Germany will let the Hispanic world reconstitute itself according to its Catholic and corporative tradition'.[6] This reactionary dream, now very distant, sometimes is revived in the much less severe expressions of Catholic fundamentalism. But what predominates is the anguished consciousness of living in a postmodern scenario – as stated by Carlos Castillo Peraza – where man is the only measure of all things and the basis of all value, with no dependency on and at times without any reference to God.[7] In the face of this situation, Lorenzo Gómez Morín has expressed his fear that opposite the growing expansion of liberal ideas, the devout end up constituting a new social stratus, that of the 'closet Catholics'.[8] This group, motivated by charity, would have to live forced to respect false ideas, even though its members believe they possess the truth and that other doctrines are mistaken. This is a very uncomfortable way to experience modernity (or postmodernity). Respect and tolerance for the ideas of others cannot be based on charity and pity felt towards those who supposedly live outside the truth.

We could think that it would be much more reasonable for these Catholics to come out of the closet and accept the alternative that is characteristic of enlightened thought by admitting that moral ideas exist that are not based on religion and that the acceptance of this evidence does not mean that one has to fall into the whirlwind of relativism, where all ethical postulates, even the strangest, most aberrant and most marginal, are equally acceptable. One example is sufficient: this relativism would view the female circumcision that is practiced in some regions of Africa as being as legitimate as the indigenous customs and traditions that marginalize women in Mexico. I will return to the subject of relativism further on, though I would like to make the following clear: it is not necessary to look within the Catholic religion to find the reasons for rejecting these ideas.

However, there is a very strong fundamentalist temptation to look for the legitimizing of Catholic truths within the baroque depths of an essential Mexican identity that would be the metademocratic justification for the political positions of the fundamentalist Right. The revolutionary authoritarianism governments did something very similar for many decades basing their legitimacy on a supposed national identity, an inexhaustible source of revolutionary religiosity that pervaded Mexican politics. The best example of a fundamentalist search for national identity can be found in the pages of the book written by Agustín Basave Fernández del Valle (1923–2006), *Vocación y estilo de México*, published in 1990.[9] The book's subtitle is revealing: *Fundamentos de la mexicanidad (Fundaments of Mexicanness)*. The spirited style of Basave, a Catholic intellectual who belonged to the political elite of Monterrey, promotes an impetuous pro-Mexican vocation in a flood of more than a thousand pages. It could be said he wanted to compose some sort of Thomist *summa* on being Mexican, a true theology of what it is to be Mexican. The first words of this substantial nationalistic torrent are symptomatic: 'There is no hiding from the fact that Mexico is in an inconcealable crisis'. He is principally referring to a moral crisis that is apparent in the lack of solidarity among Mexicans, in exacerbated individualism, and in loathsome egoism. According to Basave, at the end of the twentieth century Mexico had arrived at extremes like none ever experienced before. He picks up the echoes of Ortega y Gasset to declare that Mexico is a country lacking in strength of character. It is a genuine anxiety: Mexico most certainly was living through the cultural and moral crisis that ushered in the end of the authoritarian system. Mexico was (and still is) facing not only problems of development but also problems of civilization.

Unfortunately, many intellectuals and politicians have abandoned the discussion of these problems of civilization. The need to carry out studies on the moral constitution of Mexican culture in order to stimulate a critical analysis of customs should be acknowledged. To their credit, Catholic intellectuals such as Basave have delved into this thorny terrain of morality and customs.

Social and political criticism confronts the rational (or supposedly rational) fibres of society. But a criticism of culture generally comes up against emotional fibres, against textures of feelings, myths, and faith. We anthropologists know these risks well – they are an occupational hazard. Renan had already warned: it is better to be wrong together with the nation than to be very right with those telling the nation the bitter truth.

This brings us to the main argument of fundamentalism: the pretension that certain cultural phenomena are the crystallization of a calling, of a vocation. In the Weberian line of sociology, this idea is applied to scientific and political vocations. Modern societies develop non-religious forms of definition of the individual ego, as a call to carry out certain functions and to respect civil values. This call, the opposite of Jack London's famous 'call of the wild' that draws man towards primitive stages of animality, is the modern vocation that forces man to accept the mandates of industrial civilization.

No doubt this modern vocation has a religious origin. The Protestant Reformation developed the idea beginning with Saint Paul's image of God's saving call. Calvin's vocation ended up being converted into the vehicle that could guide the earthly life of motivated persons, not only through the religious call but also through civil secular work directed towards good deeds. This is where the sources of modern legitimacies based on national identities are found.

But Basave's rescue of 'Mexico's vocation' that is inserted in this long-established religious tradition represents a step backwards. For him, vocation is an inner voice that drives us: 'In order for Mexico's vocation to be carried out, it needed the miracle of Tepeyac' (p. 24). From this point of view it is understandable that Basave dedicated an entire section of his presentation to the criticism of the factors that I expressed in my book *The Cage of Melancholy*, which are – in his words – aberrant and offensive to the Catholic faith of the Mexican people. But the problem is not in the discussion and criticism of differences. The problem with this ardent 'pro-Mexican vocation' is that it defines its enemies with enraged fervour: 'The projection of our Hispanic-Catholic tradition has also had its fierce enemies in our homeland. They are – consciously or unconsciously – the anti-Mexico' (p. 29). He is referring directly to those he calls Frenchified and Yankee-Americanized technocrats. On occasion he brands them as ungrateful.

In contrast, from the perspective of a democratic civility, we cannot speak of enemies but rather of adversaries. Therefore we must criticize this abusive use of national identity as a religious vocation because it leads directly to war against enemies at home and abroad, against Masiosares who desecrate our national soil.[10]

What can this journey towards the sources of a popular Baroque ethos mean? Rodrigo Guerra gives us a disturbing indication: it is a search for forms of unenlightened modernity, which from Pascal to Ratzinger 'takes on all the fundamental questions of the modern project, but gives a neo-Augustinian answer to all of them'.[11] This is a very evocative statement. The Augustinian Jansenists were convinced that man, in his seventeenth-century world, continued to be immersed in the shadow of the Fall, with his spirit clouded, his reason obscured, his capacity to exercise free will greatly reduced and given over to lustfulness. The new Augustinians of today believe we live under similar conditions, submerged in a profound crisis of enlightened culture and liberalism. Contrastingly, this culture is glorified by some modern Pelagians who are enlightened by the liberal values of rational choice. The ancient heretic, Pelagius, in opposition to Saint Augustine, was convinced that original sin had not had historical consequences nor had it damaged human nature and its capacity for freedom of choice. It could be that today we are witnessing the vicissitudes of a confrontation between a traditional neo-Jansenist Right and another modern neo-Pelagian Right. The latter would be convinced that freedom of man, embodied in representative political structures allows us to choose a moral policy without resorting to metademocratic options.

I have pointed out two of the traditional threads that form the knot that hampers the modern impulses of the Right: the fundamentalist-oriented Catholic tradition and the popular Mexican identity understood as a foundation of political life. Now for the third cord: It is a well-known fact that hostile ideas towards modern capitalist development have grown within the heart of fundamentalist Catholicism and that – as I have said – these fundamentalists believe that genuine ethical positions cannot be defined within the democratic system. Luis Eduardo Ibáñez has observed that fundamentalist Catholics have opted to defend and promote traditional and rural guilds in the face of the havoc wreaked by monopolistic capitalism.[12] Fundamentalism frequently glorifies poverty. For example, Agustín Basave praises the value of poverty that characterizes the majority of Mexicans. The basic vocation of Mexico, according to him, 'proclaims the priority of the spiritual, ethical and social focus over mere economic development'. He is convinced that 'poverty is a creator of culture'; and further on states: 'Our poverty urges us to distance ourselves from the fascination with things of material worth'; and praises 'the cultural model of Mexican poverty' that can convert us into a 'humanistic society'.[13]

I believe we are facing a situation that Gabriel Zaid has admirably described in his book *El progreso improductivo* (*Unproductive progress*). In the face of the immense pyramid of the modern economic sector there is a traditional subsistence economy that must be supported. This non-pyramided sector is a vast collection of rustic governments, small businesses, self-employed workers, and non-academic forms of learning and research. Opposite the traditional sector – essentially petit bourgeois – we find the immense pyramids formed by administrative and industrial blocs, large national and international businesses, and powerful teaching and research centres. From the traditional economic perspective, the giant pyramids of modern capitalism are abominable. Progressive ideas usually illustrate the path of social ascension that only looks for equality in the pyramided sector, if even that. So, what Zaid calls the pyramidal obedience market appears. In this market privileged salaried employees, progressive university professionals, and good revolutionary consciences come together. A strange type of progressivist, surrounded by proletarians in Cadillacs – as Zaid states – that blocks the development of oppressed bicycling entrepreneurs, of *campesinos*, of reactionaries, of those crushed by industrial, political, and ideological progress. This vision is heir to leftist sociological theses that defined the so-called internal colonialism and to the proposals that E. F. Schumacher crystallized in his famous book *Small is Beautiful*, published in 1973. Schumacher had converted to Catholicism two years before the publication of his book and he attempted to recreate and broaden the distributionist ideas of G. K. Chesterton in it. As opposed to socialism and capitalism, distributionism encourages the wide distribution of means of production; the objective is, to paraphrase Chesterton, a little capitalism and a lot of capitalists.

The vigorous rejection of socialism by the Right is something that seems natural to us all. Its anti-capitalist attitudes may seem stranger; however, paradoxically, they tend to form part of the burden that ties the Right to conservative, anti-liberal, and fundamentalist positions.

It can be said that, in many cases, the more anti-capitalist the Right is the more conservative it becomes. Nevertheless, the opposite attitude of savage and blind pro-capitalism of some dictatorships – such as Pinochet in Chile – has stimulated a Right that, besides being conservative, is above all reactionary and antidemocratic. It is deplorable that this kind of Right has come into being in Latin America thanks to the support of the United States, the great democratic power. Fortunately in Mexico, this type of Right is virtually non-existent.

I have described the existing ties among three traditional expressions that hinder the Mexican Right – a triptych of Catholic fundamentalism, myths of national identity, and the defence of the petite bourgeoisie. It should be said that these three currents do not necessarily come together to form a coherent nucleus of ideas. The most close-minded fundamentalism can be fiercely pro-capitalist and Hispanicizing. The people's cult to the Virgin of Guadalupe does not necessarily harmonize with the defence of small shop and stand owners, *campesinos*, and rural businesses. Criticism of the pyramidal concentrations of economic, political, and intellectual power is not necessarily tied to the practice of a rancid and outdated Catholicism.

However, there are strong elective affinities among these three traditional expressions. Their convergence usually opens the door to the most conservative currents of the Right, those which have no faith in democracy, block scientific and technological innovations, defend traditional Catholic forms of family organization, support the teaching of religion in public schools, question certain facets of the secular State, dislike foreign cultural influence, and are averse to the legalization of abortion and the use of contraceptives. I would like to give a European example of the concrete significance of the convergence of these three traditional expressions. The Northern League, headed by Umberto Bossi, brings together a pure Catholicism, a cult to regional identity, and exaltation of the small family business. The result has been a dramatic strengthening of an aggressive extreme Right and a successful neocapitalist force.

Paraphrasing Gabriel Zaid, we could say that in Mexico there is a Right that gets around on bicycles and another that gets around in Cadillacs. There is a conservative Right and a liberal (or even neoliberal) Right. I would add that there is another Right which originally got around on horseback and ended up travelling on the authoritarian train of revolutionary nationalism – a train that ended up ploughing into the cyclists and scorning the luxury automobiles, all the while exploiting both. I feel the importance of this 'revolutionary' Right should be emphasized since it has been dominant for various decades. Its most emblematic representatives have been the immensely corrupt Miguel Alemán and the sinisterly repressive Gustavo Díaz Ordaz, who are only some of the reference points in a long trajectory of the authoritarian Right that stubbornly held back every democratic alternative in Mexico for decades. This bureaucratic Right is responsible for the construction of the imposing State pyramid of economic, administrative, union, and corporative interests that jumped from the horse to the train in order to end up appropriating many Cadillacs, so they could transport the docile salaried workers of the institutionalized revolution. This other Right – revolutionary and bureaucratic – has lost its hegemony but it still controls many regions of the country with the old style of governing: Oaxaca, Puebla, Veracruz, to name a few. A typical representative of this other Right, Roberto Madrazo, ran in the 2006 presidential election and lost. Fortunately the PRI is not monolithic: it houses open, technocratic, and modernizing currents such as those that were capable of accepting (and even promoting) the transition to democracy that began with the elections in the year 2000.

Octavio Paz used to say that the Right had only interests, not ideas. This statement underlines a very important aspect: the interests of those possessing economic power are important referents for defining the idea of Right. But interests that can be defined sociologically do not provide an understanding of the wide complexity of the political phenomenon of the Right. The political Right does not necessarily coincide with the social Right. The National Parents' Union is not the same as the Confederation of Employers of the Mexican Republic (Coparmex). The political Right frequently uses religious resources to legitimize itself, and in addition defines itself by its contrast with leftist currents. We can understand that definitions of this polarity depend on the historical moment in which they are made. Therefore, the parameters and coordinates are ever-changing and it is not easy to extrapolate situations from one country to another. In certain places and situations, the Left–Right polarity can almost disappear, whether it is because the parties converge in the Centre of the political spectrum (as in the United States) or because the conditions are so particular that definitions become almost useless (as in Cuba or North Korea).

We return to that triangular nucleus that I have signalled as a heavy burden that makes the modernization of the Right difficult. The idea and sensation that modernity has plunged us into the individualistic materialism which drowns people 'in the vacuousness and frustration of a culture of "useful" things that are more important than emotions and feelings', as Carlos Abascal says,[14] comes out of this nucleus. Since the end of the nineteenth century, the ecclesiastic hierarchy had realized that 'material progress and nihilist individualism lead to unhappiness'. The conclusion is that modernity enters into crisis, to the degree that market materialism and capitalist consumerism expand, leading to a profound dehumanization. Socialist modernity also led to horrendous totalitarianisms that it would be assumed existed in embryonic form in the leftist ideologies that deny the existence of a natural order.

For example, according to Abascal this dismal panorama finds its expression in the fact that even democratic socialism of the twenty-first century 'takes advantage of procedural democracy and market economy' in order to build 'a kind of "relativism dictatorship" that states that there are no universal ethical principles'. These ideas are at the heart of the conservative, fundamentalist vision that defines Catholic values as natural laws out of which correct and universal moral doctrines are born.

The strong argument would appear to be found in the denouncement of relativism. Most certainly we can arrive at the absurd if we declare – in the face of globalization of western values – that *all* cultural, religious, and ideological manifestations are equally valid. From the perspective of this assertion that today has crystallized into multiculturalist currents, each cultural or religious expression would carry with it its own internal rules of judgement about what is correct and what is abnormal and each one of these rules would have the same democratic right to occupy a seat in the grand world parliament. But, the relativist argument does not require the exaltation of universal and transcendental ethical norms in order to be refuted. Relativism refutes itself on its own since in order to be a valid option it must arise from a condition that does not exist: *all* cultural, religious, ethical, and ideological manifestations must be equally relativist and tolerant – something which obviously does not occur. Another condition that relativism would require in order to be acceptable would be an unproven fact: that the limits between each expression were stable and identifiable. Not even the enormous doctrinal weight of the different Christian churches has been able to specify in practice the limits of each denomination. Diversity has long penetrated its bases, especially with respect to religious expression that brings large masses of believers together.

Frequently, relativism is sustained by the necessity of fundamentalism to create an image of a chaotic, disorganized, sinful, corrupt, and decadent world. In the face of this terrifying image, the full doctrinaire force of Abascal's affirmation is expressed: 'Democracy needs absolute values in order to exist'. Of course, these absolute values are those that pertain to the so-called 'human person' defined by Catholic tradition. This fundamentalist thesis is nothing more than the other side of relativism: its absolutist side. Qualifying as relativist the ideas that search for legitimacy in the heart of the political community and democratic agreements is an abuse used to disqualify every manifestation that has managed to escape from stagnant doctrinal precepts.[15]

Finally, I ask the question: why is it important to situate and analyse the burdens of the Mexican Right? Why is it interesting, from a democratic Left perspective – which is mine – to observe and point out the conservative forms of the Right? Of course, we all feel the need to understand the Mexican situation during the turbulent transition to democracy. But I also believe it is necessary to understand that the danger of a restoration of the old authoritarian nationalism continues to exist. The threat of a return of the PRI Right is a fact that forms part of our political panorama. Only the strengthening of a liberal Right and a democratic Left can keep the political tensions of the transition themselves from leading us to a restoration of the rancid authoritarianism of the PRI. Of course, a direct return to the former regime does not seem possible. Rather, it would be a strengthening of a bureaucratic and corrupt political tradition. My fear is that we are facing the possibility of a repulsive regurgitation of the sewers of the former regime – a phenomenon that is not unknown in political history. We have the examples of Vladimir Putin's Russia and in Latin America, the different returns to Argentinian Peronism (especially hideous were those of Isabelita Perón and José López Rega in the 1970s and afterwards that of Carlos Menem in the 1990s).

Hegemony of the conservative Catholic Right can bring about the return of authoritarian nationalism that would attempt to reposition itself on the political scene as the old and faithful guardian of the popular revolutionary tradition. Seen in this light, the panorama seems devastating, dominated by different kinds of conservatisms. I am convinced that we can each do our bit, through exercising a critical and constructive attitude, in contributing to the weakening of conservative attitudes in the different parties in order to make way for more modern and, especially, democratic ideas.

2008

Chapter 6

Populism and democracy in Latin America

In Latin America, populism has been studied by the social sciences with extraordinary creativity and productiveness. Thanks to research and reflections that began more than forty years ago, we now have a rich corpus of ideas on populism available to us that allows the resurgence of this complex political phenomenon to be more easily approached. It is true that to the extent that populism had appeared to be buried or marginal, interest in its study declined. Aprismo, Cardenism, Peronism, and Varguismo seemed to be processes that had died out. Echoes of the populism of Víctor Paz Estenssoro in Bolivia, of José María Velasco Ibarra in Ecuador, and Jorge Eliécer Gaitán in Colombia stopped reverberating. But in recent years the sound of populism's footsteps is being heard once again. Since 1988 there has been a return of Cardenism in Mexico, in 1998 Hugo Chávez became President of Venezuela, and in 2006 two successful electoral campaigns carried Rafael Correa to the presidency in Ecuador and Evo Morales in Bolivia. In that same year an aggressive populist, Ollanta Humala, ran against the Aprista, Alan García. And in Mexico, the populist force of Andrés Manuel López Obrador brought him to a near victory in the presidential election. Years before, we had witnessed the resurgence of populist styles in Menemismo and Fujimorismo. Today there is no doubt that populism is back.

And so it is worthwhile to reread the texts written by sociologists in the 1960s. I will take only a quick look here at those past reflections to serve as a reminder and as an invitation to examine them once again. And I will choose some of the ideas and connect them to my interpretations and proposals. When Gino Germani referred to what he called national popular movements and the populist regimes they established, he listed their principal characteristics as follows: 'authoritarianism, nationalism, and one or another form of socialism, collectivism, or State capitalism: in other words, movements that have combined opposite ideological contents in different ways. Authoritarianism of the Left, socialism of the Right, and a slew of hybrid, and even paradoxical formulas from the perspective of the Right–Left dichotomy (or continuity).'[1]

Here Germani recognizes the influence of the ideas of S. M. Lipset on working-class authoritarianism and observes that this form of political participation of the masses differs from the 'western model'. He maintains that this situation is typical of the underdeveloped countries that are characterized by what he calls 'the singularity of the non-contemporaneous'. This formula is an adaptation of the sociologist William Ogburn's theories of cultural lag that were very influential at the time Germani was writing. This interpretation of underdevelopment as a motley grouping of asynchronous and unequal forms of economic and social development has adopted very different expressions and has become customary. Some examples of this variety are the folk-urban continuum, internal colonialism, dual society, unequal and combined development, or the articulation of different modes of production.

The singularity Germani observes is the appearance of popular movements during the turbulent transitional process of autocratic and oligarchic societies to modern and industrial forms that do not integrate into the political system according to the liberal democratic model, but instead adopt populist expressions (which Germani calls national-popular). This happens because the participation channels that society offers are insufficient or are inadequate.

Another sociologist, Torcuato S. di Tella, adds what he calls the 'blinding effect' to Germani's explanation. In contrast to what took place in the European countries, the underdeveloped world is the periphery of a blinding centre – advanced, sophisticated, and rich – that produces a demonstration effect on intellectuals as well as on the population mass. Mass communication raises aspiration levels and when the lid of traditional society is lifted a bit, the resulting social pressure looks for unpredictable ways out. Because modernization tends to be energetic and fast, social movements are sudden and excessive for a backward economic system incapable of satisfying new demands. The masses that escape from traditional society do not materialize into liberal or working-class political movements as happens in Europe, but rather they are attracted to populist-style demagogical and charismatic leadership.[2]

In addition, Torcuato di Tella defines a new phenomenon: the emergence of what he calls 'incongruent groups'. He is referring to social segments that are dislocated and out of context, such as aristocrats who have lost their fortune and position, the nouveau riche who are not yet accepted in the highest social circles, or displaced ethnic groups. These are social sectors that build up resentment and display bitter and vengeful attitudes against an establishment they feel is unjust. 'Incongruent groups', explains Torcuato di Tella, 'and the available and mobilized masses are made for each other. Their social situations are quite diverse but they have a common hatred and antipathy for the status quo that they experience in a visceral and passionate form. This sentiment is very different from that which an intellectual can develop as a result of his or her professional activities – except when this is also strongly incongruent, something that is not so unusual in underdeveloped regions'.[3]

We can understand the limitations of these approaches that insert the populist phenomenon in the framework of the transition of a traditional society to a modern condition. As such, populism would be an abnormality or an accident that occurs during a transitional process that in developing countries does not follow western patterns. However, if we do away with the lineal or developmental framework, I believe we can salvage at least three aspects of the Germani and Di Tella formulations.

First of all, we can underline the important presence of a large segment of society made up of a heterogeneous mixture of remnants of traditional forms, groups excluded by modernization, aberrant structures of failed economic projects, damaged bureaucracies, disintegrating ethnic groups, street merchants, unoccupied immigrants, hyperactive outsiders, precarious workers, and a thousand other forms. It is a population mass that exists in the incongruent singularity of its non-contemporaneousness and its asynchronism, to use the terms of Germani and Di Tella. It is the heterogeneous mass that populist leaders call 'the people', a true potpourri whose dimension and composition varies greatly in each country and each era. It is not only a characteristic of the Latin America of the 1930s, 1940s and 1950s – we can also recognize its existence today. It is not a phenomenon that is exclusively tied to transition, but rather it is a lasting situation.

A second aspect we can retrieve is the importance given to the speed and aggressiveness that is characteristic of the modernization and expansion of capitalism in Latin America. Here we can also say that it is not a process limited to the transition of backward oligarchic societies to systems of capitalist accumulation and more advanced industrialization. The arrival of new tendencies in Latin America, albeit at times somewhat delayed, occurs impetuously and blindingly, to use Di Tella's metaphor, without waiting for society to be prepared for the changes. All things considered, these changes, like those tied to globalization, have matured in central economies and quickly disseminate their influence toward the periphery, driven by the typical voracity of large transnational companies.

And so the continued presence of the variegated incongruent masses and of dizzying, blinding flows keeps producing important political effects in today's Latin American societies. On a daily basis we can confirm the disorganizing effects and the damage these blinding flows produce in the incongruent masses. As Germani explains, the mobilizations produced by the penetration of frenetic modernization flows on a motley social mass can barely be assimilated and are poorly integrated into political systems. Therefore these movements and these shake-ups turn into the breeding ground for populist expressions. But Germani was mistaken in thinking they were merely the result of the transition of traditional oligarchies to modern societies.

And thirdly, we can reclaim the propositions early Latin American functionalist sociology made about the importance of the charismatic leader in populist phenomena. The authoritarianism that usually characterizes populist movements, as well as the regimes they establish, is associated with the personal strength of leaders whose discourse tends to be an ideological mixture that revolves around the exaltation of 'the people' – a vague notion that is related to the existence of an evil social duality that needs to be eliminated. Of course, the presence of strong and charismatic leaders is not exclusive to populism. What has been observed as strictly populist is the ideological discourse of the leaders and the particular mediations that connect them to their supporting masses. It is the multi-ideological character of a highly emotional discourse that directly appeals to the heterogeneous, offended, and multiclass mass. But even though the populist discourse is aimed at the heart, so to speak, of the people it directly convokes, the movement tends to organize – especially when it gets into power – a complex clientele-type mediation network. It must also be added that the cult to the charismatic leader is associated with a generalized statolatry.

* * *

I now wish to refer to the prickly problem of the definition of populism. The tremendous difficulty in defining the term has repeatedly been pointed out and Ernesto Laclau has even gone so far as to say it is simply impossible to define. In 1978 he had correctly stated that populism could not be defined as the expression of a social class (such as the *campesino* community, farmers, or the petite bourgeoisie) nor could it be defined as the aberrant result of a transition of traditional society to an industrial society. The comparative study of movements and regimes qualified as populist reveals many inconsistencies when an attempt is made to lump them all together. Cases in point are nineteenth-century Russian populism, Egyptian Nasserism, Argentinian Peronism, and Venezuelan Chavismo. If fascism and revolutionary socialism are added to the mix, as Laclau suggests, then it becomes obvious that a definition of populism capable of taking into account such a wide and varied range of political situations is impossible.

There is confusion, to a great extent, because in order to escape from the explanations of populism that diminish its functions and the process of change it is a part of, ideological dimensions are favoured as the base of its definition. And of course it is also very difficult to make generalizations here. Laclau found the formula he proposed for explaining populism as an ideological phenomenon in the Althusserian-Marxist idea of 'interpellation'. Populism would be a discourse that interpellates 'the people' as subject, in order to oppose hegemonic power. The interpellation can oscillate between two poles: socialism, the highest and most radical form of populism that is designed to suppress the State as an antagonistic force and the opposite form, fascism, that is directed to preserve the totalitarian State. There is a range of populist ideological phenomena between the two poles, one of which is Bonapartism.[4]

According to this interpretation, even though it is understood as an essentially ideological phenomenon, populism can be expressed in very defined forms as well as in undefined and confusing manners. Therefore, practically any ideological expression can be populist. According to Laclau, the origin of populist interpellation is historically linked to a crisis in the dominant ideological discourse that in turn is part of a much more general social crisis caused by a fracture in the power bloc or by the inability of this bloc to neutralize the dominated sectors. At that moment a class or a fraction of that class emerges that has to resort to 'the people' in its opposition to the hegemonic ideology.[5]

Recently Laclau has continued, broadened, and modified his definition of populism. He wishes to offer a logical and rational platform for the different populisms in Latin America. What he calls 'popular reason' must be capable of transforming the criticism of negative aspects (the emptiness of discourse) into the exaltation of its virtues (the leader). Now he substitutes the idea of *interpellation* with that of *construction* of a popular identity. In this ideological process, the diversity of popular demands is condensed by the populist discourse into a set of unifying equivalences. These equivalences annul the signifiers that are characteristic of heterogeneity and produce a void. It is in this vacuity of populism – which has been described as ideological vagueness and ambiguity – that Laclau paradoxically finds its rationality. Populist rationality consists of being able to embrace plurality and to construct it in an empty expression: 'the people'. Here Laclau introduces an explanation of the central role of the leader: the unit of discursive formation is transferred to the nominal order. The 'naming' of the leader fills the void and gives meaning to the people. Thus, says Laclau, 'the name becomes the basis of the thing'.[6] The popular identity constructed in this manner, guided by its leader, then demands representation (total or partial) in the power spheres.

It is a merely rhetorical solution to the problem of defining populism, now carried out with the help of Lacanian psychoanalytical instrumentation. It has the peculiarity of clearly and precisely centring the problem in the empty notion of 'the people' and in the nominalist process of its invention. Here is not the place to go into the subtleties of Laclau's new interpretation, but rather to underline the fact that his alternative to the functionalist analysis consists of placing the explanation almost entirely in the terrain of ideological discourse. This is an important limitation but it allows him to escape the critical implications that the use of the term 'populism' has and to open the doors to its intellectual exaltation. However, it seems nearly impossible that the leaders of today's populism would accept the name applied to their movement. They fear the name is the basis of the criticism of the political thing they promote. It does not seem likely that a populist leader would see Laclau's proposal of using the name of the strange thing they promote as a rational choice.

* * *

The brief critical reflections I have outlined are points of support from where I can look for a different interpretation. It seems to me we can consider populism to be a form of political culture, more than the materialization of an ideological process. In the centre of this political culture there is certainly a popular identity that is not a mere empty signifier but rather an articulated set of habits, traditions, symbols, values, mediations, attitudes, personalities, and institutions. We know full well that identities, whether they are national, ethnic, or popular, cannot be defined according to fundamentals or essences. As Jacques Derrida expressed so well, 'what is proper to a culture is to not be identical to itself'.[7] 'The people' of populist culture is foremost a myth; and as we know, myth constitutes a cultural logic that allows contradictions of very different kinds to be overcome.

Therefore we can trace genealogies and traditions in the populist cultures and show influences and connections among them, but it is impossible to define a catalogue of traits common to them all. Past populisms of the nineteenth century in the United States and Russia generated traditions and patterns that we can still recognize in their distant descendants. For example, there is George Wallace or Ross Perot in the United States and in Europe there is the Italian agrarian *squadrismo* or the intellectual *Strapaese* movement, in France Pierre Poujade, and the outbreaks of right-wing populism in the post-communist countries.[8]

The same can be said of the old Latin American populisms and their relation with the new expressions: we can recognize inheritances and political lineages, but it is difficult to fix a precise common pattern that defines them as a whole. In contrast we can recognize the existence of a type of family tree of Latin American populism that, even though it has some traits in common with European and North American traditions, constitutes a trunk of a particular political culture that we can recognize, but not lock inside the cage of a definition. In this political culture we can recognize authoritarian habits, clientelistic mediations, anticapitalist values, nationalist symbols, charismatic personalities, statist institutions, and above all, attitudes that exalt the underdogs, the simple and humble folk, the people.

To recapitulate, it could be said that populism is a political culture that is fed by the agitation of the social masses characterized by their assorted asynchronism and their reaction against rapid flows of blinding modernization, a culture that in moments of crisis tinges popular movements, their leaders, and the governments that eventually form. And such a situation can occur at very different historical moments. In Latin America populism emerged during what has been called the crisis of the oligarchic States as well as, more recently, following the impact of powerful globalizing tendencies. It has emerged in large-scale political processes as well as in limited and relatively marginal demonstrations. It has influenced the formation of national governments or has filtered through only as a particular style of certain leaders.

Even though, in my opinion, populism is principally a cultural expression, it should not be thought of as a glove that can be used on either hand or as a form that can house any political content, from Nazism to communism. It is true that populism usually presents a jumble of ideological expressions that are often contradictory. Its coherence does not come from ideology but rather from culture. Therefore fascism and communism, that have been blocs of monolithic ideological coherence, are phenomena that pertain to a very different political order. This does not mean that there have not been expressions of populist culture in fascist and communist States such as in Italy or in China. And inversely we also find fascist or socialist ingredients in populisms, as in the case of Peronism or Cardenism.

Nevertheless, populist phenomena tend to lean towards the Left and occupy social territories that the progressive parties or groups strive to penetrate and represent. As a matter of fact, the most important definitions of populism came into being in the Marxist discussions at the end of the nineteenth century, and of course it is to Lenin that we owe the critical and negative perspective from which the Left tends to understand the phenomenon. As I have mentioned, very few politicians, if any, accept being described as populist. In general, populism has been viewed with much criticism by both the revolutionary and the reformist Left and it is frequently rejected by the Right. These criticisms and rejections often produce a strange blindness that hides the populist syndromes appearing in the camps of the Left and the Right.

I would like to add the fact that motley asynchronism tends to be seen as a sign of failure of the neoliberal project and the flows of blinding modernization are interpreted as the malignant effects of Americanism and globalization. Therefore it is natural, for example, that the conquests of Bolivian populism are seen by many as a process of the Left, as the transition to a fairer and more authentic democratic society. Actually, this populist project received its inspiration for that incoherent conglomeration of ideas called 'twenty-first-century socialism' from the diverse fringes of social and political unrest. And its rejection of rampant modernization is the base for promoting its characteristic primitive and demagogic anti-imperialism.

* * *

The era in which the Berlin Wall came down and practically all social-ist States disappeared coincided with the fall of the Latin American dictatorships and the emergence of democratic regimes. This coinci-dence marks the evolution of the political panorama in a profound way. Ever since political democracy has substituted dictatorships in Latin America it is possible to confirm, in the spectrums of both the Left and the Right, an oscillation towards the Centre and an abandon-ment of extreme positions. The heirs of right-wing military and pro-coup groups are in the process of becoming extinct. The map of the Left has radically changed: guerrilla and revolutionary options that fight for pure hard-line socialism are disappearing and at the same time alternatives in favour of elections are advancing. This shifting toward the Centre was verified in a conspicuous, and even spectacular manner, in the campaign of Brazil's Lula in 2002, when he finally won. And it has also taken place in Chile. These two countries are examples of the extinction of dictatorial and antidemocratic right-wing expres-sions as well. This would seem to indicate that the tendencies are moving toward a strengthening of democratic and social-democratic currents that are competing for positions in the Centre.

But things are not so simple. In Latin America the old authori-tarian political cultures that can be labelled populist, although quite different from one another, have not disappeared. Possibly the most lasting and persistent examples of this old political culture are the Mexican PRI system and Argentinian Peronism. Unlike other popu-lisms these were a statal expression, a governmental phenomenon tied to power in which a leader or caudillo with a large social base surfaced. Lázaro Cárdenas and Juan Domingo Perón, however, also exemplify the huge disparity in the political situations from which they arose.

Populist repercussions in the Latin America of today have caused unrest over the entire continent. Its important manifestations in Bolivia, Ecuador, Mexico, Nicaragua, Peru, and Venezuela have ser-iously modified the political spectrum of these countries. To my way of thinking, they have brought about a particular distortion in the currents of the Left that, instead of approaching social-democratic stances (as took place in Brazil, Chile, and Uruguay), they have been drawn to the old populism and have received the direct or indirect influence of the dictatorial culture of fossilized Cuban socialism. In Peru, the outbreak of populist nationalism was prevented by a bland and weakened form of the same political inclination (the Aprista, Alan García). Peronist populism does not seem very virulent in Argentina and in Mexico the aggressive and conservative attitudes of López Obrador led him to electoral defeat, albeit by a very slim margin.

Current populist tendencies are an important phenomenon that should concern us; a phenomenon that connects us with symptomatic and fundamental problems, as I have said. I am referring to the presence in many Latin American countries of cultural forms tied to populism that are much vaster and deeper than their strictly ideological expressions. I am speaking about a popular culture that is nationalist, contentious, revolutionary, antimodern, with supposed indigenous roots, disdainful of civil liberties, and not very tolerant. Of course, my favourite example is the culture of the PRI, the one I am most familiar with and the one I have had to endure the longest. But the significant presence of similar cultural expressions can be recognized in various countries. It is important to emphasize that this type of popular culture lives in symbiosis with a barely developed Right that stimulates it, and that is usually allied with unrefined entrepreneurs and fast-and-easy profit-lovers not inclined to long-term economic undertakings, afraid of free trade, who make their fortunes in the shadows of politics, and who are frequently cloaked in corruption. A curious variety of this populist culture of the Right developed in Mexico, driven by a revolutionary and nationalist bourgeoisie (although attached to the dictatorial institutionality of a single party).

* * *

Populism, when understood as political culture, does not usually constitute a consistent socio-economic and political development alternative. It is not even an option for a socialist model or a means of accelerated capitalistic growth. After 1989 the construction projects for a socialist State have been a genuine rarity or a tragic anachronism. There are, however, examples of this type of project in Latin America and they are related to each other: the strange Venezuelan populist socialism that Chávez proposes is connected with the obsolete Cuban revolutionary model. But we can imagine that this option is not viable and that, sooner or later, it will disappear. Venezuela's oil reserves can possibly last 200 years but the Chavista model seems as incapable of reaching modern development as the exotic project of Muammar al-Kadhafi in Lybia in the 1960s. More and more Venezuelans are noticing the deficiencies and backwardness of Chávez's project: that was why he lost the 2007 referendum in which he proposed to modify the constitution and keep himself in power. I also suspect that it will not be long before we see Cuba shifting towards the peculiar transition that is 'market socialism', as has happened in China.

On the other hand, we have populist governments that have accepted the rules of the globalization game and of the capitalist orbit while at the same time propelling some kind of social politics that is both clientelistic and welfare-based. In certain cases, as demonstrated by Alan García in the 1980s and Menem in the 1990s, they were bad administrators of a simultaneously aggressive and stagnant capitalism. An especially tragic and corrupt variant was that of Fujimori in Peru in the 1990s. We can conclude that populist political culture mixed with a neoliberal economic agenda is very costly and is not able to push the growth and creation of wealth that could be bases for social programmes in the areas of health, education, and the reduction of poverty. This failure is related to some extent to the difficulties of becoming globalized and of attracting investments, complications that are inherent in a government that is subject to populist cultural logic.

So then, what repercussions can populist cultures have on democratic institutions? This is a burning question in several countries and it is not easy to arrive at a conclusion since we are facing processes which are still ongoing. The typical coup d'état of the extreme Right, led by the military against populist governments, is probably a remote alternative. In fact, we have an example in the recent past: the disastrous evolution of the Fujimori government. Is it possible that the Bolivian, Ecuadorian, and Venezuelan processes are headed towards an authoritarian condition, similar to that of Fujimori, but in a Leftist mould? If the populist political culture is deeply rooted the answer could be affirmative and we should expect to see these countries enter into a cycle of growing authoritarianism.

But there are other possible paths for governments of the Left with solid popular bases. The most recognized and substantiated is that of social democracy, as has come about in Chile, Brazil, and Uruguay, where the governments of Bachelet, Lula, and Tabaré have clearly moved away from populism. These social-democratically oriented governments, just like the populist governments, are centred around the need to propel equal and inclusive societies that protect the poorest and most vulnerable groups. But there are big differences: on the one hand we have a defence of representative democracy and a politics that clearly accepts that globalization is currently the most important vehicle of change. On the other hand, populism promotes confrontational attitudes towards businesspersons, looks upon foreign investments with suspicion, is aggressively nationalist, and pushes forward political reforms that contribute to the continuation of the leader's authoritarian power; reforms that weaken electoral democracy in favour of alternative mechanisms of popular integration and participation of a mobilizing, clientelistic, and corporative nature.

Certainly in many cases, the party system and the political elite have exercised power – in a democratic context – in such a corrupt, unequal, irrational, and inefficient way that they have led their societies to catastrophe. Such was the case in Venezuela, whose former democracy – inaugurated in 1959 with the fall of Marcos Pérez Jiménez – was so putrefied that it fostered a huge popular mobilization against the system.

* * *

I would like to conclude with some reflections on what could be considered the longest-lasting and most stable experience of populism in Latin America. Here again I am referring to Mexico, my own country, which can be seen as an example of the high price a society pays when populist culture is so deeply rooted that it is adopted by both the political Right and the business elite, who end up being the hegemonic group Mario Vargas Llosa ironically called the 'perfect dictatorship'. This dictatorship was so perfect that for decades it was the envy of many Latin American governments and the model for some alternative politics, such as the era of Velasco Alvarado in Peru and the first Nicaraguan Sandinismo. The Mexican governments that took their inspiration from populist culture – institutional revolutionary nationalism – stayed in power for seventy years and uninterruptedly sustained what was the most difficult authoritarian regimen to put an end to in all of Latin America.

For many years one of the principal political problems in Latin America has been to civilize and modernize the movements of the Right. The Mexican Right – locked in the old populist system – was one of the most difficult to deal with, and this explains why Mexico was the last Latin American country (except for Cuba) to enter a process of democratic transition. The institutional revolutionary dictatorship, with its large popular base, was a system that seemed too perfect and secure to the political elite to be abandoned. Finally, in the election in 2000, an independent party of the Right defeated the official party and a democratic era was inaugurated under the presidency of Vicente Fox.

At the same time a current of populism led by Andrés Manuel López Obrador was enjoying great popularity. This return to populism, now channelled through the opposition of the Left – the PRD – rather than the former official party, doubtlessly had its way paved by the government of Vicente Fox, which had let itself be tempted by the apparent charms of a managerial culture as a legitimizing base. Such action fomented disillusionment in broad social sectors and rankled groups of multivaried asynchronisms and incongruities that reacted against the young democracy that had been established only a few years before. This at least partially explains the enormous growth of the alternative populist constituency in 2006. The rest of the explanation is the fact that López Obrador, from the government of huge Mexico City, weaved a giant web of clientelistic and *cacique*-like mediations that were the material and political base of his campaign. But this populist boom was ephemeral and lacked what was needed to win.

The defeat of López Obrador in 2006 can largely be understood in terms of his reaching back to the old revolutionary nationalism and the PRI style of doing things that had been the cause of so much damage over the years. He was unable to position his electoral campaign in the new democratic political culture. He took managerial culture head-on, calling it fascist in his fits of exaggeration. And despite having a lukewarm and contradictory programme, he gave the impression that he was an aggressive revolutionary that would not allow the rich to continue getting richer. He was also very offensive towards the middle class. The same incoherence of his programme led many people (many potential supporters) to believe that he was not going to really carry it out.

The Mexican example is useful for proposing a final reflection. I have pointed out the limits and even the dangers of two opposing cultures: the technocratic or managerial culture of the Right and the populist culture of the Left. Both alternatives can erode the legitimacy of the democracy that was attained with such difficulty; whether it is through the belief that politics can function by means of the relative automatism of the market economy or through wanting to substitute representative democracy with *cacique*-like, messianic, or caudillo-like forms of political control. What we need is a modern democratic culture, the same culture whose growth in Mexican society eroded populist authoritarianism, but has not yet expanded and taken root with sufficient strength. This democratic culture has been driven by the biggest political tendencies, from social democracy to liberalism, which, after the fall of the bipolar world in 1989, are in the process of renovation and require important changes. These changes must be focused on the modification and renovation of the political culture of the political parties, and not only in order to achieve the necessary legitimacy of the political system. Political democracy, as a system of representation, does not resolve the immense problems of misery, of extreme inequality, of the lack of productivity, and of backwardness. Political programmes in themselves cannot eliminate poverty in Latin America. For a long time we have known that culture is a powerful motor of economy – a fact that economists are beginning to recognize. And, of course, cultural structures undeniably can be and have been powerful burdens that hold back economic prosperity.

And so what is at stake is not merely the movement of pieces in the worldwide or continental political game of chess. Cultural processes are behind the technocratic and populist proposals that can speed up or slow down the well-being of Latin American societies. Therefore politics must be a civilizatory process. In Latin America we urgently need to civilize the political class and democratize the popular culture. If not, instead of accumulating wealth and well-being, we will continue losing for decades to come.

2007

Chapter 7

The Mexican hydra: the return of the authoritarian party

The fractures in the political currents of the Left and Right in Mexico have fostered the strengthening of the representatives and heirs of the former authoritarian regime. From the year 2000, the disastrous inability of the democratic forces of the Right and the Left – the Partido Acción Nacional (PAN) and the Partido de la Revolución Democrática (PRD) – to converge, brought about the growth of a political reservoir, apparently mediating and centrist, that was fed by the backwater of the old authoritarianism. In the face of the 2012 presidential election the consequences of these fractures are obvious: the PAN looks like a party worn out by two terms of solitary governing and the PRD appears to be a force now in plain electoral decline. Neither the Right nor the Left, for different reasons, was able to strengthen itself into a fully modern option, while in contrast, the party of the former regime has become markedly stronger.

The Partido Revolucionario Institucional (PRI), the authoritarian party, came out ahead with voters in all the polls carried out in 2011. They show that favourable opinions towards this old party have been on the rise since 2009, while support for the PAN and PRD is gradually decreasing. The PRD is in third place, at just over 15 per cent.

Why is the PRI on the rise? This party has made no apparent remarkable change, it has not essentially modified its programme, it has not publicly criticized its authoritarian past, and its leaders have kept the old style of speaking and behaving intact. The PRI does not appear to have absorbed new ideas or to have created a new and original vision of Mexico. Reading the documents of this party is like plunging oneself into the flattest greyness imaginable: there is nothing there of interest, nothing new, nothing imaginative. For more than ten years, from the time of the government of Ernesto Zedillo to the 2006 elections, the PRI suffered an obvious electoral decline. After losing the presidency in 2000, its worst moment was the 2006 election in which it was relegated to a third force. The spectacular clash between Felipe Calderón and López Obrador that same year indirectly stimulated the PRI's recovery; its two challengers – the PAN and the PRD – apparently did all the work, by not being capable of joining forces to promote a profound change in the system.

And so, quietly, and in the shadows, a very important mutation has occurred in the PRI: it has become a real political party. It must be remembered that the PRI, during the decades of authoritarianism, never was an authentic party. It was the highly centralized electoral agency of an authoritarian system, in charge of recruiting the support of the population through corporative means. It formed a bureaucratic appendix that was activated during elections and that, with varying degrees of effectiveness, administered the necessary doses of fraud. Seasonally, it became converted into the channel that the president and powerful political groups used for handing out the positions of representatives, senators, and governors. This mediating apparatus was controlled from the Ministry of the Interior. Strictly speaking, the PRI was not a government party: it was a mere government extension.

Starting from its distant origin in 1929, the official party was an instrument that enabled the unification of different revolutionary factions and the ordered channelling of power struggles. It later began to change into a simulation of a party, a hard outer covering that helped give the political system a democratic appearance. Of course it was a complicated space, intertwined with conflict and intrigue. Its worker, *campesino*, and 'popular' sections encouraged extensive mediating structures. The official party was an immense state apparatus that specialized in manipulating electoral processes.

This enormous apparatus had been steadily wearing itself out and could no longer function adequately, at least since the 1980s. But when it lost the 2000 election, the PRI suffered a massive blow and began a process of decline. Its central head – the President of the Republic – was cut off and the apparatus ceased to function as before. Suddenly the PRI bureaucracy found itself orphaned.

Wounded and weakened, the PRI became fragmented and sought refuge in the shadow of power of the many governors it still had left. These governors were like the heads of a political hydra that had gone mad from having lost the central power. The disputes were intense and rough. One need only recall, for example, the fights that led the leader of the nation's teachers, Elba Esther Gordillo, to leave the PRI, and the powerful governor of the State of Mexico, Arturo Montiel, to fall from grace, accused of corruption. But the fragmented PRI was resting on a very nourishing breeding ground: the power of the governors who, on a small scale, maintained systems that were seemingly drawn from the old national authoritarian model, as shown by Joy Langston's excellent studies.[1] The big problem with the heads of the hydra is that when one head is cut off, several grow back in its place, just as happened when Heracles fought the classical Greek monster. The mythic hero discovered a way to keep the heads from proliferating: he had to cauterize the monster's wounds with fire. This is exactly what the PAN governments could not or did not want to do.

Cauterizing the political wounds that remained open after the defeats of the PRI would have meant burning the corrupt social fabric in order to substitute it with new forms of politics. But President Vicente Fox wasted his strength and popularity as the leader of the democratic transition and abandoned the tasks of pushing a vast renovation of the political system forward. Instead, he pushed forward a rightist federalism that ended up strengthening the governors and, thanks to his administrative inefficiency, promoted a fragmentation that eroded the central government. By doing so, the regional support bases of the PRI were kept alive. Just a few changes in the apparatus were enough to restrain or channel the fights among governors, senators, and representatives and to slowly convert the old machine into a political party capable of competing in the new democratic context. These adjustments were skilfully made after the 2006 presidential election and their effectiveness was felt very soon in the intermediate 2009 elections when the PRI became the primary force in Congress.

1. Coalitions and political culture

It is symptomatic that right before the 2012 elections, a government coalition proposal is being promoted, when for two terms in office, the political leaders were totally incapable of advancing any such thing. The fact that very influential leaders of the big parties have proposed a coalition based on an explicitly programmed agreement, so that a future government without a majority in Congress can function 'harmoniously', is revealing. This was the proposal in the manifesto 'For a Constitutional Democracy', published on 10 October 2011, in which prominent leaders of the PAN (Javier Corral, Santiago

Creel), the PRD (Cuauhtémoc Cárdenas, Marcelo Ebrard), and the PRI (Manlio Fabio Beltrones, Francisco Labastida) presented the idea of building a government based on pluralism. This is something that should have taken place twelve years ago, but neither these leaders nor others showed the slightest indication of moving towards a coalition government. Who knows why they did not promote back then, what they say needs to be done now. In fact, missing from the list of those who signed the manifesto are the politicians who will be the presidential candidates: Andrés Manuel López Obrador, Enrique Peña Nieto, and Josefina Vázquez Mota. The PRI candidate, who is certain of his victory, prefers to restore the so-called governability clause in order to achieve the desired 'harmony' between the presidency and the Congress; and the candidate of the PRD has repeatedly stated his profound aversion to coalitions with parties he considers to be tied to the 'power mafia'.

Nevertheless, the idea that coalitions are necessary ingredients of politics in a democratic context has extended considerably, albeit in many different forms; from its expression as the most effective formula for defeating the old authoritarian party, to the determined effort to have the governing party gain a majority in Congress through coalitions. There is great concern over the combination of a strong but increasingly ineffectual presidential power, a weakening of the plural legislative power, and a strengthening of the power of governors. All kinds of formulas have appeared to remedy this situation, or at least to temper its most disastrous consequences: parliamentarization of the political system, consecutive and unlimited re-election of legislators, two-round voting, federalism reform, restoration of the so-called governability clause, reduction of the number of plurinominal legislators, a coalition government, cutbacks in public financing of the political parties, etc. But any one of these changes requires an indispensable previous step: The coalition or alliance of political forces to approve these and many other necessary reforms. This is not likely to occur before the presidential election.

What does this situation tell us? I believe we are facing a very precarious and fragmented democratic culture. A new civility has not impetuously expanded that would oblige the political parties to operate with tolerance and responsibility. A culture of dignity and democratic pride has not been developed vigorously enough. To the contrary, we are still oppressed by the enormous weight of the old authoritarian political culture that is deeply rooted within Mexican society. It is the rancid culture of the PRI. Even though it has receded in many areas, it has extended outside of the party that sustains it and has invaded the PAN, the PRD, and the political elite.

This phenomenon is more evident in the spaces of the Left, where a mixture of nationalism, populism, and the cult of the revolution has slowed down the expansion of modern expressions of democracy and socialism. There has been an increasingly extended influence of leaders that came out of the PRI, bringing the old authoritarian culture with them. But the governing PAN is not exempt from this type of contamination. When all is said and done, the interests of the Right have always adapted very well to the customs and traditions of revolutionary nationalism.

We are facing a paradoxical situation: even though the weight of the traditional nationalist culture is less, a new modern and democratic attitude has not been consolidated. The precariousness of modern political culture is largely due to the fact that the party that headed the democratic transition, the PAN, has not been capable of offering and propelling a new civility, because the burdens of conservative Catholic tradition have been too heavy and it has not had an influential intellectuality to light the way towards a modern Right. The consolidation of a new democratic culture has also been held back by the Left. Despite having a large group of intellectuals, it was not able to overcome the trauma of having stood on the sidelines of transition.

For all these reasons it was not possible to have a coalition of modern and democratic forces of the Left and the Right that would not only carry out substantial political reforms, but also foster the growth of an alternative culture, opposed to the nationalist and revolutionary traditions of institutionalized authoritarianism. Another of the reasons that explains the strengthening of the PRI can be seen in this calamitous situation. Now it is members of the PRI that are the most enthusiastic about rescuing the idea of the coalitions, in order to fortify their party's return to power.

2. Violence and narcotrafficking

The PRI has also been strengthened by the extraordinary growth of violence. The predominating image of Mexico in the worldwide mass media is that of a country submersed in a sea of bloody violence that has produced tens of thousands of homicides tied to the struggle against narcotrafficking. Mexico is reflected in the local and international press as a country subjugated by the disasters of an uncertain war on the drug cartels; Mexico has inherited the image held by Colombia in the past. It is regrettable that this image has coincided with the process of the transition to democracy that began at the end of the twentieth century. To a large degree, the spectacularity of the crimes has hidden the complex problems the Mexican political system faces.

A strange paradox has been observed during the first years of the transition. The sensation and belief that the country was experiencing a hellish existence of growing violence was predominant in Mexican public opinion. However, a study by Fernando Escalante showed that this was not really the case.[2] Between 1992 and 2007 the homicide rate actually made a notable drop year by year. Of course, this gradual descent of violence was not occurring in all corners of the country. There were regions and cities, especially along the border with the United States, in the northern part of the western Sierra Madre and in the western regions of Guerrero and Michoacan in which homicidal violence was contrastingly on the rise. The decrease in violence had more clearly occurred in municipalities of fewer than 10,000 inhabitants in the centre and southern parts of Mexico. Taken as a whole, national tendencies were positive and did not justify the generalized sensation of insecurity that many citizens perceived and that the press and television denounced with alarm. To a certain extent, this paradox is explained by the fact that the losers of the 2000 presidential election, both the dethroned former official party and the party of the disillusioned Left, bolstered the perception that Mexico was sinking into a morass of violence. The political currents of the opposition promoted the idea that the arrival of democracy had brought the violence and extension of narcotrafficking along with it.

The general downward trend of violence stopped abruptly in 2008. This was the year in which a dizzying and extraordinary rise in the homicide rate began, once again ascending to the levels of two decades before. There is no doubt that this brusque change was related to the intensification of the fight against narcotrafficking unleashed by President Calderón. The most conventional interpretation of this dramatic rise in violence refers to the fact that the repression executed by the army, the navy, and the federal police has upset the balance that existed among the drug trafficking groups. This has caused an increase in the competition to take over the vacant spaces, together with the resulting violence among the criminal organizations that are fighting over the territories. The high homicide rates are concentrated in regions where the war on crime is being fought the hardest – regions that already had elevated levels of violence. However, as Fernando Escalante has keenly pointed out, this only partially explains the extraordinary rise in violence since 2008.[3] There have been far more deaths than those attributed to disputes and retaliations among drug traffickers or to the extension of their criminal activities into other areas (kidnapping and extortion). In my opinion Fernando Escalante is on the right track with his explanation. He believes there is a power crisis within the municipal police that has partly been caused by the intensification of military operations. Mexico suffers the problem of a traditional complicity between criminals and the municipal police that are in charge of maintaining a certain kind of order in illegal and informal markets. The crisis of these abusive, corrupt, and inefficient police forces has left a void that compels many individuals to pro- tect their interests through violence, adding the defensive and violent attitude of these persons fighting for their illicit properties and busi- nesses to the clashes among criminal groups. The intensification of the fight on the part of the central power against narcotrafficking has accelerated the crisis of what Escalante defines as a system of political intermediation based on the negotiation of selective transgression of the law. This system is viewed by many as an onerous inheritance from the former authoritarian regime, during which the governments of the PRI made an infinite variety of pacts with criminal organizations. Seen from this perspective, the problem is that chaos and anomie are throwing organized crime into disorder and confusion during the transition to democracy.

The drama of violence triggered by the fight against narcotraffick- ing has overshadowed the democratic transition. A very alarmed por- tion of the population is leaning towards a return to that 'system of negotiation of selective transgression of the law', believing that this will bring a certain tranquillity. That is one of the reasons why the former authoritarian regime, the PRI, is presently at the head of the electoral preferences in regard to the 2012 presidential election.

It is important to look beyond the repulsive and horrifying spec- tacle of homicidal violence that has clouded the panorama. Behind the spectacle we must find the threads that move transition and that explain the deterioration of the mediating social fabrics that ensure the stability of civil society. The political analyst Ricardo Cayuela has expressed this very strongly: 'Mexico's problem is not drug traffick- ing, the ostentatious cherry topping illegality's cake [. . .] This cake is made out of a permissive society that allows the law to be broken and of authorities at all levels of government who show us that the law is an element that is, in a word, negotiable.'[4]

President Calderón's decision to escalate the confrontation with organized crime is not something that was planned with anticipation or that the government was prepared for. Nothing in the political programmes and proposals that came out during the election campaign of 2006 suggested that the winning candidate would unleash a war of such proportions. This outcome was a premature decision by Calderon's government to strengthen its legitimacy, which had been greatly weakened after the electoral process. A third of the electorate was convinced there had been fraud and the political group headed by López Obrador was determined to provoke a collapse of the government. The escalation of the war against narcotrafficking definitely strengthened the government's legitimacy but at the same time it muddied the waters of politics and created many dramatic and unexpected effects that overshadowed the problems characteristic of transition.

3. Restoration?

All the polls have shown that, in the last five years, support for the PAN and PRD has been gradually decreasing, while sympathy for the PRI has grown. The two parties that won the most votes in the 2006 presidential election have been surpassed by the PRI in the surveys on voting intention. This party is close to reaching 40 per cent of the intended votes, while the PAN has attracted 25 per cent, and the PRD a little more than 15 per cent. Many voters (between a fourth and a third) still have not decided how they will vote or say they will annul their votes, making all predictions unreliable. The support for the PRI will probably decrease in the next months and both the PAN and the PRD will see support for their candidates grow. The Left is in the most difficult situation, because its path is filled with obstacles and destruction that it has placed there itself and that caused a dramatic drop in voting intention and the highest percentage of rejection and animosity. The Left's campaign of condemning the ravages of the war against organized crime (whose homicide figures are often exaggerated) has damaged the image of the Calderón presidency, but it has also contributed to increasing sympathy for the PRI, rather than for the PRD. Their strategy has backfired; the president maintains a 64 per cent citizen approval rate while support for the Left has not grown. To the contrary, the idea that it is necessary to negotiate with the drug trafficking cartels has become legitimized and it is something the Left would obviously not do. Whereas in contrast, the PRI has witnessed the growing impression that if it wins the election, some kind of arrangement will bring peace.

If the Left does not get back on track, we will find ourselves facing the danger of a strengthened bipartisan system in which the two hegemonic poles belong to the Right. The Left will remain a marginal and residual sector that will have to accept having a critical testimonial function, embittered by the fact that it let the opportunity to become a great modern socialist party escape.

The Right that came into power in 2000 has not managed to develop the liberal traditions with enough impetus to be able to confront its conservative burdens. Illusorily committed to small-minded disputes and short-term pacts with the opposition, it stopped using the immense resources of the federal government for modernizing the political culture, transforming the archaic education system, breaking up the television duopoly, and combating the powerful hydra that has been growing under the state governments.

Meanwhile, the principal head of the hydra – the governor of the State of Mexico – grew with great force. It is symptomatic that the now ex-governor and PRI candidate for the presidency, Peña Nieto, constantly refers to the PAN and PRD as 'opposition' parties; he has never presented himself as what he really is: a politician of the opposition. For the PRI the opposition has always been the others. When he registered himself as the PRI candidate on 28 November 2011, he stated:

> 'I do not expect, nor does my party expect, the *opposition* to speak well of the PRI; lately, the *opposition* has been speaking about, signalling, and criticizing the PRI a lot [. . .] the PRI is not going to play the *opposition*'s game.'[5]

It is curious that he uses this old way of speaking while at the same time he denies that the PRI is returning to the past. Perhaps he is right: the PRI actually has never abandoned the past, therefore it cannot go back to it. He most certainly represents a large part of the country, that part that is still submerged in the culture and structures of the former regime.

For many leaders of the PRI, their party has not been in the opposition: it has conserved and broadened a solid state power bloc that today adds up to twenty governorships. In many of these places the PRI does not need to restore anything, because little has changed.

Half a dozen governors, having recently escaped from the PRI due to internal fights, were taken under the wing of opposing coalitions and rose to power without ever really having taken a step outside of the nationalist and revolutionary institutional culture. All of this shows the immense influence of the customs and traditions of the PRI. But a complete restoration of the former regime on a national scale is impossible. The PRI is now a party living in a new context and therefore its internal fractures will be all the more damaging and threatening. In the places where the PRI has been fractured and therefore lost elections, there have been outgrowths of democratic civic culture. And even the PRI factions that have abandoned their base are carriers of an authoritarian culture. They provoke new situations that, over time, can erode the old habits. In addition, it will be very difficult for a member of the PRI as president to destroy the power of the governors and place them under the executive power once again.

Together with the 2012 presidential election there will be elections for renewing governments in six places. Among them, there are some where the PRI could regain power, such as Mexico City and Jalisco. If that happens, the danger of restoration will be intensified and the political panorama will darken considerably. Under these circumstances, alliances between the democratic parties of the Right and the Left would need to be formed in order to curb the authoritarianism of the PRI, although such an occurrence at the present time seems very difficult.

4. An abstinence syndrome

The resignation of Humberto Moreira from the presidency of the PRI at the end of 2011 helps to remind us that this party is historically tied to the corruption that has corroded the political system for decades. The PRI does not have an absolute monopoly on corruption, but without a doubt, it is the party that most obviously symbolizes impunity, electoral fraud, disrespect for the law, and the simulation and deviation of government resources. The inexplicable increase in wealth of many PRI politicians is proverbial and has been converted into a typical image familiar to us all. The use of public funds for political purposes is not a legend, but a reality that Mexico has experienced for decades. There is a long history of dishonest manipulation of electoral results, and today one third of the population believes there will be fraud in the 2012 elections, according to opinion polls. Thanks to the culture of corruption that was sustained for many years by the PRI, many people today distrust all politicians and all elections. It surprised no one when the national director of the PRI was forced to resign because he was suspected of having falsified documents to hide the fact that when he was governor of Coahuila, he amassed a debt of 36 thousand million pesos that nobody can account for. Many people are convinced that corruption is a trademark of the PRI and that from Miguel Aleman in the 1940s up to Carlos Hank or Raúl Salinas de Gortari more recently, the list of PRI members suspected of embezzlement is unending. We understand very well the significance of César Garizurieta's well-known phrase that the Revolution did justice to the politicians who firmly believed that *not* living off the budget is living in the wrong.

Corruption is widely seen as the lubricating grease that keeps the machinery running efficiently, that keeps everything flowing smoothly. It is revealing that the PRI presidential candidate campaigns with the slogan of efficiency (the title of his book of propaganda refers to an 'efficient State' and to a 'democracy of results'). If we want things to work efficiently, we have to grease the system, the attorney general's office or the bureaucrats, the customs agents or the traffic police. This is how advantages are obtained, from building permits, water permits, or land use permits – even to speed up legal paperwork – or permits to set up businesses. Businesses in Mexico apparently can spend up to 5 per cent of their annual incomes in extra-official payments to public servants. Eight persons out of every ten see the judicial system as corrupt. Of course, all this is part of a complex institutional and cultural network that has existed for decades. Corruption is only one of the facets of a much greater phenomenon. In the centre of this phenomenon is the PRI political culture.

A fact that needs to be considered is whether the possible return of the PRI to the central power would actually be nothing more than a symptom of the putrefaction of the political system, a sign that the ailing system needs the old 'efficiency' that lubricates the rusted wheels of government with the customs and traditions of corruption. I wonder if the rise of the PRI is not the strange abstinence syndrome of a society that needs a dose of the old drug that had kept it tranquil. It would be the symptom of a society full of fear that, as a reflex, resists abandoning the old political culture; that resists giving up deeply rooted habits.

Many politicians will object to this conclusion. They will say that the real problem in Mexico is not cultural, but structural. I believe the same idea by which problems are viewed as structural is part of the old political culture, the same culture that blocks all change to the system's structure. In order for there to be structural changes, there has to be growth of a culture that channels social and political energies in the proper direction. Tocqueville discovered this long ago. He understood that customs give the most solid support to democracy. But the term *custom* is a translation that does not take into account the nuances of the original French concept: *mœurs*. In addition, Tocqueville explained that he used the term in the ancient sense of the Latin word *mores*, that does not simply mean customs or 'habits of the heart', but rather the mass of notions, opinions, and ideas that make up the 'habits of the spirit'. The *mœurs* take in all the moral and intellectual status of a people. It can possibly be compared to the 'spirit of capitalism' that Max Weber spoke of, in the sense of a modern *ethos* derived from Protestantism. I believe today we can translate the concept of *mœurs* as that of culture, in the way anthropologists use the term.

We received a good illustration of the backwardness of political culture from the PRI candidate, Enrique Peña Nieto, at the Guadalajara International Book Fair on 3 December 2011. He rightfully became the laughing stock of a good part of Mexico not only because apparently he has never read a complete book in his entire life, but also because he is 'incapable of activating neurons when confronted by the unexpected', as Jesús Silva-Herzog said.[6] The PRI candidate functions, as so many other politicians of his party do, with discipline and by instinct, but 'he is not a modern politician. Listening to him is like hearing an old record; seeing him is like going back to a past time', states the same author. The problem is that perhaps that time is not completely in the past and that Peña Nieto is possibly the best example of the abstinence syndrome of that part of society that is still addicted to the old structures. During the transition to democracy, that part of society has suffered unbearable tensions from experiencing the restriction of its traditional habits and customs and therefore has looked for the restoration of the old unguents that were injected into the system. It is likely that the hydra that continues to live in the territories of the former regime will win the election in 2012. But the hope remains that those still addicted to the old political culture will manage to overcome their fear and anxiety.

February 2012

Part II

Culture and Democracy

Chapter 8

Intellectuals and scholars facing democracy

While in other parts of the world intellectuals seem to have turned into a kind of species in danger of extinction, in Mexico the collapse of the authoritarian regime has been the driving force behind an enormous expansion of intellectual spaces. The age of writers' packs and intellectual caudillos has ended, bringing about an extraordinary increase in the number of voices that express their ideas, their interpretations, and their predictions. Newspapers, magazines, radio, and television accept a host of intellectuals in their spaces who, following an old tradition, are convinced that they have something to say about anything and everything, and that everything can come under the control of their inclinations and likes and dislikes. Naturally, those who consider themselves 'experts' on a certain topic watch in dismay as their traditionally specialized domains – in academia or in technocratic spaces – are invaded by an overwhelming flow of commentators that filter through the cracks. This mass of opinators that has disparagingly been called 'commentocracy' is quite heterogeneous and varied: there are writers with academic ambitions, intellectualized journalists, scribbler politicians, politicized professors, displaced artists, and all kinds of people that feed their vanity and fame with their appearances in the mass media. Nonetheless, they form a great multitude of public intellectuals that encourage political life with their discussions. I will first comment on this new massive intellectuality to then discuss the problem confronting those who work in academic environments.

It seems to me that this assorted mass of intellectuals is a product of the transition to democracy. On the one hand (the optimistic one) it is the core of the healthy critical mass that every democratic State requires. But on the other hand (the pessimistic one), this social group incorporates a particular guile, typical of democracies that lack historical tradition. It includes all kinds of characters, a veritable Court of Miracles made up of academia escapees, pretentious journalists, literary fugitives, hopeless ideologues, unemployed technocrats, foolish politicians, refined bureaucrats, and many other specimens. A middle class that is easily frightened by the challenges of democracy views these figures with alarm and the new political elites of the Right look upon them with contempt. Strictly speaking, not all of these characters can be considered intellectuals. But if indeed they are not, at least they form part of the mediating cluster that has always surrounded those who, with their reflexive attitude, *do* hold the title.

One of the most serious problems within Mexican culture is that these cunning creatures of democracy spurn or distrust their own mothers and they feel abandoned in a melancholic Mexico, burdened with suffering and sin. My point is that ten years after the political alternation strongly marked an era of transition, a large number of the country's intellectuals believes that democracy has still not arrived, that it came into the world deformed, that it is merely an empty form, that it is paralysed, that it is of poor quality, that it is blocked, that it is covering up an oligarchy, or that it is stuck in the past.

This peculiar melancholy manifests itself in very different ways; from the most basic complaint against democracy for not freeing us from poverty and backwardness, to the over-elaborate political reform proposals designed to return us to a situation in which the president has a majority in Congress, as was the case in the days of the authoritarian regime. Unfortunately, this melancholy is tainted with a vague longing for the past in which both a supposed benevolent protector that was the State and a comprehensive hegemonic official party were very carefully guarding the well-being of the citizens.

Many believe that we have gone from a superficial, opportunistic, mafia-like, and solid intellectuality to a postmodern, marginalized, depressive, fragmented, and incoherent one. This vision is perhaps an exaggeration, but it reflects aspects of the new reality, which gives rise to the question: how is the new intellectuality connected with those in power?

I have already described the most obvious manner: a stream of commentators flows from this intellectuality that pours ideas out over a part of society and over the political class through the mass media. Its purpose is to directly or indirectly influence the organisms of power. But now there are new problems: the political function of intellectuals becomes uncertain due to the peculiarities of the democratic electoral struggle which oblige them to increasingly substitute the old

intrigues and political scheming with more or less clear public definitions. This forces many of them to maintain a more forthright and
open relationship with the political power. An intellectual of the Left
can no longer simply chronicle events in code, full of cryptic references, or publish brilliant analyses full of structuralist riddles that only
the initiated can understand. The writer of deep right-wing leanings
can no longer make nationalist and revolutionary speeches in order
to then charge under the table for consulting services and for round-
ing people up and transporting them to political meetings and to the
polls, as was done in the past. And furthermore, the old co-optation
mechanisms are broken or lifeless, even though many regional governments have managed to revive them. Today the most autonomous
critical intellectuals are definitely able to operate in more spaces, but
not without having to endure the traditional quotas of marginality
and indifference.

Under these new conditions there was a significant phenomenon,
the consequences of which we are still not able to measure. I am referring to the irresistible attraction of getting close to political power
that captivated a great number of intellectuals in the last presidential
election. The magnet of the powerful Mexico City government and
the fascination for being very near the person who was considered to
be the certain winner of the presidential election produced a great
whirlwind that sucked in an important segment of the nation's intellectuals. This strange phenomenon can be attributed to the fact that
intellectuality had been immersed in dismal black humours, leading
it to attempt to repeat the actions of the old intellectuality during the
authoritarian regime. But now this had to be done in the light of day,
in public, and under the spotlights of the media. Instead of establishing hidden and discreet connections with those in political power, as
was done in the past, now it was necessary to actually plant oneself in
the Zócalo in support of the one all saw as the future president.

The difficulty that there was in understanding defeat, combined
with the discovery that they had been bedazzled by the stale populism of a *cacique*, has sunk many intellectuals into a desperate political gloom. The worst has happened: attracted by power, they were
left empty-handed after having sacrificed their ideals on the altar of
a withered myth. The bitterness of failure has been dominating the
anger about an electoral fraud whose existence was never convinc-
ingly proven.

It seems to me that this bitterness is one of the motors that is pump-
ing a dense flow of deception and melancholy towards an important

sector of public opinion. In addition, there is the distress created by the dramatic confrontation with the drug traffickers, by the inability of the leaders, and by the incongruence of the political parties. And the economic crisis has brought more bitterness to the panorama.

Due to all this, it may seem strange that someone would dare say that at the beginning of the twenty-first century Mexican intellectuals have incurred very serious irresponsibility by not pushing forward pride, or at least pleasure, in the fact that the country managed to escape from the authoritarian webs in which it had been held prisoner for nearly the entire twentieth century. A majority of intellectuals – who to a great extent propelled the democratic changes with their critical attitude – refused to collaborate on the construction of a new democratic political culture. Fear seized many: a terror of being assimilated into the Right that was at the head of the first governments after the arrival of democracy has paralysed those who should have rationally promoted democratic pride as a substitute for authoritarian patriotism. The rational impulse has been very weak, which explains why too many intellectuals continue to be looking backwards. I sense that they are not communicating with the new generations and that they have been left stranded in the past century.

* * *

I now wonder whether the academic intellectuality, especially that which is tied to the social sciences, is in any condition to offer us keys for understanding the transitional reality in Mexico and in the world. I want to make one thing very clear: it is extremely difficult for the social sciences to perceive their own condition and to assess the development, the limitations, and the insight of studies that are carried out in Mexico. This lack of ability on the part of social science to recognize advances made in its name is an adverse signal, intimating its critical condition. For a good number of years now, many persons have suspected that the social sciences are in a difficult situation. People have spoken of the breakdown of anthropology, the crisis of sociology, the sterility of history studies, the corruption of law practice, the backwardness of economic analyses, and the uselessness of psychology. However, these perhaps excessively pessimistic views cannot be easily sustained since we lack the instruments for measuring the condition of the social sciences in Mexico. But nevertheless, we can suppose that this same lack of critical studies on the social disciplines is an indicator that we are facing an abnormal situation. Many of us who work in the social sciences feel discomfort and perceive preoccupations around us. The uncomfortable question is being asked: is there a serious shortage of critical analysis in Mexico that causes worthwhile works to be ignored, while afterthoughts or even stupidities are overrated? With the avalanche of opinators and commentators stimulated by the democratic transition, the valuable work of many scholars certainly runs the risk of being buried. At the same time, in this new situation, much research is seen under a new light, oftentimes exposing investigations as irrelevant and of poor quality. I believe there is a consensus in this respect: the social sciences do not tend to examine their own condition and they do not seem to measure up to the democratic transition that demands a critical and creative attitude. This situation becomes obvious if we consider the fact that academic journals review very few studies and there is practically no discussion of the researchers' ideas. Critical analysis in the non-academic press – supplements and cultural magazines – is somewhat erratic and often depends on ideological criteria or on group interests, even though controversy is more frequent there. It is very rare to find review articles that evaluate the advances made in a particular subject. Likewise, books do not tend to critically present preceding studies that refer to the subject being dealt with.

What is it that inhibits critical evaluation and analysis? We can point out several immediate causes: the influence of persons in academic positions of power that block the work of those who do not share their interests or ideas; the excessive presence of a mediocre, sterile, bureaucratized sector that is indifferent to what goes on around it; a lack of funding to the social sciences due to the dominance of the so-called hard sciences; the equalizing potlatch effect that blocks support to those considered to excessively stand out above the rest. Added to the stunted nature of critical analysis is the fact that the excessive praise of a given work is often due to the fact that the author exercises or has exercised powerful bureaucratic or governmental functions. Here we come up against the complex problem of creation models for students and young researchers. If the models to follow are empty and unsubstantial works, a multiplying effect of mediocrity is established and a low creativity level is institutionalized. This excessive worth given to expendable works is usually strengthened by the defence of local glories in the face of foreign currents. Instead of raising the bar to compete on an international level, it is lowered in the local arena so that competitors of doubtful quality are protected and promoted. The result is the formation of bureaucratic clots in the network of communicating vessels that should be irrigating and nourishing intellectual and academic work.

This does not mean we should favour the work of those who study the researchers rather than stimulate the direct study of social reality. Prolonged immersion in one's own ink and the practice of contemplating the navel of the discipline itself frequently results in those typical texts of theoretical and methodological recommendations that ask others to do precisely what one himself or herself is not doing. Nor should we focus on the production of exegeses and hagiographies of authors in the social disciplines. Incentives to carry out research and opening up the results to criticism can be more interesting and creative. It is necessary to escape from the vicious circles of excessively carrying out historiographies of historiography, sociology of newspaper clippings, political reconstructions of ethnic ruins, psychology of abstract entities, or hermeneutics of economic and legal texts. At a given moment these closed-circuit exercises can produce something of interest, but in general they contribute to the asphyxiation of the social sciences.

All the factors I have pointed out (and other similar ones that could be added) are important and should not be minimalized. But I think we can detect certain problems behind them that let us assume that a kind of transition appears to be starting in the social sciences. I am only referring to certain subjects I can reflect on that are linked to my interests as an anthropologist and sociologist. I am not attempting to generalize my conclusions or criticisms here.

Since the 1950s – or perhaps before – the social sciences have revolved around the real or imagined needs of the national State. Anthropology and sociology in particular were trapped in a contradiction: despite relying on the nationalist mythology, they looked down on the study of cultural symbolism and the institutions that legitimized and sustained the national State. They focused on certain themes: economic inequality, dependency, underdevelopment, the backwardness of the rural and indigenous population, marginality, dualism, the national character, the national bourgeoisie, demographic growth, etc. By looking for greater scientific support in economics, the social sciences found a dead end and were unable to dispel the mystery they were obsessed with: the causes of backwardness and underdevelopment. In a brief evaluation of social studies that I made in 1997, I came to the conclusion that the sociologists who inherited and continued this tradition believed that dependency and globalization (or, as some prefer to call them, underdevelopment and neoliberalism) had kept Mexico from developing a consistent and strong civil society. The process had been catastrophic; fascism or chaos threatened the system, and the solution, if there were a glimpse of one, would have to come from supporting the soft forms of authoritarianism – semi-democratic and populist forms – or from a more or less revolutionary national salvation alternative that would pave the way for a new type of economic development. Globalization was naively expected to weaken the imperialist forces of the United States.[1] In this tradition, other perspectives were taken into consideration such as the cultural and symbolic dimensions of socio-political reality, resulting in opposing ideas: the Mexican system had its roots in a solid civil society that contained keys to explain the backwardness and nationalist authoritarianism.

In Mexico the social sciences were at times an incoherent amalgam of Marx, Durkheim, and Weber – a difficult-to-digest mixture that was recycled with variable doses of Leninism, structuralism, or functionalism. In the tendencies that were obsessed with the problem of dependency, Tocqueville's great theme, democracy was conspicuous by its absence and was sidestepped even in those texts that supposedly were studying it. A book that was symptomatic of the social science situation in the 1960s is *El perfil de México en 1980*,[2] which put together the presentations of a symposium organized in 1970 by the UNAM (National Autonomous University of Mexico) Institute for Social Research to illustrate the future of the country. In this reunion two themes were virtually non-existent: democracy and the 1968 crisis. How could the social sciences develop if they servilely submitted to a State that wiped the repression of Tlatelolco and the existence of a non-democratic authoritarian system off the map?

During the long crisis of the Mexican political system, the social sciences were opening new tendencies and currents that were sometimes qualified as postmodern. It became increasingly clear that society could function with, and be governed by, new democratic norms and it was confirmed that they would not result in the collapse of the country's structure. These processes would require new explanations. The ideas revolving around the theories of dependency and its derivatives were now obsolete in this new reality. These tensions caused a fragmentation of the social sciences that coincided with a disinterest on the part of students to enrol in careers linked to research (notably sociology). Another disturbing factor was the invasion of scores of commentators in the mass media whose analyses tended to substitute the dry and often sterile results of academic research. In addition, there has often been an excess of theorizing welter and a shortage of empirical references in articles in the academic journals.

From this fragmentation, small groups of social scientists were formed that adopted the cryptic language of 'rational choice', of institutionalism, of semiotics, of econometrics, of relativism, of phenomenology, of structuralism, and of other currents of thought. There have been frequent, somewhat frustrated, attempts to resemble the physical and natural sciences by using terms that are incomprehensible to the layman. Anthony Giddens has pointed out that those declaring that 'the discoveries in the social sciences do not say anything new and are only disguised in technical language that everyone can express in everyday terminology',[3] need to be taken seriously. This has contributed to the separation of the social science that appears in academic publications and that which is circulated in newspapers, magazines, cultural supplements, or in commercial publishing houses. It is also worth mentioning that the translations of important books written by social scientists from other countries are almost always published by private, non-academic publishing houses.

Academic journals are not usually the result of the work of an editorial board. The majority function as reception counters for article and review proposals that are then processed by very formal selection systems. Journals obtain material in a rather random manner, even though they usually target the production of the research centres they have connections with. They operate with confidential filters that are not always reliable. These journals seem destined to pile up in libraries or in digital archives and serve the purpose of thickening the curriculum of their authors. They operate without a precise guide and circulate abstruse styles.

We face a double problem: in the first place, the social sciences, paradoxically, distance themselves from the society that surrounds them. And secondly, the social sciences, fragmented, are isolated from one another. Academia moves away from society and produces very few studies based on direct research, but it produces too many speculations: not much empirical study but plenty of theory. In addition there is the disturbing fact that researchers pay little critical attention to what is produced outside their own circles. I purposely indulge in exaggeration to encourage reflection. The excess of theorizing and the lack of communication are leading the social sciences into a difficult situation. But these imbalances are not expressed in the same way in the different disciplines. There are factors in each area that shape the problems I have pointed out: the greater importance of professional practice (law, psychology), the empirical traditions (anthropology, history), the ties with governmental administration (economy), and the academic influences (sociology, political science). In each discipline we observe differences in their relation to the governmental political agencies or to the mass media, in their importance in university academic spaces, and in the influence they receive from business spheres.

The time has come for researchers to face up to uncomfortable questions. Who is doing the best work in social science? Where are the best studies being carried out? In what areas does social research successfully compete with the best science carried out in other countries? The search for answers will make them take a very close look at their own work, and thoroughly evaluate the substance of their disciplines. Each researcher will look for his or her own answers, but it will be a very difficult task if done in a context lacking critical stimuli and good communication channels. Or perhaps, given the difficulties, she or he will simply refuse to look for answers and will remain thwarted in the presence of intellectuals and scholars who do ask questions and audaciously (sometimes excessively so) answer them. Who in Mexico has produced a better study of our environment, writers such as Octavio Paz or university professors writing in journals that are read only by academicians? In the following chapter, I share my thoughts and reflections on questions that Octavio Paz asked more than half a century ago.

2010

Chapter 9

The labyrinth and its map

Octavio Paz began his journey through the Mexican labyrinth by drawing a large question mark. He knew that the answers to his questions would be fleeting and illusory. The questions themselves could become impenetrable mysteries. Right at the beginning of his reflections, in the fourth paragraph of *El laberinto de la soledad*, Paz addresses us – inhabitants of his future – in order to cast us a challenge: 'The questions all of us ask ourselves now will probably turn out to be incomprehensible within fifty years'.[1] More than half a century later we find ourselves doubting: do we understand Paz's questions? I believe the poet was right: we do not understand them.[2] But Octavio Paz introduced, more than a doubt, a slight hope: his hand most certainly trembled when he added the word 'probably'. Perhaps, just maybe, someone would escape from his or her circumstances and succeed in deciphering the enigmas . . . Paz set himself up as the devouring Sphinx of the passing travellers who cannot answer his questions. And they cannot answer them because they do not even understand them . . . It will take many passers-by and many years, more than fifty, for the questions of Octavio Paz to again be fully intelligible.

With what kind of attitude can we approach the Pazian Sphinx? Some have thought the safest manner of confronting the Sphinx's riddles is to adopt a mocking position. For example, a postmodern and ironic Oedipus could confront the Sphinx who terrorizes all Mexicans with its puzzle: 'What is', asks the Sphinx, 'the creature who has but one voice and is successively no one, someone and everyone?' 'The Mexican,' answers our parodic Oedipus, 'who first is no one of any worth, then is a solitary *someone* behind the mask, and finally becomes the contemporary of everyone!' And at this moment our Aztec Sphinx flaps its turkey wings, tenses its coyote body, and runs towards the precipice in search of certain death. And so the problem is eliminated by the parodic and mocking murder.

But there is another way to face up to the Sphinx: in a herme-neutical spirit we can attempt to translate the questions and advance explanations and interpretations, in a mimetic ritual in the presence of the liminal monster who has set himself up as the guardian of the Mexican identity. The ceremony can adopt the form of a paraphrase, with the movements of the ritual drawing the map of where we lose our way: a distorted image of the labyrinth which, unlike the trad-itional maze, has no way out.

I would now like to show the way in which these two alternatives regarding Paz's work were revealed in an amiable discussion with the person I am certain will become the great biographer of the Mexican poet. The critical edition of *El laberinto de la soledad*, prepared in 1993 by Enrico Mario Santí, contains a documented and creative introduc-tion by the Cuban essayist that Octavio Paz himself had revised. In 1995 in a letter, I commented to Santí on an opinion of his that in my book *La jaula de la melancolía* (*The Cage of Melancholy*) I had para-phrased *El laberinto de la soledad* (*The Labyrinth of Solitude*), making it a kind of interpretation or translation.[3] In his answer, Santí correctly pointed out to me that he had not spoken of paraphrase: in effect he had written that the title of my book was a parody of Octavio Paz's title.[4] In other words, upon naming my book I had made a burlesque imitation of Paz's text. The Cuban critic was not correct in thinking I had wanted to make fun of a serious text. In my letter to Santí I explained the origin of the title.

Tocqueville had been my inspiration for the idea of melancholy, which he applies to the United States. In *La democracia en América*, he refers to this new disease of democratic nations: there men never obtain the equality they desire, although they easily obtain relatively equitable conditions. The equality they desire is always just out of reach: 'They feel they are always about to grasp it, but it constantly slips away from them. They are close enough to see its charms, but too far away to enjoy them and they die before they have been able to fully taste their sweetness. This must be the cause of that strange melan-choly which frequently haunts the inhabitants of democratic nations amidst their abundance and of that displeasure with life that takes hold of them in the midst of a comfortable and tranquil existence.'[5]

From this idea I jumped to Max Weber, who described the modern capitalist condition as an iron cage. I thought: Mexican modernity is also a cage, but a cage of melancholy rather than of iron. I immedi-ately realized that it could be taken as a paraphrase of Paz's book, but I liked the idea too much to abandon it. Sometime later I found out

that the fortunate metaphor of the iron cage had also been a paraphrase that Talcott Parsons permitted himself when he translated *The
Protestant Ethic and the Spirit of Capitalism*. Max Weber spoke of something like a box or a house as hard as steel (*ein stahlhartes Gehäuse*); the
great German sociologist never spoke of a cage or of iron.

The epistolary discussion does not end here, for when in 2000 – in
a round table discussion – I gave a public account of the exchange
between Santí and myself, my Cuban friend read an inaccurate newspaper review of it and promptly wrote to me again to reiterate that he
had never considered my book, *The Cage of Melancholy*, to be a parody;
just the title: 'I do not think', wrote Santí, 'that you can deny that
your title is a parody, in the same way that, for example, the title *Sor
Juana Inés de la Cruz or The Traps of Faith* is a parody of *Justine, or The
Misfortunes of Virtue*. Furthermore, as my compatriot Cabrera Infante
said, to parody is not to hate, but rather it is an homage from one
writer to another.'[6]

I insist – and I said so to Santí – that my title is not parodic, nor do
I believe that the 'traps of faith' parodies the Marquis de Sade's title. I
agree, to parody is not to hate. But it certainly is to make fun of. And
if I reject parody, it is not to make a public retraction or self-criticism,
but rather to send out an invitation to the paraphrase: to explain,
amplify, criticize, and translate with liberty. 'It is possible that my dis-
crepancy', I wrote to Santí,

> is simply that I have a narrower and less lax concept of parody than
> you do. My intention, on touching upon the theme of parody, is part of
> an attempt to clarify my intellectual relationship with Paz. Neither the
> 'hard core' followers of Paz nor the 'pure Left' understood my position,
> which is fully expressed in *The Cage*. From the start, my book was very
> poorly received by the extremes, even though it was given a very good
> (silent) welcome by a wide audience that continues to read it.[7]

Santí continues to believe he is right, according to what he wrote me,
but that he is 'rethinking' his point of view. The same goes for me.

As a homage to Paz, more than half a century after *Laberinto*, I wish
to vindicate, paraphrase and reject the idea of a parody. I believe it
is the same thing Paz did when he recognized the melancholy rever-
berations that the idea of solitude produces. Modern society has promoted, according to Max Weber's beliefs, man's solitary confinement,
surrounded by a mechanized and massive petrification of goods and
merchandise. In his hard steel box neither puritanical asceticism nor
the ideas of the Enlightenment console him. I wish here, in a brief

interlude, to point out that the idea of an iron cage shares an intimate history secretly linked with melancholy; it is a history that does not begin with the singular paraphrase of Talcott Parsons. In fact we can locate at least two precedents, both known by Max Weber, that connect us with the notion I am interested in paraphrasing: melancholy. I am sure Parsons took the expression from John Bunyan's *Pilgrim's Progress*, a Puritan text well known to Weber, in which there is an important passage where the pilgrim, Christian, is led to a very dark room and finds a man locked in an iron cage, plunged into despair. I have no doubt that Parsons, who was the son of a Congregationalist preacher, remembered the expression from *Pilgrim's Progress* when he translated the German sociologist's text.[8]

The image of the iron cage to refer to the melancholic condition of the solitary individual who has lost his *raison d'être* was used in another text, also known to and cited by Weber, and which equally stems from melancholy: in Baudelaire's two celebrated prose poems, known as *Paris Spleen*, a wild woman confined to an iron cage (*'cage de fer'*) is spoken of.

Puritan desperation that cannot endure the weight of original sin and the oppressive tedium of modern *spleen* draws the map of a labyrinth with no way out, and thus it is no longer a labyrinth. It is the map of melancholy, a map that does not offer answers since it does not even ask questions. This is why I say that behind the labyrinth of solitude lies the map of melancholy. We know that Octavio Paz had thought of writing a book about melancholy and its relation to poetry. I hope that among his papers the first drafts of that book will someday appear.

So, in order to glimpse the underlying map, I would like to refer to two of the different melancholic threads with which the *Laberinto* is woven. The first leads to Sor Juana Inés de la Cruz and its background is the Golden Age and the Renaissance. The second takes us to the melancholic spirit of the Spanish Generation of '98. I will not take on the critical analysis of the Mexican expressions of identity as I have already done so in other texts: *The Cage of Melancholy* and *Oficio mexicano*.[9]

* * *

When in *El laberinto de la soledad* Paz refers to Sor Juana Inés de la Cruz, he says there is 'something unfulfilled and undone' in her life and work and that there is 'an awareness of the melancholy of a spirit that never succeeded in forgiving her daring and her status as a woman'.

A bit further on he says that the image of Sor Juana 'is that of a melancholic solitary figure who smiles and is silent'.[10] As we know, Paz did not abandon the subject, and in his study of Sor Juana he believes that the soul that travels in *El Sueño* feels the same anguished uneasiness that the angel drawn by Dürer in his engraving *Melencolia I* felt, because it cannot transform the contemplation of the cosmos into form or idea. The soul's journey in Sor Juana's poetic dream would be like the melancholy flight of Dürer's angel.[11] The soul's intellectual night flight benefits from the dismal pyramidal shadow coming out of the silent earth and that rising, trying to reach the stars, is pushed upwards by the black humours of war. Dark melancholy spurs the mind on to elevate itself, like the radiating pyramids, towards the heavens. However, the sight of celestial chaos blinds the soul, which retreats to the shadows where it can watch, from the semidarkness, the grand world theatre: an impossible illusion, since, when the body awakes, the peregrine soul returns to its abode without having accomplished its purpose. After its journey, the soul returns, like the poet, to its carnal residence, and Sor Juana describes how the vapours of fantasy vanish with the arrival of the sun that wakes the world. I have no doubt that for Paz, Sor Juana's poem is a great metaphor for comprehending the crisis of twentieth century Mexican culture.

But Octavio Paz was not always convinced that the solar light of dawn could wake the world. In *La llama doble* (1993) he wonders if the second half of the twentieth century will be illuminated by the crepuscular light of melancholic Saturn and no longer by the ambiguous but violent light of Lucifer that illuminated the first half. 'Perhaps,' says Paz, 'although Saturn loves nuances. Mythology paints him as the sovereign of a spiritual Golden Age weakened by black bile, melancholy, that humour which loves chiaroscuro. In contrast, our time is simplistic, brief and brutal.' So, we would have a melancholy dispossessed of its poetic nuances and erotic tonalities: a melancholy trapped in an iron cage, and not the magic, sad, and dark humour that the Renaissance and Romantic poets invoked.

Octavio Paz absorbed the saturnine and baroque inspiration of the Spanish Golden Age thanks to, among other figures, the poetic presence of Sor Juana. In fact, the Spanish Empire seems to have begun and ended under the sign of Saturn: the myth of melancholy is present at its birth in the Golden Age as well as at its death at the beginning of what has been called the Silver Age.[12] This Silver Age, in whose heart we find the Generation of '98, had a stimulating influence on the creation of *El laberinto de la soledad*. I wish to point out the fact that

Octavio Paz protected his *Laberinto* under the melancholy shadow of Antonio Machado. The initial quotation is an obvious reference to the spirit of the Generation of '98, which was personified by the great Spanish poet and which made melancholy an emblem for referring to the ill-fated national identity in fateful times – the end of the nineteenth century, when the decline of the once great Spanish Empire was lived through. The *Laberinto*, like the anguished reflections of Unamuno, Ganivet, Ortega y Gasset, or Azorín, offers a lucid but bitter critique of a political culture whose impetuses are extinguished as the revolution becomes institutionalized and to the degree that the revolutionary nationalism empire adopts the most authoritarian forms.

I do not wish to speculate about the Generation of '98 or the final collapse of the Spanish Empire. There is abundant literature on the subjects (in fact, a genuine avalanche of publications). My intention is only to sketch the map of modern Spanish melancholy, the one that Octavio Paz vitalized and, to a certain degree, paraphrased. To begin with, it is important to point out that there is not a void between the old Baroque melancholies and the modernistic ones or those of '98, as Guillermo Díaz-Plaja's book *Tratado de las melancolías españolas* has shown, albeit somewhat inarticulately. For example, an important link in the chain of sullen, paralysing humours is without a doubt found in the writing of José Cadalso in the eighteenth century. In his *Cartas marruecas* (1773–4) he describes the mediocre, boring, and repetitive life of some Spanish courtiers who by not even aspiring after posthumous fame, are submerged in the everyday tedium of those who suffer great despondency when they realize that, upon death, they will be the same as the lowest of their slaves.[13] The despondency to which he refers is melancholy, even though he does not call it that. His ideal is that men renounce their thirst for posthumous fame and that they look upon heroes and great writers with 'tedium'. Further on Cadalso rectifies his scorn for the thirst for transcendence, since he realizes that tedium plunges the Spanish into that horrendous lack of willpower later denounced by Ganivet. It should be parenthetically pointed out that the subject of melancholic tedium was also taken up again by Mariano José de Larra in his curious essay from 1833, entitled '*Vuelva usted mañana*', in which Spanish idleness is contrasted with the enterprising spirit of the Frenchman Monsieur Sans-délai, who wants things done with no delay. Octavio Paz carried out a similar counterpoint between American optimistic utilitarianism and Mexican contemplative mistrust.

In another text, *Noches lúgubres,* Cadalso lets us see how the gloomy exaltation of death and wandering through the cemeteries is not an exclusive attribute of the '98 melancholiacs. Are we perhaps not facing the complicated process of the creation of a tragic and ill-fated imperial consciousness? Is not the bleak world vision being shaped here of a dominant class that does not succeed in navigating the national ship through the turbulent waters of modernity, and so resorts to melancholy as a way to attenuate its hardships?

The Spanish Empire, as has repeatedly been stated, ran into great pitfalls as it entered into modernity. The dominant Spanish culture adapted to modern times with difficulty and it is possible to perceive certain symptoms of this problem in the way in which ideas are woven around melancholy. The cultivation of melancholy propelled the creation of a modern consciousness of individuality in all Europe and provided models of controlled suffering for resisting the terrible ills of mechanization, industrialization, and massification without losing heart. At the same time, romanticism was both a vehicle of and a sieve for melancholic feelings: it brought back the old tradition of sad humours but to a certain point filtered its most disorganized effects (utopian and revolutionary). It can be supposed that in Spain a relatively precarious romanticism did not sift out the most miserable aspects of black humour and amplified its negative features in such a way that at the end of the nineteenth century we ran across many bitter, hardened, furious, and blind Don Quijotes, obsessed with rescuing a damaged national identity or one in danger of disappearing due to the lack of unity in Spain. Baroque melancholy was poorly assimilated by nineteenth-century Spanish culture, especially by the Generation of '98, to the point that it became dissociated with the irony and humour belonging to the Cervantine tradition. And without those ingredients, it has been difficult to assimilate the so-called decadence of Spain and the collapse of the Empire. Modernity needs melancholy, but excessive doses of that black humour turn into a conservative and reactionary burden.

This obsession of searching for pathways that is so typical of the Generation of '98 should not be surprising. Antonio Machado expressed this anguish in his very famous verses: 'Wanderer, there is no road, the road is made by walking'.[14] But the inexistence of pathways was also the traditional threat of the famous 'noonday demon', anguish, which paralysed wills. Rosalía de Castro, whose extraordinary poetry was a fundamental link in the long chain of melancholy, refers to it in 1884:

> In the summer, the hour of noon,
> could well be called
> night-time when man, struggling wearily,
> more than ever is irritated by
> the imposing force of matter
> and the infinite anxieties of the soul.[15]

The Generation of '98 inherits the sadness of the romantics such as Rosalía de Castro and Bécquer, but their melancholy, Maurice Cranston has said, is neither sweet nor pleasant, but rather bitter and profound, as Spanish romanticism lacks that tearful quality which drove Rousseau and enchanted many Germans.[16]

In addition, the Generation of '98 lived and suffered the idea of a typically Spanish melancholy. Antonio Machado, in well-known verses, alluded to the bitter melancholy that inhabits the sombre solitudes of Castile. His brother Manuel, in a poem entitled 'Melancholy', exhibits his own dismal sentiments:

> At times I feel sad
> like an old autumn afternoon
> of nameless nostalgias,
> of melancholy sorrows so full . . .

He describes the typical wandering next to the tombs of the dead in romantic tones. Azorín, in his well-known book about Madrid, described similar sentiments: 'We wandered among old tombs in the silence of the night. We felt attracted by the mystery. The vague melancholy that this generation was impregnated with converged with the sadness emanating from the graves. We felt Spain's unfortunate destiny, defeated and battered beyond the seas, and we promised ourselves to exalt her to new life. Everything became logically connected in us: art, death, life, and love of the homeland'.[17]

Azorín's appreciation takes us directly to the theme of the 'decadence' and 'defeat' of the Spanish Empire, and of its link with melancholy. I believe that towards the end of the nineteenth century a complex and peculiar cultural fabric had been consolidated which succeeded in converting adversity into strength of spirit, failure into identity, and decadence into patriotism and *casticismo*. In order for this fabric to develop, a long process of historical decantation was necessary that was able to develop the archetype of melancholy to the point of reaching the perverse but effective forms that are usually associated with the Generation of '98. This historical process must be recognized and analysed in order to stay away from the simplistic idea that the political and economic setbacks, which came to a head at the end of the nineteenth century, were the cause of justified sentiments of melancholy and sadness for the Spanish.

To conclude this rapid archaeological excursion through the ruins of Spanish melancholy, I would like to quote Ángel Ganivet. In his conservative defence of Spanish identity in the face of the power of the United States, referring to a Latin American musical genre, he wrote:

> the 'habanera' alone is worth all the production of the United States, including the sewing machines and telephonic apparatuses, and the 'habanera' is a creation of the territorial spirit of the island of Cuba, and brings out in our race those profound feelings of infinite melancholy, of pleasure that pours out in torrents of bitterness and that would not make the slightest impression on the race that inhabits the [American] Union.[18]

It is curious that Ganivet did not perceive the contradiction between this exaltation of Spanish melancholy and the condemnation of its expression in the form of collective apathy, which is nothing more than another morbid symptom of the black humour called anguish in the Middle Ages. Ganivet was a bundle of contradictions, hence our interest in him: for example, despite criticizing the Spanish lack of will, he wishes to appease the Spanish obsession with unification. In an ironic comparison with the famous dilemma of Omar, to justify burning the library of Alexandria, Ganivet maintains that if we believe that men are prone to unity, we should be patient in the knowledge that this idea will end up triumphing; and if to the contrary men are prone to differentiation or to pluralism, it would be useless to go against the tide. Neither does he believe men walk aimlessly, waiting for a genius to guide them. In conclusion: do nothing.

Nothing . . .That is the melancholic key to those situations in which men do not want to do anything, but in which many things occur: many tragic events that bloodied the history of Spain and that ended, not with a genius, but with a leader who believed himself destined to be the guide of all uncompromisingly unified Spaniards.

* * *

El laberinto de la soledad is part of that immense cultural arch which unites the Golden Age with the Hispano-American twentieth century, that links the Quijote with Juan de Mairena and Sor Juana with Octavio Paz. A long vein of literary culture can be defined as an existential baroque labyrinth. I start from the fortunate expression of Manuel Duran, who, in a brilliant anatomy of a sonnet of Quevedo, defines what he calls an 'existential Baroque', a vast network of themes and attitudes that covers several centuries and many Spanish writers.[19] One of the constituent stones of that existential baroque labyrinth is precisely Quevedo's sonnet that begins like this:

> I looked at the walls of my country,
> if once strong, now fallen to pieces,
> tired from the race of age . . .

What do the old walls of the country hold in, walls both of the nation as well as of the person? It is the anguished question – the enigma – of the poets who venture along the paths of the baroque labyrinth. Quevedo's answer is premonitory:

> and I found nothing upon which to set my gaze
> that was not a reminder of death

Octavio Paz asked himself the same question in *El laberinto de la soledad*. His book has the immense power of capturing all the secular force of a culture that has woven troubling answers to the labyrinth's enigma. Could Mexico and Latin America be an overseas continuation of Spanish decadence?

It must be said that the age of the labyrinth is over. The walls have crumbled. It is true that the Mexican Revolution and the Spanish Civil War – in addition to the two world wars – stoked the embers of the old questions. *El laberinto de la soledad* was born out of the revived flame and was converted into the great work that closed the doors of the existential Baroque. To do that, it creatively collected new forms of expression, such as surrealism and existentialism that were mixed with nationalist, Marxist, and Freudian ingredients in order to creatively confront modernity. The result seems to me part of what Bolívar Echeverría has called the 'baroque ethos': a peculiar way to experience modernity, that recognizes its inevitable ravages but that carries out a desperate criticism looking for the opening of a poetic and dramatic dimension.[20] Of course, existential baroqueness, in *El laberinto de la soledad* and in Paz's texts continuing his reflections on national identity, was tempered by a curious spirit which was at the same time stoic and gothic, that permitted the acceptance of authoritarian nationalism combined with a structuralist anthropological interpretation. I believe that the specifically Spanish and Latin American form of existential baroqueness is sealed by *El laberinto de la soledad*. And in a circular effect, the labyrinth itself is closed, even when we can hear the echoes of voices and phantasmal murmurings coming from its interior. We hear them but we do not fully understand them. We have no choice but to paraphrase them from outside the labyrinth, rephrase them and reinterpret them, knowing our translation will be a betrayal.

One of the muted echoes that resounds the most is the one that insistently repeats the word 'all'. The *Laberinto* opens with an assertion: '*All* of us, at one time or another, have had our existence revealed to us as something particular, transferable and precious'. The book's final phrase, before the appendix, which has been widely cited and repeated, maintains that we are, for the first time, contemporaries of *all* men'. An entire pyramid made of large blocks of collective voices has remained buried within the labyrinth: we, them, the others, the Europeans, the Indians, the North Americans, the *pelados*, the *pachucos* . . . The labyrinth's echoes insistently repeat a counterpointing (Paz would say, a rhythm) of the choral voices of the conglomerates with the poetic chronicle of the personal discovery of individuality. We know that this counterpointing contains a guide placed there by Paz to orient us in our mythic and historic anxieties, but its keys have remained buried. However, even though those collective voices do not correspond to the preoccupations of our postmodern era, without a doubt they draw us a map of twentieth-century Mexican culture. This map does not show the escape route but instead is a poetic portrait with a moralized landscape of post-revolutionary Mexico. It does not give us Ariadna's thread nor a therapy to cure the labyrinthine solitude, as Paz would have liked. Because – and once again I paraphrase Paz – more vast and profound than the labyrinth of solitude lies melancholy.

There are some privileged travellers – like Paz – who upon suffering the perplexities of melancholy have left us, besides a labyrinth, an immense open, lucid, bare, and frank cartography. It is the ancient map, torn and fractured, that shows us how the labyrinth would be if it had been, so to speak, gutted and turned inside out, so that its sinuous entrails remain outside, exposed for all to see, like intimate viscera in the obscene market of postmodernity.

We can imagine that, like a benevolent Minotaur, Octavio Paz has remained outside his labyrinth, condemned to exile but endowed with a new vitality. From outside his great work, Paz now lives among us with more strength than ever.

2001

Chapter 10

Ethnographic sonata in Nay-flat

As an ethnology student in 1963, I formed part of a commissioned ethnographic expedition to acquire pieces for Mexico City's new anthropology museum that was being built in Chapultepec Park. The group's intention was to provide the halls of the museum with objects used in the Day of the Dead Celebration in Michoacan. To go to the beautiful island of Janitzio in Lake Patzcuaro as common tourists was out of the question. We were to find a more 'authentic' and 'typical' domain of the indigenous otherness. So, on 1 November we disembarked from a motorboat onto the island of Pacanda, a place where we would supposedly find more genuine and less contaminated forms of the syncretic rituals celebrating the dead saints. It was terribly cold and on this flat island of Lake Patzcuaro nothing held back the wind that blew furiously through the streets and the cemetery. The lugubrious ringing of bells invited the souls of the dead to visit their relatives and they were offered food and drink to draw them to the temptations of this world. We engaged in buying the offerings of *pan de muerto*, braided flowers, candles, and copal burning incense holders from the inebriated Indians who were happily chatting alongside the gravesites. Perhaps the expedition director believed he was penetrating into the deep Mexico, according to the expression he used years later,[1] but the students recruited to buy ethnographic pieces assigned to be laminated and exhibited in a museum showcase suffered more from the absurdity of our work than from the discomfort of submerging ourselves into the depths of that icy night of the dead. To ease our distress, we ended up joining the Purepecha Indians in their invitation to drink a toast to the deceased.

The ethnographers seemed to us to be actors in a theatre of the absurd. Paradoxically they were looking for barely contaminated syncretic rituals, that is, infected, hybrid and impure by definition. They wanted to rip out some fragments of a live ceremony in honour of the dead to crystallize them and exhibit them outside their context: like killing the dead. They wanted something profound but they were only scratching the surface. The curious objects, equally syncretic, that were sold in Janitzio to satisfy the tourist taste for *kitsch*, would have served the same purpose.

This was a most revealing experience for me about Mexican ethnography, which had been converted into the symbol of a nationalist and revolutionary society that received indigenous culture through the front door (the museum), but made the real-life Indians use the servants' entrance to then be swallowed by modernity. Ten years later, as a result of my work in the Mezquital Valley of the Otomí region, I wrote about the indigenous condition, still under the lugubrious light of that Night of the Dead on the island of Pacanda. I maintained that the State needed the cultural cadaver of the Indian in order to feed the myth of national unity and I described the official indigenist institutions as permanent funeral homes for the indigenous people, holding a perpetual wake over the Indian's corpse.[2]

These old memories of my experiences with Mexican ethnography compel me, more than to intone a speech, simply to sound some instruments in an openly negative key. However, with the passing of time, I have felt it prudent to lower the critical negative a half-tone.

* * *

In those years, indigenism was dominated by revolutionary nationalism, the dominant ideology manipulated by the authoritarian government that has subjugated Mexico for decades. Indigenism has displayed different faces within the revolutionary nationalist space. It has worn paternalistic, functionalistic, technocratic, populist, liberal, fundamentalist, Marxist, relativist, and guerrilla expressions.[3] But there is a common keynote in them all: it is an ideology which revolves around the State, it is a protestation in the name of the indigenous peoples to demand a government policy geared towards normalizing and directing the relation between ethnic groups and dominant socio-economic and political structures. At the base of indigenism one usually finds the ethnographic activity of different schools of anthropologists who – some with better luck than others – reconstruct and invent identities of pre-Hispanic origin. But it is not only a process promoted by social scientists: in many cases we find the political incorporation of the indigenous population into corporate-style structures, be they union, bureaucratic, *campesino*, of a political party, or military. As is well known, indigenism harbours an interior contradiction that blocks its development: it is an ideology that exalts cultural difference and then reduces it to politics. The result ends up damaging the cultural dynamic it is hoping to stimulate or rescue.

The first indigenism integrators recognized this contradiction and tried to take advantage of it to stimulate the formation of a national State. From Manuel Gamio to Gonzalo Aguirre Beltrán, indigenist ethnology accepts and even promotes the integration of indigenous peoples into national society, although it tries to rescue cultural elements of the ethnic groups and protect them from the worst forms of exploitation. In the 1970s there was a peculiar turn of events in Mexican anthropology: it was recognized that the integrationist policy had failed, whether it was because by becoming assimilated, indigenous peoples cease to be just that, or because racism has kept them marginalized. A new generation of anthropologists arrived at the institutional *establishment* who were also considered to be revolutionary and nationalist, like their predecessors, but furthermore, they were guided by a mixture of fundamentalism and relativism. Therefore, they proclaimed that anthropology should be at the service of indigenous groups more than at the service of science, that it should denounce modern imperialist interference, purge Western culture, and form a new national project. The Barbados Declaration of 1971 represents this attitude that clamours for the liberation of the native Indian, who must be the protagonist of his own destiny.[4] Nevertheless, for these anthropologists the State is the true driving force of the 'radical rupture', the *deus ex machina* that guarantees the indigenous peoples their identity, recognizing rights that existed prior to their rights of national civility; it is responsible for all crimes committed against them, it must offer assistance or protection and appoint authorities in charge of establishing relations with the ethnic groups.[5] The statism of the new indigenists is vehement and obsessive. Its social base is formed by the corporative structures of institutional revolutionary authoritarianism that firmly control indigenous organizations and communities through a complex pyramidal system of *cacicazgos*. The obvious contradictions and paradoxes of the new forms of indigenism are part of the fascinating mysteries that characterized the institutional revolutionary dictatorship that dominated Mexico until 2000. This mystery was extended to the enigmatic relationship between the Zapatista National Liberation Army (EZLN) and the PRI governments of Carlos Salinas de Gortari and Ernesto Zedillo.[6]

* * *

The revolutionary obsession which drove twentieth-century Mexican anthropology placed ethnography practitioners in an anguished position: their activity was on the whole geared towards discovering and conserving ancient traditions within a context of accelerated change and revolutionary progress. In political mythology, revolutionaries are portrayed as the personification of the new and so their greatest nightmare is to be left behind and not to have kept up with the new modern and postmodern times. The final stretch of the twentieth century definitely changed the world political panorama. First of all, capitalism had woven an immense global network, put together with the decisive help of spectacular scientific and technological advances in computation, genetics, conductors, etc. Secondly, another process occurred: a formidable expansion of political democracy in Latin America and Europe had swept dictatorships of different designs off the map. Dictatorships were replaced by democracy – first in Spain, Greece, and Portugal, then in the South American Southern Cone, followed by the Soviet Bloc and finally, just before the end of the twentieth century, in Mexico.

I wish to briefly refer to some of the more relevant aspects of the new post-modern challenges faced by the concept of revolution. In its most radical version, it confronts a brutal erosion of hope in a progression that should have led capitalism to a revolutionary collapse or, at least, to a grand renovation led by popular forces; in contrast, new political dimensions, cultural forms of legitimacy, and moral demands have come to the foreground. It is evident that the idea of revolution – the banner that had confronted the typical right-wing positions that wanted to conserve the established order and traditional privileges – has been eroded by the new political culture. Gradually, the idea of revolution is being converted to a certain extent into a reactionary culture – habits that react against the new democratic tendencies. It can rightly be said that social democratic currents had long surpassed revolutionary tradition. However, in many parts of the world, especially in Latin America, the illusion was kept up that a qualitative and revolutionary transition to a new situation was possible, with the direct or indirect help of the socialist bloc. That illusion began to be shattered in 1989, and not much of it is left today. In Mexico, not even Subcommander Marcos wants to be called a revolutionary: he prefers to be a rebel. The drama of the conversion of revolution into a retardatory symbol has been seen in many places, not only in our 1910 revolution. The nectar of the revolution in Russia, China or Cuba has been soured with the arrival of an unacceptable antidemocratic Thermidor.

A new observable phenomenon, connected with a clear setback of revolutionary and statist theses, is the gradual exclusion of economic topics from public opinion concerns. When qualitative change in the economic structure and nature of the State ('revolutionary' changes) is not possible, financial, fiscal, or labour management tends to become ramified and above all specialized and technocratic. Political alternatives find relatively little to hold onto within the economic sphere and more and more they shift towards symbolic and metaphoric planes that are related to the cultural and ethical consequences of governmental administration. I believe that, even though it seems paradoxical, this tendency is as strong in the so-called Third World countries – with their terrible economic deficiencies – as it is in the richest and most prosperous regions of the globe. This happens because political experiences of the twentieth century have demonstrated that the fundamental influences of industrial development are more cultural than economic in character. Of course, I do not mean to imply that the grave problems of economic backwardness are going to be resolved with cultural programmes. What I do mean is that civil society understands economic and financial programmes less and less if they are not accompanied by a translation into cultural and moral terms and symbols. This political shift towards cultural terrain is a phenomenon that is closely tied to the creation of new forms of democratic legitimacy.

* * *

To briefly explore this movement, I shall refer to the link between nationalism and the emergence of a neo-indigenism that glorifies ethnic identity symbols. As is known, examples of national borders coinciding exactly with ethnic boundaries are very rare, if they even exist. A certain degree of cultural violence and violation of ethnic delimitations is usually implied in the definition of a national space. The reason of state usually imposes itself over ethnic reason, although with the passing of time, ethnicity can avenge politics and provoke difficulties. Even apparently well-defined national states such as France bear the scars of old ethnic wounds: the Pyrenees are a political border that divides ancient cultural conglomerates formed by Catalans and Basques. The latter still produce a certain breeding ground for violent conflict on both sides of the Franco-Spanish border.

The interests of the big imperial powers, upon accepting decolonization, have provoked even greater tensions by almost always ignoring ethnic geography. The definition of national spaces usually contradicts the pre-national geography of the formerly colonized regions. In any case, be it in Bosnia or in Kurdistan, this dislocation usually promotes violence and terror. At the same time, national identity has frequently recurred to ethnic symbols in order to define itself. This is evident in Mexico, where the name of the entire nation has its origin in the name of one of the most powerful ethnic groups the Spanish came up against in their conquest of the region: the Mexicas. In its large central hall, the National Museum of Anthropology was designed precisely to present the Aztecs as the symbol of national identity. And the national emblem is a symbol clearly exhibiting its ethnic origin, being a reference to the mythological founding of Tenochtitlán. Of course, the ethnic nature of the symbols and names of the nation is erased by the clearly centralist intention of their use. The emblem is obligatorily associated with the flag, and both symbols have undergone many changes and alterations. They have frequently been linked to devotional imagery, as much to the Virgin of Guadalupe (the colour white) as to the supposed purity of the Catholic religion. The Virgin of Guadalupe's own image has been converted into an indigenous and national symbol despite its obvious Castilian origin.

These paradoxes lead us to recognize the irrational character of national symbols. Could there be any greater evidence of this irrationality than the national anthem, another of the most cherished national symbols? The aggressive, bellicose, and traditional tone of the national anthem makes its irrationality obvious, together with the outdated and decrepit nature of its references to archangels, the fingers of God, laurels of triumph, blood-soaked flags, celestial destinies, and the rest of the symbology of an origin obviously far removed from that of aboriginal ethnic groups.

Of course, symbols do not emerge in cultures as part of rational processes, nor can they be understood with arguments extracted from Aristotelian logic. Pointing out the irrationality of national symbols is neither a disqualification nor a criticism, but rather the verification of a cultural event. That same irrationality is crystallized in traditions that glorify the atemporal (or so to say eternal) nature of national symbols. In this way, the act of exalting nineteenth-century patriotic war values against audacious enemies should not affect the nationalist identity cult, since this profound dislocation between metaphors and the present reality is in itself the proof of the perennial nature of national values. The more absurd the exalted values, the more their abstract and atemporal nature grows, to the degree that there are those who end up believing in the eternal existence of a threatening anti-hero named Masiosare.[7]

The ethnic symbols of Mexican national identity have been powerful myths nourished by post-revolutionary nationalism that grew in strength throughout the past century. Like all myths, they stimulated diverse rituals and cults to heroic indigenous personalities (such as Benito Juárez) or semi-divine ones (such as Cuauhtémoc). With the passing of time, however, cult rituals and acts began to lose their substance and became converted into boring and very bureaucratized official processes. It can be said that we are witnessing the transformation of symbols into signs. Symbols are dynamic images that influence and reorganize their surroundings and do so by representing an idea in a plastic way. By contrast, signs constitute a fixed and abstract relationship between the signifier and the signified. This is why algebra and mathematics require signs, but they are incapable of functioning with symbols.

National symbols become converted into signs when they lose the life they once contained. Today, for example, the national emblem is a sign that, printed on paper, on a wall, or on a piece of cloth, indicates the official nature of an action or space. The same has happened with the flag and its colours. The indigenous or pre-Hispanic content of many symbols tied to national identity has become an abstract sign alluding to dead values and defines petrified spaces of official culture. They are no longer symbols, but signs adorning the acts of transfer and investiture of power and marking ceremonial sites to distinguish them from civil society's own common spaces.

So, if we ask ourselves about the future of ethnic symbols of national identity, it can be said that the destiny of many of them is to be converted into signs. Sooner or later, the future of patriotic symbols will possibly be to pile up in the storage rooms of museums and official archives. Of course, in the same way the death of many ethnic symbols can be seen, it is also possible to observe their birth or revitalization. And one need not look too far. The indigenous guerrilla movement in Chiapas, coming into the public eye in 1994, took up an image again that had become a rigid sign. The figure of Emiliano Zapata, with his moustache, cartridge belts, and sombrero, was little more than a sign used by some sectors of political bureaucracy to allude to a long-buried revolutionary vocation. The EZLN recycled the sign and converted it into a symbol of the Indian struggle, together with the balaclavas borrowed from mountain climbers and bank robbers, which are not precisely part of the ethnic clothing of any group. But that does not take away from its impact. Just the opposite: it provides it with an attractive mysterious halo and a romantic aura.

Of course, the birth of Zapatista ethnic symbols was not a stimulus for the strengthening of national unity and identity. To the contrary, it was a very clear signal that the dominant nationalist political culture was in a deep crisis. And one of the most visible consequences of this crisis was the collapse of the dictatorship of the Revolutionary Institutional Party (PRI) and the beginning of transition to democracy. It is now obvious that the legitimizing structures based on the nationalist and post-revolutionary identity have ceased to function.

The void left by nationalism cannot be filled simply with renovated nationalism. There are leaders who are attempting a rescue mission and who propose a type of political Esperanto with strong doses of populism. But this language is as poorly efficient as the national technocratic language of Salinas that attempted to renovate the old revolutionary nationalism. On the other hand, the subject of a pluri-ethnic and multicultural nation has been emerging strongly. There is an avalanche of demands coming from marginal minorities or subcultures and long-discriminated-against ethnic groups. A nationalist rescue operation would consist of choosing a few symbols coming out of the ethnic mosaic in order to add them to the showcase gallery, and at the same time attempt to co-opt the groups that encourage them, and integrate them into the parastatal mediation system. I do not see much of a future in such an operation. It is no longer possible to simply offer ethnic morsels to the old hungry nationalist ogre so it can renew its strength. Actually, the new ethnic tensions form part of immense transnational and post-patriotic cultural networks. The strengthening of a new democratic legitimacy is found in the connection of these networks with a solid fabric of radically autonomous civility where new rules for the democratic game are developed.

What function could ethnic symbols have in this new context? We can see that a flow of symbolic imagery spills out towards these cultural networks, where symptomatic processes take place, from the crudest manipulations of a popular environmentalism or an outrageous militancy bolstered by pseudo-aboriginal cosmogonies, to creative phenomena such as indigenous language literature inspired in ancient metaphors or the artistic rebirth of pre-Hispanic symbology in the hands of able artisans. However, I do not believe that these events are especially useful in de-fragmenting national identity. New hordes of symbols of very diverse origins will strengthen the idea that Mexican identity is a changing flow lodged in democratic coexistence, in diversity, and in harmony with the most disparate sectors.

The epoch of the dissimilar has arrived, leaving behind the political anxiety for symbolic unification.

* * *

One of the problems deeply affecting ethnological research is a result of its profound immersion into government political and bureaucratic institutions. This situation has affected the scientific and academic aspects of anthropology practiced in Mexico, because it has been exploited by (and has become dependent on) the legitimation mechanisms that the State has required in order to reproduce the institutional despotism of the revolutionary nationalist elite for decades. The result has been that areas of anthropological activities – especially archaeology and ethnology – have been converted into spectacular appendages of governmental political action. The condition of dependency is not exclusive to anthropology. It has been a characteristic of all cultural activities – of painting and literature, film and folklore, music and arts-and-crafts, intellectual culture, and popular culture. The relationships between culture and politics have been part of the governmental fabric that has given cohesion to the authoritarian system that crystallized after the 1910 Mexican Revolution.

Since indigenism, after all, is an ideological proposal which attempts to define the relationships between the spheres of power and the cultural forms of indigenous ethnic groups, I believe it is necessary to address a very basic problem contained in the idea I am putting forward: what is the relationship between democracy and culture? And here I will lump together ethnic group culture, popular culture, and intellectual culture. I do not think it is constructive to maintain the separation between non-Western ethnic expressions and artistic and literary forms coming from European tradition. We anthropologists must not limit ourselves to describing marginal and 'primitive' cultures: ethnography of the dominant culture must also be carried out. In the following lines I will take a quick ethnographic look at governmental culture.

The relation between culture and democracy is a controversial and thorny theme. Saying we must attain a political culture that allows us to live more democratically is an insufficient assertion that refers exclusively to what culture can bring to democratic political spaces. This approach alludes to the utility of culture (of art, literature, traditions, customs): used well, culture increases the democratic values of politicians and realms of power. But what can even the most democratic of political systems offer culture?

It is very difficult for politicians and their parties to avoid the temptation to utilize culture for their own ends. Beyond the good intentions all politicians announce, about liberty and cultural diversity, we discover in many of them their intention to manipulate cultural spaces and to use cultivated individuals, who at times accept now familiar lamentable roles: the reprimander in the name of a superior morality, the organic intellectual informer of the vices of others, the persecutor of everyone or thing that attacks the profound identities of the national essence, or the revealer of the hidden intentions of his or her adversaries. Since there is no lack of corruption, confusion, and superficial morality in the political milieu, these 'culture workers' are never without work. I am convinced that some indigenist anthropologists stand out among them.

But the correcting of certain malformations of some intellectuals and politicians is not a problem of political will. The presence of a thick, socially prominent scab of 'culture workers' is part of one of the most intricate problems bequeathed to us by the long domination of institutionalized revolutionary nationalism.[8] It is about the close union – a true symbiosis – between the administration of the immense cultural patrimony and the support mechanisms of creation and research. The situation has had, in the long run, some negative consequences. In the first place, in the cultural field it has produced power forms that Max Weber would certainly describe as patrimonialist; that is, the enthronement of administrative sectors that appropriate the management of cultural patrimony and, by extension, of the institutions that support research, creation, or diffusion. Secondly, it has favoured the dominance of cultural expressions that seem to naturally emanate from the administration of the 'national' patrimony, tending to stamp them with a predetermined ideological orientation and expositional function.

Cultural patrimony has been understood to be a mine whose exploitation generates something like a national rent feeding the Mexican identity and strengthening State sovereignty. And when seen from that point of view, cultural patrimony, like oil or the *ejido*, needs to be guarded by commissioners and administered by an extensive bureaucracy that monopolizes the management of creation and research stimuli.

* * *

As I have said, one of the effects of having creation, teaching, and research be an appendage of cultural patrimony management is the tendency to concede privileges to large-scale spectacular productions and nationalist tendencies. Cultural patrimony exploitation is a constant motive for theatrical celebration, in the most diverse forms. So festivals, ceremonies, fiestas, and rituals tend to substitute for the profound and permanent creation stimuli. The official calendar of festivities overpowers, and frequently suffocates, the cultural processes themselves. Octavio Paz had warned of this when he pointed out that the important dimensions of the fiesta serve to interrupt the passage of time. The quantity of reunions, conferences, festivals, celebrations, discussions, tributes, and street displays is amazing. The tendencies that renew the idea that culture is a grand theatre where the magnificent spectacle of our plural democracy is displayed have recently emerged.

The result is that the spectacle and the fiesta absorb, so to speak, pharaonic amounts of resources, whereas the extension, modernization, and construction of institutes of study, libraries, museums, galleries, publishing houses, or cultural centres receive less attention and are left in the hands of an inefficient and not very imaginative bureaucracy. Privileges are bestowed upon the volatile and showy to the detriment of support for prolonged actions that lead to the creation of solid institutions. Governmental publishing houses shrivel or become converted into public relations companies for their directors.

Cultural banquets are frequently justified by the idea that they stimulate massive consumption of the arts or that popular participation in the celebrations injects vitality into the environment of the intellectual elite. This vision has contributed to separating the circuits of 'high' culture from the 'popular' art forms. The result of this contra position – popular culture versus refined culture – on more than a few occasions has resulted in a general impoverishment of all cultural expressions. The promotion of the popular has taken away from many cultural manifestations, while elitist seclusion has deteriorated less known artistic expressions. In this way, many massive spectacles turn out to be degrading and the avant-garde becomes hardened and cloistered. For many years populism has stimulated elitist reactions and has not promoted an elevation of cultural levels.

We are arriving at the end of a long epoch of government interference with culture: political interference marked by patrimonialism and populism. Actually, the official cultural policy of the last few years has moved away from these traditional forms, in order to adopt more plural attitudes and diversify options. But it has not managed to find a new path.

However, starting from changes in all governmental management, a new attitude has slowly been making way that stimulates efficiency, quality control, the hiring of specialized businesses, and decentralization, to name only a few of the features of a *managerial culture*, as it is called by some. It is clear that the government led by Vicente Fox has created expectations (fears as well as hopes) that this culture is extended to all spheres of politics of the State. The challenge facing the government is for the old revolutionary culture to be defeated by a new governmental culture. The old revolutionary culture is expressed in connection with symbols of authoritarian nationalism, of redeeming indigenism, of an institutionally rebellious people, of constant agitation to gain benefits, of social movement co-optation, of *cacique* and leader prestige, of the fear of repression. The symbols of governmental culture with managerial aspirations are efficiency, professionalism, supervision, civil service as a career, benefit accounting, and management quality.

Actually a new culture and a new ideology are being built: at times the president is proclaimed to be a superintendent capable of honourably and efficiently administering the governmental shop where correctly applying manuals and supervising operations is all that needs to be done in order for everything to run smoothly. This assessment reflects a lack of respect for the democratic figure of the executive power, which cannot be reduced to a managerial function. And it also overlooks the fundamental fact that President Vicente Fox is the symbol of transition to democracy. Political life requires something more than a manager in Los Pinos. Cultural sectors and the governed are not shareholders of a governmental corporation, although they do have interests and they wish to obtain benefits. The new symbology will attract ample sectors of the population that no longer live under the umbrella of the Mexican Revolution. But there is a wide range of voters, organizations, and movements who still live in the shadow, so to speak, of General Plutarco Elías Calles and General Lázaro Cárdenas. In Chiapas we have the shadow of General Emiliano Zapata. That part of Mexican society – rough, agitated, contentious, and frequently corrupt – will not easily respond to major managerial surgery.

Up to what point can the new modern and managerial pragmatism function in political culture? This question takes us back to the problem of culture's political usefulness. I have no doubt that the introduction of some rationality into cultural management can effectively combat corruption and vice. To give an example, when manufacturing a pair of trousers, it is necessary to know (through anthropomorphic and ethnographic studies) the size distribution of the consumer population and its tastes; decisions must also be made about quality and manufacturing time, for reaching an optimum balance and producing the highest dividends. But the components, measurements, and parts of cultural apparatuses cannot be programmed in the same manner. It is true that if the new clothing the cultural entrepreneurs produce for the politicians is made using inadequate manuals and instruction guides, there may be problems. It might not seem essential to the factory managers to invest in the best quality zippers, and they may prefer instead to spend the money on English cashmere. But if the trousers do not zip up properly, Mr Minister will not be able to go out in public.

* * *

Ethnologists today find themselves trapped between two critical situations. In the first place, their relationship with political and governmental spheres is quite deteriorated, due to the transition to democracy and to the degradation of the traditional forms of national identity.[9] This weakening, which implies a loss of meaning for indigenist action, was accelerated in 1994 with the Zapatista uprising in Chiapas, and it came to a critical head with the defeat of the PRI in 2000.

Secondly, during the last decades of the twentieth century, the process of dissolution, integration, and liquidation of indigenous cultures was accelerated. The picture painted by Carlos Basauri in his voluminous ethnographic compilation published in 1940 was not at all promising.[10] More than half a century later, as can be verified in another extensive recompilation of ethnographic data carried out by the National Indigenist Institute, the erosion of ethnic groups has continued.[11] A loss of the indigenous peoples' own profile and their consequent integration into the dominant society is obvious, a situation which no doubt is graver than that shown by these ethnographies, in which I fear a naive affection for the ethnic groups hides the degree of destruction of their cultures.

This dramatic situation leads me again to the image with which I began: some practically dead ethnic groups that certain anthropologists and many politicians wish to push towards society's showcases, so that they walk like authentic living corpses, true zombies. The ethnography that has studied the rituals of the Caribbean population of African origin tells us that in the beliefs associated with *vodun* (or voodoo), zombies appear – living dead whose souls have been stolen and who are obliged to work as slaves. It is a metaphor that describes the situation of many indigenous peoples. But it seems to me to be an especially excellent metaphor for the indigenisms that have re-emerged in Mexico and Latin America in recent years. In closing, I will turn my thoughts to this peculiar situation.

Some would be pleased to exclaim: a ghost is travelling across Latin America, the ghost of indigenism! They would like to believe that a new force has been born against which the old oligarchs join together in holy alliance. But indigenism is really a political zombie pampered by social forces reacting against the expansion of democracy in Latin America. We can understand – but not justify – that a large part of left-ist movements that were orphaned after the fall of the Berlin Wall are hoping to find a substitute for lost revolutionary subjects in the new indigenisms. But it is obvious they are playing with a dangerous polit-ical creature that has left tragic tracks in the history of the continent. I am referring to Latin American populism, which from Argentinian Peronism and the Mexican PRI to Chávez in Venezuela has perversely impregnated a political stage already plagued by dictatorships.

Fortunately, Latin America has ceased to be a mosaic of dictator-ships, and democracy has extended itself to nearly all the countries (with the grievous exception of Cuba). But the transition to democ-racy, although propelled by forces of the Left, arrived in the hands of the Right. Unfortunately, large sectors of the Left have not assimilated the new situation and are promoting a restoration of the old popu-lism with strong doses of indigenist ideology. The multiculturalist wave promoted by the now outdated confines of American and British political correctness, strengthened by anti-globalization phobias and multiplied by the despair of the poorest, is taken advantage of by some politicians to stimulate populism's resurrection. On not a few occa-sions, paradoxically, the exaltation of ethnic identities is interwoven with archaic forms of nationalism. And, to complicate things even more, there are conservative sectors (even in the Catholic Church) that support the indigenist zombie, which has been seen to create corrupt and antidemocratic – and in some cases (as in Nicaragua), clearly reactionary – fringes.

In Europe, the revolutionary voyage to Cancún, to Chiapas or to Cochabamba to vigorously confront globalization in the company of indigenous *campesinos* may appear very appealing and liberating. But the after-effects of these impulses to lend support to the good savages can be terrible. One of the consequences is an alarming political phe-nomenon: the growth of a reactionary and conservative Left armed with a populist, indigenist ideology. The key to this process is found in the rehabilitation of an indigenism fortified by a blood culture that exalts identities, homelands, and revolutionary war. Mexican *neozapatismo* is a friendly face of the indigenist zombie, but some movements for indigenous autonomy in Central America and in the Andes region have a more sinister countenance. One of the extremes is the sanguinary Maoist populism of the Shining Path in Peru.

The indigenism travelling across Latin America like a zombie is much more than a praiseworthy defence of native cultures and of the unassailable right of Indian ethnic groups to escape from misery, exploitation, marginalization, and the contempt to which they have been condemned. The new indigenism claims that not only is neo-liberal capitalist economy the enemy to defeat but that Western culture as a whole is responsible for the evils suffered by the marginalized and miserable people of the world. Their alternative is no longer socialism, which was buried at the end of the last century, but rather the restoration of indigenous traditions supposedly based on the community and direct democracy. Actually, more than an alternative, it is the glorification of a point of view that is situated in the traditional past and legitimizes a conservative reaction. In the name of customs, traditions, and values of a mythical past, the global threats of Western modernity are rejected. Indigenism usually shuns every attempt to seek possible alternatives within globalization and prefers to vindicate the conservation of supposedly pre-Hispanic customs that are actually, almost all, of colonial origin.

The forms of government defended by indigenism are usually based on male *caciques* that merge civil and ecclesiastic power; normally they exclude the participation of women and the young. It is a question of residues of political-religious colonial forms of exercising authority in which the survival of pre-Hispanic elements can barely be detected. In Mexico, for example, the defence by Subcommander Marcos of autonomous forms of indigenous government is famous. But it is not usually admitted that actually the immense majority of this type of 'autonomous' governments does not have the neo-Zapatista seal but rather that of the PRI. In Oaxaca very many municipalities function with governments based on 'indigenous' customs and traditions, which was the way that the leaders of the most backward wing of the PRI prevented opposition parties from advancing in the rural zones. Some indigenism theorists have even declared that the great example to follow are the autonomous regions along the Atlantic coast of Nicaragua, which in reality constitute an alarming case of reactionary conservatism and corruption.[12]

It is a fact that democratic political spaces are blocked by this conservative and authoritarian indigenism. Contrary to what many believe, indigenism is not only a danger to authoritarian governments. This and other reactionary populism currents threaten the advancement of democracy, and could even destabilize not yet fully consolidated transitions to democracy. Latin American democratic movements are just learning to move in the new postmodern globality and they encounter many obstacles. One of them is the spectre, not of an agile and innovating ghost, but of an opaque and heavy living corpse pulled out of the closet of social movements.

* * *

This zombie also wanders through the halls of the new National Museum of Anthropology built fifty years ago in Chapultepec, a museum that was born as a great symbol of the Mexican identity.[13] As such, it houses the very contradictions of nationalism, but it is also based on the exposition of the extraordinary pre-Hispanic cultures, whose originality and creativity were the expression of a complex and marvellous historic process. The exhibition of the riches of the ancient Mesoamerican cultures is a spectacle that stands on its own merit and can be damaged by any manipulation that tries to force connections between the past and the present. The builders of the new National Museum of Anthropology let the indigenist ghost enter the halls, in an attempt to insinuate that the spectacularity of the pre-Hispanic past was connected with the greatness of the modern national revolutionary State. They sent the cultural expressions of the surviving ethnic groups to the attics of the museum, to the halls of the highest floor, to suggest a correspondence between the past and the present. What they managed to do was to make the terrible catastrophe that has destroyed the indigenous societies since the Spanish conquest obvious, but without explaining the process. In some way the ethnography in the National Museum of Anthropology ended up being a melancholy sample of a multi-ethnical relativism that attempts to show that each surviving cultural niche represents values similar to those that are contemplated upon in the large halls. But the museum cannot be a kind of multicultural parliament of showcases where diverse ethnic groups, connected by imaginary stairways to the impressive archaeological spectacle of the great halls, are represented. It is necessary to rethink the relation between ethnography and archaeology. The connections between the ancient and the modern must be rethought in order to escape from that nationalist vision which only sees the past as manipulatable survival. The problem has also been presented on other continents: how is the link between the rich Mediterranean ethnography and the ancient Egyptian, Greek, and Arab cultures to be understood? Can we believe that the grandiose character of ancient Greek culture requires a folkloric supplement to demonstrate its importance to the modern world?

The ancient Mesoamerican cultures enrich us without the need for inventing nationalist umbilical cords or ethnographical survival supplements. The extreme complexity of the relations between the ancient and the modern is due to their insertion into the history of Christianity. This is an uncomfortable and complicated theme that I only wish to point out here. In the same way that we cannot understand modern Greece without Byzantine, we cannot understand today's Mexico if we jump directly from the Teotihuacanos, Mayans, and Aztecs to the ethnic folklore of the modern Indians, without passing through the Conquest, colonization, the Christian Renaissance space, and Western modernity. In order to do that, it would have to be admitted that an ethnography of modernity can be made.

With my reflections I have wanted to say that the new National Museum of Anthropology confronts us today with the necessity of integrating ethnography into a rational and scientific analysis of the ancient history of Mexico and of its modern consequences. If the museum stops being a spectacular gallery of the signs of national identity, the function of ethnography can change substantially. It can stop being the guide for the indigenist zombies that pass through the museum like tourists and be converted into a discipline capable of deciphering not only exotic survivals but also the signs of modernity and postmodernity.

2004

Chapter 11

1968: Defeat, transition, counter-culture

1968 is a sign of defeats. It is also the signal that marks the beginning of an age of transition. In addition, it is the symbol of an attractive cultural crystallization that began at the end of the 1950s and lasted to the end of the 1960s. The defeats were the Soviet invasion of Czechoslovakia in August, the failure of the French insurrection in May, and the crushing of the Mexican student movement in October. The Prague Spring was destroyed, the Paris rebellion was repressed, and the Mexican students were massacred in Tlatelolco.

The period of transition that began in 1968 culminated in the fall of the Berlin Wall and in the disappearance of almost all the Latin American dictatorships, including the Mexican regime. The world that had been split into two politico-military blocs disappeared and democracy spread out to large portions of the planet.

The culture – or perhaps better said, the counter-culture – of the 1960s signified an injection of vitality, of iconoclastic energy, of sexual experimentation, of musical and literary inventiveness. It was the age of rock and the Beatles, of sexual liberation, of the Cuban revolution and guerrillas, of Beat poetry, of the rejection of conventional standards of dress and appearance and conservative morals, of middle-class Maoism and the libertarian explosion, of the new Marxism and structuralism, of Third-World exoticism, of abstract art and the baby-boom, of the exaltation of youth and the expansion of the number of students.

The year 1968 has left us a triple inheritance: defeat, transition, and counter-culture. I realize that to say that the movement of 1968 signifies defeat will irritate some. José Revueltas said that the experience was extremely positive, although he immediately added: 'under the condition that we know how to theorize the phenomenon' (*México 68: juventud y revolución*, p. 21). But the theory Revueltas was thinking of did not save the student movement, which he had conceived as a political representation of a (temporarily) absent proletariat. For many years, more than a few 68-ers have refused to admit defeat. After going through all kinds of Leninist or Maoist juggling, the memory of '68 was transformed into a glorious epic that had only transitorily retreated so that it could look for new revolutionary channels. Unfortunately, those new channels culminated in a dirty war that put tough and dogmatic guerrillas face-to-face with cruel and often illegal repression. In this second turn of the screw, the guerrilla descendants of '68 lost again.

Dogmatic Marxists who reacted against the new ideas also criticized the student movement. Perhaps the most extreme example of this position was the principal leader of the Popular Socialist Party, Vicente Lombardo Toledano, who on 1 October 1968 published a pamphlet entitled 'Youth in the world and in Mexico'. At the age of 74, the most renowned leader of the Left in the country, who had dedicated his life to strengthening the revolutionary institutional State, felt the need to lecture the youth. He sharply criticized the young persons who 'slander Marxism by calling themselves Marxist reformers' and who wanted to bring about a new revolution and make way for a new Left 'but who do not follow the Marxism-Leninism path'. With creative imagination, those young people, like their fellow youths in many parts of the world, were looking for new paths for socialism: but Lombardo – and with him a large sector of the Left that was sheltered under the wings of authoritarian nationalism – was not able to understand the students' rebelliousness. The day after the publication of Lombardo's pamphlet against the student movement, thousands of young people gathered in Tlatelolco, where they were fiercely repressed by the army in a barbaric act that left a lingering bitterness in the very depths of the Mexican political system. The young people naturally did not listen to Lombardo. And he did not wish to let himself 'be carried away by the eloquent words or brilliant and audacious phrases' of the 'ideologues of the new revolution'. Six weeks after the Tlatelolco massacre, Vicente Lombardo Toledano died – in the odour of Leninist sanctity – without having wanted to understand that the cries of the young students were not 'an antinational provocation'.

In contrast, from prison, the great intellectual stature and intelligence of José Revueltas converted him into an example of political honesty. In jail, Revueltas was convinced that the repression of 1968 would have the same historical function as the killing of the Río Blanco workers in January 1907: it would give way to revolution.

The repressive efficiency in Río Blanco – he said – was circumstantial, illusory, and fleeting. In the same way, the deadly violence in Tlatelolco would be ephemeral and blind. The repressive government's blindness showed – according to Revueltas – that it was defeated, as in ancient history when it was believed that the gods first blinded those they doomed to perdition. History had accelerated its rhythms and the new revolution was approaching.

But the revolution never arrived. And more than thirty years had to pass before democracy did. Those who governed, despite their blindness, continued to stumble along the road for a very long time. The ferocious efficiency of the repression of Tlatelolco was not able to stop those same wounds of defeat from receiving the seeds of a slow political transition. The authoritarian system was indeed injured, but the political putrefaction process lasted for twenty years. The 1988 presidential election made it clear that authoritarianism was agonizing: the system had split, the PRI was divided and the majority of Mexicans voted in favour of the new political alternative represented by Cuauhtémoc Cárdenas. Electoral fraud – endemic in Mexico – denied the triumph of the Left. It would take another twelve years before the country was able to completely enter into a democratic phase. Although the Right won in the year 2000, the remote causes of transition are found in the distant student movement of the Left.

And so, the authentic initial impulses of transition were not sectarian Marxism-Leninism, aggressive Maoism, or guerrilla Guevarism. The embryo of change was contained in the modest democratic demands of those six points in the 1968 student petition that demanded freedom for political prisoners, abolition of the crime of social dissolution, and the renunciation of various police chiefs. One of these law enforcement officers was the despicable general Raúl Mendiolea, known by everyone who had ever been detained for political reasons. I cannot resist introducing a personal note here, remembering when this officer (at that time a colonel) interrogated me in his office when I was held under arrest for a week for handing out propaganda in the street that criticized President John F. Kennedy's visit to Mexico at the end of June 1962. The image of this fat policeman with a shaved head who harassed me with questions while he played with a gold coin on his desk has remained etched in my memory. He was one of the officers who conducted the harsh repression against the students of 1968 and was personally responsible for torturing many.

The democratic demand to stop the repression characteristic of the Mexican authoritarian regime was slowly growing within society, shaping the comprehensive process of transition to democracy that culminated in the year 2000. With the passing of time, the defeat that had been inflicted upon the students was gradually metamorphosing into a solid democratic idea inserted into the Mexican political reality. Behind this process is the change of a generation that began with a radical revolutionary attitude and ended in democratic liberalism.

And so the president who assassinated the students in Tlatelolco – Gustavo Díaz Ordaz – was wrong when he said in his memoirs that 'Mexico will be the same before and after Tlatelolco, and perhaps continues to be the same to an important extent, because of Tlatelolco'. For we now know that nothing – after Tlatelolco – was the same as before.

There was a significant phenomenon behind the defeat and the slow transition: a counter-culture with worldwide ramifications that lasted many years and whose influence can still be felt at the beginning of the twenty-first century. Perhaps counter-culture is not the most adequate term, but I do not have a better one at this time. I am not referring to the hegemonic culture of the sixties or to the literary or musical expressions of the best-known creators of the era. This counter-culture, impregnated with an attitude of rebellion, was like the strange new air breathed by youth in the 1960s and 1970s, it was a particular way of consuming, reading, and making love. It is therefore difficult to say that novels such as *La tumba* by José Agustín, *Farabeuf* by Salvador Elizondo, or *Gazapo* by Gustavo Sáinz are representative of the counter-culture. They are, only to a certain extent. However, they are a good example of Mexican works that were read then, and were absorbed with a counter-cultural attitude. But *La región más transparente* by Carlos Fuentes was also read at that time, and he is an author who can hardly be labelled as counter-cultural.

The counter-cultural attitude in Mexico was more a kind of consuming, of diversion, and of criticism, than it was a current of ideas or a literary style. Preppy rock groups such as the Teen Tops as well as more aggressive groups such as Three Souls in My Mind (later known as the Tri) were listened to with the same spirit. Perhaps the theatre of José Luis Gurrola and Alexandro Jodorowsky could be considered to have a more counter-cultural characteristic than the poetry of José Emilio Pacheco or Jaime Sabines, but they all fed an audience that let itself be saturated with these works with a critical, insubordinate, and even insolent willingness. The counter-culture was a dissonant mixture of various ingredients: a ritual and intellectual use of drugs, guerrilla warfare, rock, Marxist treatises, La Onda narrative, abstract art, folk and revolutionary songs, Maoism, liberation theology, existential-ism, hippies, pornography, Guevarism, beatniks, and a long et cetera.

Of course, decades later, the Mexican counter-culture dispersed and the more radical attitudes softened. But it is important to note that the counter-cultural attitude marked the entire generation of 1968, the generation that at the beginning of the twenty-first century is in hegemonic positions or has the capacity to strongly influence the political course. This influence is found in two very different ideo-logical locations – the Left and the Right – both of which coincide on the absolute necessity of pushing democratic transition forward. It is therefore fundamental to understand the counter-culture of 1968 not as a closed corpus of ideas and works but as a rainbow of critical and rebellious attitudes.

2007

Chapter 12

Memories of
the counter-culture

On a certain occasion I had been a little lost in the library of the University of California at Berkeley, looking for information on the counter-culture and marginal groups – a subject in which I have always been passionately interested – when a disquieting book fell into my hands. A shock ran through me as soon as I picked it up – I had known the author over thirty years ago. She was Bonnie Bremser, the wife of a Beat poet, who had lived in my house in that far-off time when I was living immersed in the same counter-culture currents that were now the subject of my research. The title of the book struck me as strange: *Troia: Mexican Memoirs*. I did not really understand the reference and had to consult several dictionaries until I finally found it: *troia* is the Italian word for sow or bitch. But it also means whore or slut. An image flashed through my mind. I suddenly remembered how Bonnie had survived in Veracruz and in Mexico City as a prostitute and her husband had participated in soliciting customers for her. Bonnie was not especially pretty, but she was a nice girl. She was slightly dark-skinned and on the thin side, and when she wasn't out on the street, she dressed really terribly. Her husband looked like a criminal. His expression was bitter and he hid his eyes behind sunglasses. He could have escaped from an American film noir.

The memories began to come back to me as I leafed through the book. It was the spring and summer of 1961. I had just returned from New York, where I had gotten to know several members of the Beat movement. My friend, the painter Josep Bartolí, had asked the owners of an art gallery in Greenwich Village, the Barons, if they could put me up. And thanks to them I met many poets and artists, all of whom were very intimidating for a boy who had just turned 18. I remember Elaine, a painter, and wife of the famous artist Willem de Kooning;

I also met the great poet Paul Blackburn and the young writer Margaret Randall, who a short time later moved to Mexico. Parties, cocktails, poetry readings, the new art exhibits, marijuana, young beatniks . . .

I returned to Mexico on 7 April 1961, with my head full of new ideas and sensations, to live alone in my parents' apartment – they had stayed in the United States – in Plaza Citlaltépetl. And so began a genuine carousel of strange visitors who lived at the house, that went on for months. Some stayed only a few days, others for several weeks. My address had passed from hand to hand and nearly every day some-one new arrived: persons from the north, painters, radical leftist mili-tants, hopeless writers, young aggressive poets, inveterate pot-heads, drug-addicted or lunatic intellectuals, and a genuine variegated fauna of more or less revolutionary individuals.

One fine day, Ray Bremser, Bonnie, and their baby, Rachel, arrived at the house. He had spent six years in a New Jersey prison, accused of assault with a deadly weapon. When out on bail, he married Bonnie without permission from the authorities and was put away again. After being released once more on bail, he ran away with his wife to Mexico. She sometimes went out in the evenings to look for customers and he stayed with the child; when the baby cried and was not able to sleep he gently blew marijuana smoke in her face. After a few days they moved on to Veracruz.

In the library at Berkeley, the further along I got in reading Bonnie's memoir, the more my own memories continued to return. And suddenly an idea struck me: was I not exploring those commu-nicating vessels that link the intellectual life of an individual with the spirit of an era? Many writers worry about their work reflecting, in some strange way, the period in which they live. As an essayist I have always been bothered by the doubt: are we free to express our ideas or are we prisoners in the bubble of our era, our culture, and our social condition? Obviously we are not completely free. How is the influence of our environment filtered? And if we knew the paths of these flows, could we manipulate them to expand the space of our freedom? As I was going through the pages of Bonnie Bremser's book I felt that three decades earlier, a door in my consciousness had been opened, letting the gust of the 1960s' counter-culture enter. That year, 1961, marked me forever. It seemed very strange to me that no one in Mexico had translated and published this pathetic testimony of a young woman trapped in the web of the counter-culture.

Apparently, the Mexican police had gone after Bonnie and Ray in Veracruz and he had escaped to Laredo. Some time later, Bonnie fled

Veracruz, where she left the baby in someone's care, and headed for Mexico City by taxi because she was afraid the police would be watching the bus stations. I continued to go through the book, somewhat distracted by my own memories, when I suddenly jumped at seeing my name on page 90. Was that possible? Yes, without a doubt:

> Once in Mexico City, rather at the edge of it, my driver is now turning back to Veracruz, and having taken 50 dollars he gives me back 50 cents so I can continue into town, I am going to Roger B[artra]'s house where I think I will be safe from the police until I get my papers straightened out – Plaza Citlaltépetl, homeless and passionless I get no expired papers. (pp. 92–3)

At the end of the book, Bonnie's recollections end with a date: 11 October 1964. What she writes about had to have taken place in the spring and summer of 1961. A note in the book (published in New York by Croton Press in 1969) says the author was born in 1939 and has plans to 'find a jungle in South America where she and her husband and daughter Georgina can live'.[1] This story reminded me that a decade earlier another beat writer had escaped a trial in New Orleans, accused of drug dealing and theft, and had arrived in Mexico City. William Burroughs established himself there in 1949 and then made a trip to the Amazon jungle in search of the exotic drug, yagé. He lived in Mexico completely drugged and alcoholized. In 1951 he shot and killed his wife Joan at a party. He had wanted to play William Tell, but the bullet missed its mark. Things did not turn out quite so badly for Bonnie, the wife of Ray Bremser, although she lived her life on a very precarious path. In her memoir she describes how she felt after arriving at my house:

> I am out in the hot Mexcity muggy afternoon, more determined than before to have things my own way, and nothing inspires me better than resistance at this point. I am still reading [Fidel] Castro and know that all petty shifts and loopholes that end up in favor of the government are always illegal. So, down the street, swinging it only in rebellion, my head goes up even higher. (p. 93)

At that time – I thought when reading these lines – the association between the rebelliousness of the counter-culture groups and the Cuban revolution was not so surprising or strange as it might seem today. Marijuana was linked to Marxism, the unconventional forms of eroticism were running along the same lines as the guerrillas. Beats as well as aspiring revolutionaries met together at my house; those in search of artificial paradises as well as those who wanted to bring down oppressive systems. Several of us formed part of a political group that worked with Rubén Jaramillo, the *campesino* leader from Morelos. We even had what was fortunately a frustrated guerrilla experience. In 1961 we travelled to Arcelia, on the Costa Grande of Guerrero, to organize an armed group. A cold chill ran through me remembering that event, as I was reading Bonnie's memoir in the library. I recalled how, with my Central American and Mexican companions, we had run through the steep streets of Arcelia announcing the meeting with loudspeakers, how we had made a call to insurrection at that meeting, how the *campesinos* had agreed with our ideas. We had supposed they would rise up with their own arms. We had none and I had never even fired a shot or had a rifle in my hands, except a totally useless one that had been lent to me for marching in the army when I had done my military service a few years before. I remembered that at that time Guerrero was a region that was strongly affected by great tensions: the governor (Raúl Caballero Aburto) had just fallen from power, after having very violently repressed the *campesino* civic movement headed by Genaro Vázquez Rojas. I remember how the army had been alerted that some guerrillas (us) were organizing a subversive group. Terrified, we left Arcelia and when we got to Chilpancingo, the state capital, the next morning, a newspaper announced that the army was looking for dangerous guerrillas in Arcelia. I remembered that in May of the following year Rubén Jaramillo, the leader who had motivated us to fight, and his pregnant wife and three children had been assassinated by the military.

During that summer of 1961, in the hot afternoons before the rain, we got together to discuss the coming revolution, and at night we were joined by the gringo Beat friends, some teenage 'existentialists', and classmates from the School of Anthropology. A lot of drinking and smoking went on. Margaret Randall and a pair of strange Americans, Diane Bakus and Howard Shulman, who were headed for Cuba had arrived at the house. She had just been released from a mental hospital and he was injecting himself with heroin every day. I remember that I was very attracted to Diane and that she did not reject my caresses. Bonnie had abandoned her little child, Rachel, forever; she had given her up for adoption, and she was desperate:

> I am in a perpetual state of sweat, the elements have met my arrival in Mexcity with a burst of heat. I do not look or wish for pleasant weather, have no prospects of pleasure and so continue this soul drive in the

withering heat, but do not wither. Back to Roger's I mail, or package
to mail, an extract of promise from M that she will promptly mail Ray's
manuscripts to him in Laredo [. . .] frantically I try to think my way out
of it. This is the situation: Ray is in Laredo, I hope (I have had but one
letter dated five days earlier), the baby and home are behind me, I have
no money to go backwards or forwards or even to move around in the
city, no money, so I am left the alternative of asking for help. (p. 93)

Bonnie tells how she would look for friends and people she knew,
tell them about her misadventures, appeal to their pity when she con-
fessed that she had had to prostitute herself to survive, and would get
money from them. I remember that at that time everyone had problems and was looking for a way out, an alternative, a change, a revolution . . . And when we did not have enough problems we looked for
more by living on treacherous and uncertain paths. Most definitely,
one of the things that most disturbed me in Bonnie's memoir was the
dramatic contradiction between the liberating spirit of the Beats and
the lamentable condition she lived in, tied to domestic and maternal
chores that she escaped from in a certain way when she prostituted
herself. But by doing so, in order to support her poet husband, she
accepted a degrading condition. However, she also explains in her
book that she was looking for sexual pleasure. It bothered her to work
in a brothel in Mexico City but she tells what happened one day: 'It is
a hot afternoon and all I am thinking of is myself, within reason, got
to get money, but it is natural pleasure and this cat is O.K.' (p. 140).
But she became disenchanted when they had group sex with her and
in addition to not paying her the agreed amount, lacked imagination
as they timidly penetrated her, one after the other. The descriptions
of her sexual encounters are crude, almost cold, but powerful. They
are every bit a complicated act, difficult to decipher, and one that
feminists who have read the book have clashed with. With a hint of
bitterness, Bonnie tells how others saw her:

> My mistake was later to get high at Roger B[artra]'s house (mistake to
> be myself? What am I, a statue?) and spill the beans about how we have
> supported ourselves these months in Veracruz. Maybe I bait M a little
> for she has been shocked already at R's house, and I am surprised at her
> disapproval and so continue to lay more of the whole story on her than
> I should have, bitterly boasting not at all reconciled at things, wonder-
> ing at the necessity of the past myself, this present necessity being so
> much greater. Anyway, I pour out a confession that burns their ears and
> covers up my human tracks. I have begun to erect a reputation that will

make my personality and my love a recluse, though both are there to
be seen. (p. 94)

Bonnie Bremser, so wrapped up in her own problems and anxieties, had no idea what was happening in Mexico, and surely did not
care. The counter-culture intellectuals from the United States saw
Mexico only as a wild and backward space and were never interested
in its political and intellectual manifestations. Neither Ray Bremser,
nor Allen Ginsberg, nor Jack Kerouac approached the Mexican intellectual and artistic milieu. Burroughs had not had the slightest con-
tact with Mexican culture either. Looking back at that time, I can
remember very few signs of interest in Mexico shown by the Beats
who passed through the country. The one exception was the poet
Margaret Randall, who stayed to live in Mexico and founded, together
with Sergio Mondragón, an interesting and unjustly forgotten magazine, *El corno emplumado.*

That afternoon in Berkeley as I continued to read Bonnie's book,
I remembered that during the summer of 1961 I had come into con-
tact with two worlds that I would later focus much of my attention on
as an anthropologist: the rural world and that of the counter-culture.
The *campesinos* of the Costa Grande of Guerrero and the rebellious
spirits of the Beats left an underground mark on me. I remembered
how on those summer nights we would get together to conspire and
at the same time to practice a ritual of rejection of everything established. With the *campesinos* and ethnic groups we wanted to make a
revolution; with rituals and drugs we wanted to explore a new reality.
Molotov cocktails as well as packets of marijuana were in my refrigera-
tor at home. We were just as ready to go to Cuba and fight against the
United States invasion (the counter-revolutionaries had just disembarked in the Bay of Pigs) as we were to read the poetry of Lawrence
Ferlinghetti out loud. I remembered how months later I told a friend,
the film-maker Paul Leduc, about my revolutionary furies. He was
alarmed by my radicalism and convinced me that rather than continuing agitating in the student and 'petit bourgeois' environments
I should join a serious leftist organization, the Communist Party.
That saved me from a sterile, dangerous, and childish rebellion but it
placed me in a world in which for too many years we futilely searched
for the proletariat class that should have opened the doors for us to a
new society. But that is another story . . .

The images that Bonnie evoked in her memoir jarred me, and even
though I read them protected by the walls brimming with books in

the library of Berkeley, I felt vertigo when looking back at that era. She relates:

> I was finally admitted to Roger B[artra]'s house and invited to stay, in fact M was staying there then. Roger's house was full of people and bed-bugs. I poured out to them my whole story and they reacted variously. Roger was very sympathetic. Blonde Spanish Roger, Ray and I have stayed with him on a previous trip to Mexcity, a lark, an explorative journey to Mexcity to initiate me to hustling there, but I was sick the whole time and had to go to a local clinic to be treated for a kidney infection, on a street where other doctors' offices were located, one where I had my abortion, not wanting to have a baby so obviously belonging to the streets, our matrimonial vows already so abused. (p. 95)

I remember my apartment jam-packed with people. I remember the bedbugs but I do not remember how understanding I was. Living together for a few weeks with Bonnie and the rest of the personalities from the Beat world had to have been a potent injection of tolerance. I liked them very much, in part because they took me back to my childhood, when for a few years I had become a free and happy gringo boy who ran around with his little band of friends through the forests and along the ponds of Newton (New Jersey) and the long beaches of Bayville (New York). It was my original paradise, where myths such as that of Huckleberry Finn lived. With Bonnie once again I spoke my rudimentary childhood English, and even though her audacity frightened me, I sensed that she was exploring new attractive but dangerous ways of living. I do not remember her speaking to me of her abortion and how much it upset her. She explains it in her book:

> I am hardly yet able to face this specter of murder, and how much better would things have been if I could have accepted the fruits of my labor, good and bad, since I am not much of a judge of which is which now. But Roger was nice enough to be able to understand my frantic state, and that night I was introduced to the first taste of something called Acapulco Gold, which was not the real thing; I did not run into the authentic item until three years later in New York, and it is something like wheat grain, beautiful healthy high, but these kids at Roger's were smoking something good, and I helped them, and sat up through the night writing a huge slow letter to Ray including as much encouragement and love to him as I could. (p. 95)

Upon reading this I remembered how the distant and long puffs of smoke had connected me forever to a fascinating alternative world.

The strangest thing is that in those reunions of 1961 I firmly and naively believed that I was riding atop the new waves of the century, that I was getting high into a history that some day would open a more productive path for us. But something else happened: the swells of that counter-culture ocean became fixed in my memory and, from some dark corner of my consciousness, have continued to rock me ever since.

2007

Chapter 13

Street life and politics

To talk about life on the street is to deal with a strange singularity, although at first glance it might seem somewhat banal. To explain what I mean, let me make a little detour. The movement we associate with street life makes us think too quickly in organic terms, imagining an urban body criss-crossed with arteries and veins that send energy to the different organs and to extremities that are articulated neighbourhoods. A street body has even been imagined that is equipped with an enormous belly made up of a central market and large excretory canals. But in reality we are clearly concerned with non-organic social life forms.

When speaking of non-organic life forms, it is very common for doubts and discussions to come up. The idea that non-organic systems capable of self-organization can exist – they have been called bioids – is viewed with uneasiness and even with suspicion. Ilya Prigogine has polemically pointed out the importance of physical phenomena that exhibit spontaneous self-organization – such as the so-called chemical clocks or solitons – that do not reach a stable balance but maintain regular rhythms. Reactions that change colour in an orderly sequence or waves that travel unperturbed for many hundreds of kilometres (tsunamis) are examples of such events.

Some scientists think there could have been chemical systems in the primeval soup from which organic life emerged that were capable of maintaining an identity similar to homeostasis, were sensitive to environmental fluctuations, and were capable of evolving.

In contrast, when other non-organic forms are spoken of, such as social, cultural, or political life, these concepts are not usually met with the same resistance. We are so accustomed to thinking of literature or music as life forms that we do not stop to think about the fact that they actually are non-organic forms, albeit supported by those biological entities, us humans. Of course, biologists are familiarized with these types of phenomena in which, for example, the genetic information involved in the development of an embryo does not direct the entire process but rather triggers self-regulation and growth mechanisms that are not predetermined by the sequence-initiating DNA.

In social life this phenomenon is much more apparent. Even though the initial spark of an individual's life obeys biological impulses, non-organic self-regulation processes determine the growth and ramification of social life.

If we feel there is life in institutions, in financial markets, in novels, or in symphonies, it is not because they are founded on millions of biological organisms. We think there is life there because we recognize structures that are capable of reproducing, evolving, and regulating themselves according to codes and symbols that do not come from the organic environment of individuals.

So social life adopts different forms, some of them more orderly than others. To begin with let us think of three of its most organized expressions: private life, economic life, and public life. Private life revolves around family and crystalizes in homes, in houses. Economic life materializes in factories or offices (and in rural zones, in cultivated fields). Public life is expressed in different ceremonials, some of which take place in churches, theatres, government dependencies, schools, or auditoriums. All these are non-organic life forms that in the course of centuries make up the huge conglomeration of constructions that are cities, and that do not seem to have an organic existence. But they do seem to be a new species of large monsters endowed with organs and a great capacity for self-regulation. However, no matter how popular biological metaphors have become for describing modern life, we know that we are dealing with phenomena that do not function in the same way living organisms do.

Nonetheless, in the social life forms I mentioned, there is a high level of organization and a very complex mechanism that regulates the processes. But, as we know, not everything in social life occurs in such an organized and orderly manner so as to prevent dramatic setbacks. In fact, societies appear to be characterized by a mixture of order and disorder. Sometimes order is not very coherent and disorder is not as chaotic as it first appears to be. To get closer to the topic I wish to comment on, let us think about how private, economic, and public life forms materialize in cities. According to the era and culture, houses and all kinds of buildings that are the sites of different activities are built in a relatively orderly fashion. Obviously it is necessary to leave spaces for people to be able to get around from one place to another and so another life form arises, that of life on the streets. Streets are a means of public communication.

The street, which has been turned into a powerful symbol and into one of the most important arteries of modern life, is nevertheless a social phenomenon that is notoriously different from the private, economic, and public expressions that are its origin. The street is a phenomenon tied to the growth of necessary, but residual, interstices and spaces. Of course, the street goes counter to the place where family life occurs. In contrast to the street, the home is where it is assumed that, under ideal circumstances, order prevails and customs and traditions reign that are subject to relatively rigid norms and codes. The same occurs in the workplace where rules and hierarchies are strictly enforced and measured by chronometer. The public life that I referred to also takes place in schools, churches, government buildings, auditoriums, and similar places. Streets are public spaces too, but they are strips designated for the traffic of vehicles and persons where a heterogeneous mixture of extremely different activities occurs. These spaces are not designed for definite and specialized public expressions, such as those that take place in theatres or churches, and they usually have very few constructions built for specific functions (such as kiosks or plazas created for political manifestations).

Life on the streets offers a first paradox. Looked at from the supposed tranquillity and order of the home, the street appears symbolically as the kingdom of disorder and commotion. But at the same time the streets of every city form a perfectly organized set, each one with its name, its code, and its place in a neighbourhood and a political circumscription. If we consult a map we will see no symptom of anomie. And nevertheless, upon leaving the hierarchized order of the office and the factory, the street seems to be a chaotic and menacing place where one can run into any type of person imaginable. To be thrown out onto the street, whether by a boss or an infuriated spouse, is a considerable threat. In this sense the street is a space of vulnerability and abandonment, of noise and filth, of danger and transience.

The enormous heterogeneity of street life is obvious. The road of the forsaken is also the place of strolls, cafés, shopping, restaurants, and parks. Each city and each neighbourhood has its own personality, its identity, from the boring streets of the upper class zones to the vibrating centric neighbourhoods; from the numbered grids of many modern cities to the gothic labyrinth of old cities.

When the great thinker George Steiner was asked to define his idea of Europe, he first thought of the cafés, the leisurely walks, and the streets. Later he added the double inheritance that originated in Athens and Jerusalem, and the European fears of an approaching decline of civilization, the end of history. 'The café', says Steiner, 'is a place for assignation and conspiracy, for intellectual debate and gossip, for the *flâneur* and the poet or metaphysician at his notebook.' The stroller gets up from the café and walks through streets bearing the names of statesmen, illustrious military men, poets, artists, composers, scientists, and philosophers. It is the sovereignty of recollection, the self-definition of European streets as places in the collective memory that includes the commemoration of killings, suffering, hate, and human sacrifice.[1]

Steiner is heir to a tradition that was strongly propelled by Walter Benjamin, who realized that walking along the streets and through the commercial arcades was a penetrating exercise that aided in understanding the peculiarities of an age and a culture. One of Benjamin's most interesting books is *Einbahnstrasse* (*One-way street*). This unsettling philosopher always behaved as if he lived on the street, like a *flâneur* who wandered by chance through various European cities. His life was a one-way street travelled by a thinker who was not sure if life had any meaning . . . so when he saw there was no way out of this street, he ended his life. Yet Walter Benjamin taught us that street life does have meaning. 'Not to find one's way around a city', he wrote, 'does not mean much. But to lose one's way in a city as one loses one's way in a forest requires some schooling' ('Tiergarten', *Berliner Kinderheit um 1900*).

By no means is it easy to decipher street life. The signals of what takes place there are so mixed that it makes their translation into an intelligible language very difficult. The space itself is a texture of asphalt, brick, cement, and earth traversed by cables, autos, bicycles, motorcycles, and gutters. Here there is a bewilderment of voices, noises, and music that becomes enveloped in an incongruent mixture of smells and lights coming from puddles, filth, traffic lights, the selling of food, advertisements, headlights, shop displays, and windows. Even in cities of very developed countries with sophisticated civic cultures – let us say Switzerland – the streets give a sensation of unpredictability and chance. This sensation is greatly multiplied in the big cities of the Third World. A writer described the city of Lima in the 1960s in dramatic tones: 'a city where two million beings bump into one another in the midst of loudspeakers, savage radios, human congestions, and other contemporary insanities, in order to survive'. Those two million 'move around making their way . . . among the beasts that agglomerating underdevelopment turns men into'. This author, Sebastián Salazar Bondy, in his book with the symptomatic title *Lima la horrible* (México, 1964), speaks of 'civil chaos produced with cancerous speed by the starving urban throng' (pp. 16f). And what this writer saw is nothing compared to the Lima of today or – still more monstrous – Mexico City. I do not want to be an alarmist. I am interested in pointing out that the random and at times chaotic heterogeneity of street life is like a sensitive sponge that absorbs, so to say, the mood of a society. This seems of the greatest importance to me since it means that careful observation of street life can reveal aspects and dimensions of social life that are hidden to the casual observer. The streets are like a type of theatre where the forces of order and chaos come face-to-face. On the one hand there is a mob of actors that brings chaos, some more than others, into street life: street vendors, beggars, peddlers, pickpockets, squatters, homeless children or adults, neighbourhood lunatics, gangs, uncivil drivers, prostitutes, and many more. On the other hand we have the forces of order that try to fight the entropy: mayors, the police, guards, mail carriers, garbage collectors, couriers, and behind them an army of bureaucrats, architects, functionaries, and engineers dedicated to the tasks of all kinds of urban administration, from naming the streets to regulating the traffic lights.

Facing the wild entropy of daily life on the streets are the domestic forces driven by the spirit of Baron Haussmann, the powerful functionary who drastically modernized and remodelled the city of Paris in the second half of the nineteenth century. One of the motivations of this urbanizing baron was to eliminate everything on the streets that could be used in connection with popular uprisings and in that way provide security for the Parisian bourgeoisie.

The resulting effects of balance from this permanent confrontation between social order and chaotic dynamism are reflected in daily street life. There we can contemplate the scene of countless accidents, correlations of forces, negotiations, and routine violent acts. The rhythms of this street life and its equilibriums change hour by hour, going from the morning workday frenzy to the tranquil and sometimes threatening night. The cycle is both routine and mysterious – the inconceivable, the strange, and the dangerous are hidden within the creases marked by the flows of daily monotony.

Humanity's destiny is probably only rarely determined on the street. But nevertheless Henri Lefebvre was right when he said in 1963 that the street is 'the micro-world of modernity'. He added: 'With its mobile appearance it publicly offers what in other places is hidden, carrying it out on the stage of an almost spontaneous theatre'. For this sociologist the street is a kind of 'social text' where the signs of diversity of classes and conditions, of things of beauty and of ugliness are mixed together. The street is a spectacle where our wandering ego is part of the set in a world full of strangers. 'An overpopulated desert,' says Lefebvre, 'the street fascinates but never takes too long to disappoint [...] Overpopulated, the street becomes the place of the crowd, and each individual becomes lost in it or avoids it. Abandoned, deserted, the street becomes attractive because of its emptiness.'[2]

The future of society is not determined on the street. But in contrast the street is the mirror of its present condition and sometimes of its future. The way in which the street responds to important events at times reveals their ulterior consequences and the mood of the population. In this sense, the street is a mediation network that captures the peculiarities of contradictory poles, of social paradoxes, and of political incongruities. Streets reveal the fabric of what I have called imaginary networks of political power, mediating and legitimizing channels that every society requires.

Therefore, streets are a very sought-after setting for political forces. Movements and parties become a part of street life and invade it. Many persons believe these invasions of the street spectacle can change events and influence governmental powers to accept their demands. Political manifestations in the form of taking to the streets to protest are certainly an important ingredient of political life. However, it must be recognized that only on exceptional occasions do the street irruptions of movements produce important effects (sometimes positive, other times disastrous). The manifestations of 1968 are a prime example; and in 2006 the invasion and occupation of the centre of Mexico City by the parties that did not accept the results of the presidential election of that year. In fact, the latter was a poor imitation of the famous 'orange revolution' that took over the streets of Kiev in 2004 and pushed the transition to democracy forward in Ukraine.

Careful observation of this confluence of urban civil society with political society is very interesting and uncovers aspects of the social fabric that are often hidden. When political society spills over into civil society's street life, both an unsettling and a revealing mixture of the sensibilities of the population are produced. Politicians frequently become disoriented in these situations and come to incorrect conclusions. The mass meetings convoked by the neo-Zapatistas showed something more than sympathy for the indigenous rebels and their subcommander. They revealed the fact, and this was not always understood, that society particularly supported peace and the insertion of indigenous peoples into civil and political life. The Zapatistas of the EZLN did not understand this and they ended up marginalized.

Another example: a careful observer of the lengthy occupation of streets in Mexico City in 2006 by López Obrador and his followers would have realized that the chemistry in the relation between the political activists and the inhabitants of the city was not good. The *cacique*-style political structures and the mass of people driven to demonstrate hid the fact that the majority of the city's inhabitants felt that the semi-permanent occupation was an imposition on civil life by the political spheres. Only a few intellectuals close to López Obrador realized that, but no one listened to them. Many people living in Mexico City felt that the demonstration was an arbitrary obstruction of the city's free flows. This protest looked like a rigid governmental and bureaucratic structure installed in the street, with its sheiks lodged in tents, blocking traffic and shielding its leaders from any type of urban contamination.

Mexico City has been increasingly saturated with these political intromissions. Life on the street is disturbed more and more. Political order is imposed too frequently on street life. The result is more chaos and less trust in the political forces that interrupt the flow of street life. It is very possible that these instabilities could be the beginning of the downfall of the politicians who, in the name of the Left, govern Mexico City.

I hope that these reflections are taken as an invitation to carefully observe life on the street, and to pay close attention to the contradictions between order and flow, between stability and change. One more example is a paradox between urban nomenclature and social reality that strikes me as somewhat ironic. In Mexico City there is a poor district called Political Reform and its streets are named after almost all the reforms imaginable – over fifty. They go from the management reform and the youth reform, through the scientific, sports, and geographic reforms, to the customs, political, and constitutional reforms. And yet in Mexico we know it is precisely a reform of the State that is sorely missing. When a street finally does have that name, it will surely be when this reform, too, has come to a standstill.

In this case order was enforced by a so-called Nomenclature Commission of the Government of Mexico City that is in charge of assigning, reviewing, approving, modifying, and recognizing the names of the streets, districts, and free spaces that exist in the city.

Without a doubt the incessant logorrhea of this commission, possessed by nominalist furore, solemnly ignores all relation with life on the streets. It would be useless to ask the nomenclators why there are so few revolutionary streets, in fact there are only three: revolution (plain and simple, which is the name of a long avenue), social revolution, and agrarian revolution. And of course the revolution is embodied in the numerous streets that are named after heroes.

* * *

The street is an intimidating place, especially in certain big cities of the Third World. Many people avoid the street out of fear of pollution, accidents, muggings, and traffic jams. Functionaries and politicians abandon the streets in direct relation to how high they are on their climb to powerful positions. They take shelter in their mansions and they move about encapsulated in limousines or even in helicopters. The political elite distance themselves from the streets that they occasionally send their hordes of activists to. Since the leaders stop circulating through the streets they eventually lose the feel for their environment and no longer recognize their habitat. Politicians end up immured in the high spheres or on the upper floors of urban reality, hardened and insensitive to what is happening on the ground floor and out on the asphalt, while accompanied by a jet set of businesspersons, movie stars, and famous personalities from different walks of life.

And finally, one must ask: is life on the street in danger of extinction? Is street life being damaged by the insensitivity of government leaders and the new tendencies in urban development? Cities as we know them are certainly endangered, paradoxically threatened with drowning in the swell of massive urbanization. Cities, as an old form of culture, are invaded by enormous masses of floating immigrant populations. Uncivil and illegal forms of survival are extending. New technologies foment the disaggregation of employment and fragment work places as well as work processes. With increasing frequency it is no longer necessary to go out of the suburban building, take some means of transportation or walk, in order to get to work or to go shopping. Now we use the computer or the telephone more than the streetcar, the bus, or the metro. City life is being substituted by distance correspondence: the new forms of communication allow not only for tele-amusement, but also for teleshopping, tele-information, and above all, teleworking. City life on the streets is now invaded by floating crowds and tends to be substituted by social telecommunication networks that are overwhelming the old territorial forms. And the territory that is affected most is the street. Closed ghettos develop, whether they are residential islands for the upper class or poor slums, each of them impenetrable to strangers.

Yes, the street is endangered. If we wish to stop its extinction, it is necessary to promote forms of civic self-management revolving around renovated forms of identity that civilize, so to say, the daily struggle for survival and that domesticate the aggression towards strangers migrating to urban zones. This sounds like a utopia, but perhaps making it a reality is a worthwhile endeavour.

2008

Chapter 14

The shadow of the future

The future is uncomfortable and dangerous. It provokes intense discussions and bitter confrontations. Some even kill for the future. George Orwell's classic text on the future, the novel *1984*, has provoked intense controversies. In 1949 Orwell described a terrible socialist future, capable of destroying all hope. When the fateful date arrived thirty-five years later, it was obvious that the horror predicted by Orwell had indeed been embodied by real existing socialism. That was how Julio Cortázar saw things at the time, when in an essay written in 1983 on Orwell's novel, he criticized the situation in Cuba and Nicaragua and clarified that he did so *pro* those liberating processes and not *against* them. He distanced himself from criticisms against socialist processes and explained: 'how to not take into account the criticisms of an Octavio Paz or a Mario Vargas Llosa? Personally I share many of their reservations, with the difference that in my case I do so to defend an idea of future that they only seem to imagine as an improved present, without accepting that it has to be fundamentally changed.'[1] But actually it was the socialist *present* that did not improve, and that to the contrary, worsened, that did not have a future: it was fundamentally changed less than ten years later. The future that Julio Cortázar envisioned did not arrive. Socialism collapsed and left a battered utopia. In a few places, such as in Cuba, the ruins of the chimeric experiment remained in a terrible state, as a reminder of a past that came to nothing.

The future is disobedient and deceptive. Thanks to the Greek tragedians we know that the road to destiny is soaked in blood, cruelty, and violence. The future is unruly and does not obey the mandates of the prophets. It shows us one face, but when it arrives, it has changed and wears a different countenance. Cortázar, in his critical reflections on the year 1984, took on the theme of the 'new man', that future being that the engineers of the soul had to begin to build. Cortázar asked himself: 'How can the new man be created? Who knows the parameters? There is an illusory diagram that quickly degenerates into sectarianism and the impoverishment of the human entity: the desire to create a permanent revolutionary type, considered a priori as good.' In Cuba this idealization meant, says Cortázar, 'the condemnation of the homosexual temperament, of intellectual individualism when it is expressed in critical attitudes or in activities apparently unrelated to the revolutionary effort, and it can take on religious sentiment in its repudiation, considering it a reactionary flaw'. At that time Cortázar was convinced the future would correct those vices. Cortázar died very shortly afterwards, precisely in 1984. He was not able to see how the malevolent ravages of that threat, embodied symbolically in the year 1984, ended up shattering the future he had imagined and desired.

I have wanted to begin these reflections remembering Cortázar, the great writer I so admire, because with the example of his contradictory and anguished relationship with socialism we can understand that for many the future projects disturbing shadows onto the present. The socialist future contemplated by Cortázar firmly fixed the dark shadows of Orwellian 1984 onto his life. If we go back half a century, we arrive at a text whose title I have reintroduced in order to give a name to these reflections. I am referring to the book written by Johan Huizinga, the great Dutch historian, published in 1935: *In the Shadow of Tomorrow*. Huizinga was known for his marvellous exploration of the past in *The Autumn of the Middle Ages* (1919). His sombre book of 1935 warns against savagery and points out that culture is soaked in a spirit that holds *myth* in a position higher than *logos* and places *existence* over *intelligence*. The book's subtitle is revealing: *A Diagnosis of the Spiritual Distemper of our Time*.[2] We can suppose that Huizinga was influenced by the triumphs of Hitler and the Nazis in Germany, although he makes no direct reference to them in the book. He could not predict that he would die a prisoner of the Nazis ten years after the publication of that work, a few months before the Second World War came to an end.

Huizinga's book helps us understand that we cannot explore the future. What we can study are the shadows the future projects in the present. Huizinga states that as a historian he can only foretell 'that a great change in human relations is never produced ending in what has previously been thought. We know for certain that things take a different course from the one we might think'.

Huizinga's shadows are similar to those that many thinkers have contemplated in times of crisis. He observes symptoms of decadence, he believes a cultural crisis is being experienced, that a process of intense and radical imbalance is taking place in which the bases of ethics are put in doubt. It is a disease that places the value of notions above scientific values, that promotes an excess of the printed word or words tossed into the air, and that confronts humanity with intellectual challenges for which the anxiety-filled organism is not prepared.

When we observe the shadows of the future we can explain their presence in different ways. These shadows can be produced by the intense darkness of tomorrow that is projected onto the illuminated present. The future is also bleak when the evils of the present are seen as they expand and there is little hope in sight. That is what Huizinga did: he observed the diseases that affected the culture of his era and warned of the dangers that threatened society.

The perceptive Chilean sociologist Norbert Lechner gives another explanation in a book with a title very similar to Huizinga's: *Las sombras del mañana* (*The Shadows of Tomorrow*), published in 2002. Lechner stated there: 'Not only the past casts shadows, so does tomorrow. They are the forces that keep us from imagining the new, another world, a different life, a better future.'[3] Here, the light of the future is blocked by obstacles whose shadows extend towards us. One could think that, to catch a glimpse of the future, all we would need to do is remove those obstacles, those forces that inhibit our imagination.

I have wanted to cite these ideas on the shadows of tomorrow because they remind us of the sad tone of those who look to the future in moments of restless transition. And Mexico is passing through these moments precisely due to a difficult transition that gives the sensation that we are living on the brink of disaster, submerged in a profound crisis and facing a dark and threatening tomorrow. One of the obsessions that usually prevails at critical moments is the idea that the country is losing character and identity. With the arrival of democracy and the defeat of revolutionary nationalism the country is supposedly on a downward slide, pushed by the ruling Right towards a loss of character, towards a fusion with foreign values that belong to the English-speaking world. In the face of this national character crisis, right-wing tendencies emerge that long for the PRI to return to power, in the hopes of restoring the supposedly authentic profiles of the Republic. Other tendencies, equally conservative but leaning towards the Left, promote a populism that would strengthen the national features of what is called a 'true' democracy.

The same conservative inclination that becomes alarmed at the possibility of a loss of character has emerged in various European

countries and in the United States. The impetuous growth of the
foreign-born population and the flow of immigrants have caused the
forces of the Right to hit the ceiling. They fear that their national
profiles are becoming blurred by the invading torrent of aliens. In
Mexico the invasion of foreign cultural values penetrating through
pores opened by globalization is feared.

It continues to be disturbing that only ten years after the initiation
of the democratic transition, a majority of organized political forces
were leaning towards a restoration of the nationalist culture characteristic of the former authoritarian regime. Some politicians invoke
the hackneyed phrase of Heraclitus and exclaim: 'Character is destiny'. If there is no character, they say, we will have no future. Long
ago Walter Benjamin explained that if there is character, destiny is
constant, and therefore *there is no destiny*. That is why it is important to
clearly separate character and destiny. The former belongs to comedy
and the latter belongs to tragedy.

When Mexico had character, we lived immersed in the revolutionary comedy: there was no destiny, everything was institutionalized in
the eternal return of authoritarianism. Now with democracy, we have
a destiny: but we live without knowing how it will end.

In the era of the revolutionary comedy, the authoritarian character
of a permanent national identity was the dominating force. With the
arrival of the democratic tragedy a multitude of contradictory and
changing characters has appeared, but no one knows how the political confusion will end and many fear it will not be a happy ending.

It seems to me that Mexicans have been gradually abandoning the
national character that the political comedy had assigned to them.
From the time I wrote *The Cage of Melancholy* I thought that the crisis
of archaic superpatriotism would sooner or later bring about the end
of authoritarianism and the advent of political democracy. And that
did take place – later rather than sooner – and now Mexico is in the
uncomfortable situation in which government legitimacy is no longer
based on the old nationalist tradition, but a new democratic civic
culture that would stabilize the system has yet to be consolidated.
And therefore the future is projecting long and disturbing shadows
over us.

What alternatives for the Left can we find in the presence of this
critical situation? Of course, we have the old formulas, beginning
with the most visible ones on the Latin American political horizon:
populism and statist protectionism. These alternatives cast sombre sil-
houettes from the past and threaten the immediate future with their

dangers. They are the shadows of Hugo Chávez and his partners in the opaque Bolivarian socialist enterprise.

Although they have Fidel Castro's blessing, this new edition of populism is not attempting to implant the Cuban model, which is one of the few remnants left of the dictatorial socialism of the past century. Rather it is a vaguely anticapitalist authoritarian statism that tries to strengthen regulating and interventionist governments with a shrill but inefficient nationalist and anti-imperialist vociferation.

For its part, the Mexican Right is immersed in the interests of the elite and lacks the imagination and intelligence necessary for doing something other than letting itself be carried away by global tendencies, and in fits and starts, choosing among the alternatives that arise. What the Right *does* continue to do with tiresome insistence is to denounce the evils of the growing moral crisis. From its perspective, said crisis is revealed by a lack of respect for the authority of ethical laws of absolute validity, inspired in Catholic values that are considered immovable. The most obvious sign of the moral crisis that alarms the Right is the dysfunction or fragmentation of the family as society's unifying nucleus, causing a massive proliferation of crime, drug-trafficking, and violence. This thesis gives way to the conservative ideas of limiting secular education, rejecting the use of birth control, the legalization of abortion, and same-sex marriage. The Right frequently establishes a causal relationship between the erosion of ethical values and the dissolution of national character, since Catholic morals are supposedly deeply rooted in the essential Mexican identity.

Another large shadow projected onto Mexican society is that of the return to power of the descendants of the former authoritarian regime. These descendants are found in all parties and are deeply embedded in the political culture. Social sectors captivated by populism, but disenchanted with the Left that is lost in its internal struggles and its corruption, see the PRI as an alternative. Business and finance groups that have become disoriented in the labyrinth of the new democracy also see the PRI as a last resort. It must be recognized that the PRI is an assortment of contradictions, a very fragmented space. I see it as a cracked desert of dried-up ideas where the pragmatic attitudes that unite its leaders and barons grow like cactuses.

The political situation in Mexico at the beginning of the second decade of the twenty-first century is ambiguous and contradictory. The right-wing PAN in power is convinced that it is riding the most advanced waves of the democratization and globalization process. In contrast, the Left believes the country is living a terrible decadence caused by the group in power, made up of a small band of corrupt politicians and pseudo-businesspersons that are no more than influence traffickers. The PRI tries to present itself as always having been society's defender of democracy, giving the impression that it will now arrive, free from corruption, to save Mexico from the conservatives and populists that have plunged the country into chaos. In the empty spaces that separate the three big parties lives a horde of parasitic parties whose opportunism is only surpassed by their incoherence and corruption. Of course, these are the extremes, but they certainly reveal the fact that Mexican political life is deeply fragmented and each fragment seems to have come from a different planet.

I believe that this particular situation can be described with the formula the Argentinian sociologist Gino Germani used when he referred to Peronism and other populist phenomena in Latin America. Germani says that these peculiar situations arise from the 'singularity of the non-contemporaneous', in other words, from the motley collection of incongruent situations that proceed from different eras. Undoubtedly he retook the expression that Ernst Bloch made famous when characterizing Nazi Germany: the 'contemporaneity of the non-contemporaneous' ('die Ungleichzeitigkeit des Gleichzeitigen'). Bloch used this expression in his book, *The Heritage of Our Times*, published in 1935, the same year as Huizinga's book. Parenthetically, it should be remembered that in the 1930s Bloch publicly excused Stalin and openly justified the famous and sinister trials that condemned many communists to death at that time. But this should not prevent us from seeing that Bloch's expression reflects important tensions that disturbed the intellectuals and politicians of his day and that continue to do so today.

In his book Ernst Bloch said that the Left in Germany had been wrong to condemn 'non-contemporaneous' social groups and had not understood that utopian hopes stemmed from these precapitalist segments. This error had enabled Nazism to monopolize utopian images capable of attracting the masses. Bloch believed the success of the Nazis was sustained by the disproportionate survival of anachronistic institutions and attitudes in such a way that irrational tendencies inherited from the past led the popular masses to identify with Hitler. Gino Germani believed that Peronism in Argentina was a similar phenomenon.

Certainly it can be said that in Mexico we have endured the simultaneousness of premodern, modern, and postmodern planes that have become intertwined in a fascinating spectacle. As Bloch said:

'Not everyone lives in the same Now'. And so not everyone imagines the same future. This has helped the populist political culture to become deeply rooted within Mexico. Today Mexico is still experiencing a profound fragmentation and a threatening simultaneousness of non-contemporaneous situations, as are other Latin American countries.

I would say that in Mexico we are confronting a strange situation. Socio-economic structures have been becoming uniform to the degree that capitalism has extended, the market has penetrated every corner, and urbanization is growing energetically. Nevertheless, while globalization penetrates the pores of the economy, we observe cracks and fractures in political life that go beyond ideological differences separating the parties and political currents. Mexican politics does not offer that panorama characteristic of modern democracies in which the party system functions with a certain coherence and in relative harmony. Under these advanced conditions, political forces are contemporaneous, that is to say, they share features of the era in which they live, they live in the same Now.

I purposely exaggerate here to express myself more briefly in saying that in Mexico the parties and political forces currently make up an incongruent cluster of absurd attitudes. The problem is not that each one is pulling in a different direction, since it is understandable that the struggles of each party are in accordance with their postulates and interests. The problem is that the parties and political forces are themselves internally incongruent and are pierced by enormous fissures.

The components of the Mexican political system simultaneously coincide in the electoral and ideological struggle, but they are not contemporaries. One of the fundamental aspects of democratic politics lies in the ability to and habit of *contemporizing*, in the sense of knowing how to live in the same era, to know how to live at the same time. And therefore to contemporize is also to adapt, to compromise, and to reconcile. But if there is something that characterizes many Mexican politicians it is the fact that they are unadapted, uncompromising, not very conciliatory, and upstarts. We can say a corrupt PRI politician from Puebla or Guerrero is not a contemporary of the President of the Republic. Televisa is not a contemporary of the EZLN, and union leaders are not contemporaries of tax department technocrats. Business leaders are not contemporaries of the rebellious teachers of Oaxaca. Those in control of the ecology party do not live in the same dimension as the Catholic Right in Guanajuato or Jalisco. The populists of the PRD do not contemporize even with the leaders of their own party. The small political bosses of Iztapalapa are not from the same era as the municipal president of a northern state.

And nevertheless, they all form part of the same system and are all aboard the same ship. But with their corruptions, intransigencies, and intolerances, they can seriously damage the ship and cause it to wreck. I wish to emphasize that I am not simply stating the obvious: that politicians must negotiate, make pacts, and establish alliances. Clearly they must do those things and they are, even though far too often the negotiations are accompanied with corruption.

What seems fundamental to me is that the most important political forces be capable of living in the world of today, that they understand the codes of our times, and that despite the fact of holding opposing positions, that they be capable of reading the historical moment in which they happen to coincide. Few things are worse than a politician who does not know how to read the lines that define the world around him. An illiterate politician is incapable of living in harmony in the same world with others; he cannot understand his adversaries and understand that they are not his enemies. If a politician of the Right really believes her adversaries of the Left are dangerous subversive conspirators that constitute a potential communist threat or masked terrorism, it will be very difficult for her to live together with such persons without trying to wipe them out. On the other hand if a politician of the Left thinks that the Right is quasi-fascist, essentially abusive, absolutely incapable of being modern, and is nothing more than a conspiracy of the rich to sell the country to foreigners, I do not see how he will be able to accept living under its government without trying to bring it down. It also has to be understood that the PRI is not simply a completely putrefied authoritarian machine that can only take us back to the authoritarian past, that it is incapable of reform, or of becoming a party that accepts the democratic game. What is more, it must be accepted that the small parties that I looked down on a few paragraphs back could undergo mutations that turn them into alternatives.

The maturity of a modern politician lies, among other things, in his or her capacity to understand that the adversary is not an enemy. Of course, things get complicated when there are political positions in the party ranks that *do* consider the adversary to be an enemy that needs to be eliminated. When this happens, as is the case in Mexico, fractures appear that impede the political parties from being true contemporaries and from sharing the same space in the simultaneousness of our present.

Undoubtedly it can be said – following Reinhart Koselleck – that singularity in a single time does not exist, but rather there are different temporal rhythms characteristic of political and social units, of concrete men that act, and of institutions and organizations. So there is not one sole historic time but rather there are many times that are superimposed, one on top of the other.[4] This does not mean that *space of experience* and *horizon of expectation*, to use Koselleck's terms, do not crystallize in society. The problem in Mexico is that the spaces of experience are frequently limited to the municipality, to the state (and on occasion to the nation), and to factions of the party or institution. To put it more bluntly: many politicians cannot see past the ends of their noses. The same thing happens with the horizon of expectations: it does not go beyond the next presidential election. The complexity of the world and the image of a somewhat distant future elude the Mexican political elite.

Why is the Mexican political class submerged in incongruence precisely now that we have finally passed into a democratic condition? Norbert Lechner, whom I have already cited, offers us important indications made on the return of his country, Chile, to democracy, after the long dictatorship of Augusto Pinochet. He found that the political process lacked a mental map with which to orient itself. The new democratic landscape turned out to be unknown territory: 'A world that had been familiar to us', said Lechner, 'came down and we found ourselves with no instruments to guide us'.[5] In Mexico, during the last decade of the twentieth century, the political elite was so immersed in the tensions that shook the system that it did not realize the world had changed. Even though it was the time of the country's entry into a peculiar type of economic community with Canada and the United States, the crushing political process – affected by dramatic assassinations, the Zapatista uprising, the increase in drug-trafficking, and a strong economic crisis – brought Mexico towards an unexpected democratic transition that paved the way for the change of political power in the year 2000. Not even the principal transition actors fully realized what was happening in the country, and much less understood that the transition had taken place in a new world context. The Right that came into power did not have enough intelligence to elaborate a new mental map of the democratic space. National authoritarianism was on the verge of collapse and could not believe it had lost the presidency. The Left was still digesting the fact that democracy had entered by way of the Right.

I am afraid that instead of elaborating a new map, the political class is recycling the old cartography. But each group, each party, and even each leader is reconstructing a different map: none of the plans seem to have come out of the same atlas. One might think that the different ideologies that separate the parties, the forces, the leaders, and the intellectuals explain this fragmentation. But they do not. Democratic political struggle usually confronts groups with at times very opposing visions and that offer divergent solutions to dilemmas that can be located on the same world map. But when the incongruence of non-contemporaneous groups predominates, each one responds to dilemmas and problems that belong to very different eras and worlds. In Mexico, those who think democracy has existed for a long time, those who believe democracy arrived at the end of the twentieth century, those who believe democracy has not yet arrived, and those who simply do not believe in democracy are all confronting one another. So, while some believe in a certain return to the former regime, which – they say – was not so bad, others want a finally 'real' revolutionary change. And still others are convinced that Mexico is already going down the right road and only needs to perfect political and economic mechanisms. But the first group does not know exactly what they want to return to, the second has no idea what kind of revolution they want, and the third group wants to remain in power and let the road they are on take them to who knows where.

But there is a problem in all of this. As has been observed repeatedly, throughout the twentieth century the counter-culture and avant-gardism have promoted the erosion of the old unifying canons characteristic of capitalist society that revolve around scientific progressivism, nationalist humanism, political equality, and bourgeois ethics. Industrial society's own evolution has contributed to this erosion by stimulating globalization, the loss of significance of the national states, and the precariousness of work. Like it or not, this process of destruction of the old capitalism is very advanced. I ask the question: is the creation of coherent spaces and horizons, so that the elite can act on the globalized stage without constantly stumbling and chattering senselessly, desirable or even possible? Let me be very clear here. I am not pushing for a total reconstruction of coherency spaces such as those the enlightened spirit has aspired to since the eighteenth century. I am not proposing a return to coherency propelled by the revolutionary nationalism that has been the Mexican materialization of the modern bourgeois tradition.

I believe it is necessary to promote the growth of a coherency sphere that contains the parties and political forces. It is not a matter of unifying all of society, but rather of developing a civic culture that encloses politics in a sphere that the parties cannot easily fracture, and so cannot pour the mire of their contradictions, their babbling, their corruption, and their inconsistency over everyone. It is necessary to enclose the parties in a civilizing circuit, but at the same time taking care that civil society does not remain trapped in the orbit of politics. Outside that sphere, society must maintain a healthy fragmentation that impedes totalizing unification in accordance with patterns determined by the power circles. I am not describing a utopia: that is now occurring in places of the more economically developed world, where there are coherent democratic political systems encapsulated in a sphere that does not include its contour, a social surrounding that Zygmunt Bauman calls 'liquid' and that is full of risks and dangers, as pointed out by Ulrich Beck.

Of course, I do not laud the idea of an impermeable political sphere that is isolated from society. That would signify the decadence and putrefaction of politics. In a certain sense that is what happened during the long era of authoritarianism that was hidden behind the so-called 'institutionalization' of the revolution, and that in reality was the hardening of a political cyst that became more and more isolated from society. After many years the cyst split into fragments and we are still suffering the consequences of that rupture. It is not a matter of fostering the growth of a sphere that is closed to the tendencies of social life. It is about promoting a new political culture that will civilize the party system and will encourage plurality in civil society.

What alternatives can we envision? We are facing the possibility of returning to a populist, nationalist, and hazily revolutionary past, by way of a PRI that is allied with a disabled Left and supported by sectors of the social Right. It would not be a true return, but rather a painful prolongation of a backward and unwell political culture being extended due to the lack of new alternatives. It would be jeopardizing the future for a stillborn option.

The main alternative of the Right gets its support from the subject of security; or better said, the growing lack of security, whose confrontation is leaving the politics of prevention, contention, and repression behind to unleash, in the words of Luc Ferry, 'an authentic war against the proliferation and extension of zones of anomie where 'normal' citizens live literally terrorized by gangs capable of carrying out an extraordinary level of violence'.[6] This is the logic of the modern Right that, faced with the moral crisis crouching behind the lack of security, justifies political options centred around the defence of private life and the family, seen as the only refuge left standing after the postmodern flood. This logic takes us directly to potentially postdemocratic political systems in which legitimacy is based on the stimulus of imaginary networks, that is to say, on structures that are centred in a battle between the silent normativity of the majority and a threatening hyperactive marginality.[7] For at least fifteen years these types of political processes, which have included very different groups, have existed in Mexico. First it was the neo-Zapatistas and then it was the drug-trafficking mafias who carried out the function of marginal, but symbolically very powerful, threats that stimulate social cohesion around government.

Faced with this sombre future, we can wonder if there is an alternative from the Left that is not a populist derivation of the old revolutionary nationalism. In my opinion, yes, we can catch a glimpse, however faint, of some encouraging signs of a modern social-democratic option. I am referring to what we can call a cosmopolitan Left. I take the expression from the German sociologist Ulrich Beck, when he refers to a new Left that strongly takes up the theme of equality once again to place it in a global, not a national, context, as a concrete proposal to politically limit the damage caused by global capital flows.

This signifies carrying out politics in the global environment for the purpose of establishing supranational finance and bank controls, stopping the fiscal competition between states, and stimulating collaboration ties between transnational organizations. It is necessary that the large transnational companies be made to face the democratic solution to problems of legitimacy so that they do not ignore the political consequences of their activity. As Beck points out, it is necessary to control the delocalization and dispersion of the workforce and provide basic social protection for those thrust into the flexibility of precarious jobs.[8] A cosmopolitan attitude means recognizing globalization as the process that will inevitably envelop us over the next decades, abandoning the narrow anti-imperialism of a remotely Leninist inspiration, entering the tidal flow that is turning the world of work into a miry unstable place whose flexible character seems necessary but whose effects can be disastrous. A cosmopolitan Left faces up to problems for which there are no known remedies and it is obliged to use great imagination to be able to plunge into the globalising torrent without drowning, and once on the inside, find new ways to fight for equality. It is necessary to accept that we are living through critical problems of insecurity that must be directly confronted, without running away in the direction of an undefined struggle to eradicate its social causes, but without falling into the useless military escalation against crime. It is important to modernize the tax system to provide the State with sufficient funds and it is fundamental to find a short-term solution for the huge problem of poverty and implement egalitarian mechanisms that do not inhibit industrialization and the expansion of an advanced capitalist economy. The anticapitalist incivility of traditional and corrupt unionism only serves to hold back economic efficiency.

In the presence of the new forms that capitalism assumes and the peculiar expressions that crises adopt, the options that invoked a supposedly inevitable revolutionary outbreak have failed and populist remedies have only managed to bring the economy to a halt. But it should be pointed out that the traditional social-democratic policy of welfare fomented by the so-called State has arrived at an apparent dead end, as can be confirmed in Europe. It is true that the technocratic tendencies associated with the 'Third Way' in England and the 'New Centre' in Germany were relatively successful for a few years, to the extent that they invaded the spaces of the Right. But today they are discontinued options because globalization has impoverished the workers, inequality has risen, projects of educational reform have been sterile, and the model of a multicultural society has been a total failure.

The formation of a cosmopolitan Left cannot be defined with a few formulas such as those I have mentioned and the many more that are too numerous to list here. The fundamental problem is the consolidation of a political culture capable of being constituted on fertile ground so that new ideas can emerge. It is a new culture, but one that is supported by an old concept: that of citizens of the world. This perspective does not imply a call for the global unification of lifestyles. To the contrary – as Kwame Anthony Appiah has explained so well in his book *Cosmopolitanism* – it is an affirmation of interest in the life of others, of those who have different ideas and different practices. At the same time, cosmopolitanism maintains that we have obligations in regard to others, obligations that go beyond family, local, or national circles. Of course at times universal commitment contradicts a respect for diversity. But it is precisely in this difficult give-and-take of respecting differences and of fulfilling obligations as a world citizen where cosmopolitan convictions are consolidated.

If ever there were a place in need of developing a cosmopolitan culture, that place is Mexico. We Mexican citizens are descendants of a rich southern European culture, neighbours of the greatest world power; our country has a marginal, but tremendously important, ethnic diversity – it has received thousands of refugees from all over the world, and millions of our countrymen are living in the Anglocultural context of the United States. And, nevertheless, Mexico has lived through a good part of the twentieth century tied to an authoritarian nationalism and a superpatriotism culture, immersed in the suffocating cloud of smoke that is a supposed emanation from the revolution begun a century ago. This does not mean that twentieth-century Mexican history should simply be tossed aside. To the contrary, it is necessary to closely and intelligently examine the growth of a terrible political malformation throughout the past century.

This needs to be done if we wish to scrutinize the shadows of the future, to take on the study of this malformation from a cosmopolitan perspective. What better stimulus is there for sharpening this perspective than to look to Julio Cortázar, possibly the greatest of Latin American cosmopolitan writers? For this very reason I began my essay by invoking the author of *Rayuela*, who shortly before his death exalted a universal idea of the socialist future at the same time that he demanded a respect for diversity. He was enthused by the revolution in Nicaragua that had brought down Somoza's murderous dictatorship. In Managua in 1980 Cortázar wrote several passionate verses:

> So many women, so many children and men
> at last shaping their future together,
> at last transfigured into themselves,
> while the long night of disgrace
> becomes lost in the disdain of oblivion.

In 1982 Cortázar exaltingly compared the Sandanista revolution to the beauty of Greta Garbo: perhaps her feet are too big, as he had heard someone say in his youth, but everything else belongs to a goddess. I can imagine the sombre melancholy that would have overcome Cortázar had he lived to contemplate the future. The feet of the revolutionary Sandinista goddess were not too big, but they were corrupted and caused the collapse of the dream. Nicaragua ended up going down an authoritarian road similar to that of Mexico, and not along the cosmoroute Cortázar travelled on.[9]

I would like to believe that by travelling along Cortázar's cosmoroute the doors to the future would open. But I know very well that is not the case. The future is unknown and hazy. We can only decipher its shadows in the hope that predictions will be something more than a mere expression of our desires. Predictions usually reveal intentions. Not even politicians that act with planning, premeditation, and advantage can make predictions come true. And still something constantly drives us to invent projects, purposes, or proposals and to discuss prophecies, predictions, or probabilities.

Of what use is the observation of the intellectual or the social scientist in the face of the pirouettes of those who promise the ascent towards a brilliant future – if we follow the path they show us – and who – if we do not – threaten us with falling into a failed State full of social flare-ups? The use of intelligent rationality should help us to foresee the future development of our society. But there have been so many failures in the attempt to predict the future of capitalism and of modern society that we have learned our lesson. We end up resigning ourselves to scrutinizing the present as if it were the dead past, but without the advantage the historian has of knowing what happened after the era being studied. Perhaps the future can be used in the way Niklas Luhmann suggested, to introduce uncertainty in the present and to stimulate the system so that it oscillates between hopes and fears.[10] Whoever wishes to understand the tendencies of a society can attempt, as a physician does, to diagnose a disease, to locate the affected organs, and – in the best of cases – to prescribe the medicine to stop or slow down the malignant progression in the social system. This is what Huizinga did in his book about the shadow of tomorrow. The method is useful, but it has one big defect: while the doctor knows that his patient will have to die one day and tries to prolong her life as long as possible, we are completely unaware of what the future will be for the society we are diagnosing. If the diagnosis is correct, which is more often not the case, we would be the ones to have the merit of signing the death certificate of an era or of its institutions. And if luck prevails and the advice given results in a certain kind of recovery from the social disease, then we would only have contributed to extending the present.

If we wish to understand the society we live in, we have no choice but to immerse ourselves again and again into the shadow of the future. We are condemned, like Sisyphus, to toss a heavy stone towards the future, missing the mark, only to pick it up and throw it again. Every once in a while we will throw it correctly, but we will not know right away if our good aim is just luck or if it is because, little by little, we have fine-tuned our predicting instruments and our intelligence.

2009

Notes

Chapter 1: The Dictatorship was not Perfect

1   The first pages of this essay were published as a postscript in my book *Blood, Ink, and Culture: Miseries and Splendors of the Post-Mexican Condition*.

2   Lázaro Cárdenas, *Obras I: Apuntes, 1913–1940*, p. 334.

3   Fernando Henrique Cardoso, 'Las clases sociales y la crisis política en América Latina', in *Clases sociales y crisis política en América Latina*.

4   Roger Bartra, 'Las clases sociales y crisis política en México', in ibid.

5   Roger Bartra, *El poder despótico burgués. Las raíces campesinas de las estructuras políticas de mediación*, p. 118.

6   I expressed some of these ideas in a second text continuing the discussion with Cardoso. Although the material from the second round was published, my contribution was strangely excluded by the editor and did not appear in the book. Cardoso's response to my criticism, however, was published: in a display of bad taste he ended by insinuating that my provocations were the kind that got comrades sent to Siberia. But the only thing that went to Siberia was the text of my answer, which remained frozen, perhaps under suspicion of being part of some conspiracy.

7   Roger Bartra, *El poder despótico burgués*, pp. 147–8.

8   See the corrected, revised and expanded edition, *Las redes imaginarias del poder político*.

9   Roger Bartra, *Agrarian Structure and Political Power in Mexico*, p. 162.

10 Luis Villoro, 'Roger Bartra: Estado y sociedad civil' (1980), in *México, entre libros*.

11 Roger Bartra, 'Una discusión con Octavio Paz' (1980).

12 *La democracia ausente*.

13 Roger Bartra, *The Cage of Melancholy*.

14 I expressed this idea for the first time in a discussion with Jorge G. Castañeda (later Secretary of Foreign Relations in the Fox government) and Claudio Lomnitz (at that time professor at the University of Chicago, today at Columbia University), organized by the magazine *Fractal* and published under the strange title 'La transición: esa metáfora calva' ('Transition, that barren metaphor').

15   A summary follows of the arguments and proposals that I presented in the State Reform Study Commission, headed by Porfirio Muñoz Ledo, and whose conclusions apparently were accepted by Vicente Fox in November 2000, when he was about to take office as president of the republic.

16   The 'white night of oblivion' is a reference to the metaphors used in a brief exchange of letters between subcommander Marcos and myself. In August 1994, a short time after the neo-Zapatista uprising, the EZLN convoked the so-called 'Democratic National Convention' in Chiapas, inviting many politicians and intellectuals of the Left. On that occasion subcommander Marcos wrote me a letter of invitation (14 July 1994). I answered saying I would attend and added an invitation of my own for him to put down the weapons, leave the jungle, and abandon the white night of oblivion to make a jump towards the shadow of democratic civility (1 August 1994).

17   With respect to this, see my essay 'Derechos indígenas: imaginería política e ingeniería legislativa', and my book *Blood, Ink, and Culture: Miseries and Splendors of the Post-Mexican Condition*.

18   Jonathan Swift, *A Tale of a Tub* (1704), preface.

19   Here again I take up my written exchange with Jesús Silva-Herzog Márquez published as '*Reparar o sembrar: una conversación sobre política mexicana*', pp. 18–22.

20   This essay has had various incarnations, the latest of which was published in *México: Crónicas de un país posible* (coordinator José Antonio Aguilar Rivera). Here I present a corrected and extended version.

Chapter 2: Mud, mire, and democracy

1   This article was published in the magazine *Letras Libres* two months after the 2006 presidential election. It generated much controversy and innumerable commentaries. It is published here without modifications.

Chapter 3: Can the Right be modern?

1   Participation in the meeting organized by the National Executive Committee of the PAN to celebrate the 68th anniversary of its foundation, 14 September 2007.

2   See chapter 2, 'Mud, mire, and democracy'.

3   See my article 'Journey to the Center of the Right', in the book *Blood, Ink, and Culture: Miseries and Splendors of the Post-Mexican Condition*.

4   Rodrigo Guerra López, *Como un gran movimiento*, p. 39. An interesting precedent to these ideas can be seen in Agustín Basave Fernández del Valle's book, *Vocación y estilo de México. Fundamentos de la mexicanidad.*
5   Alonso Lujambio, *¿Democratización vía federalismo? El Partido Acción Nacional, 1939–2000: la historia de una estrategia difícil*, p. 93.
6   See Carlos María Abascal Carranza, 'El futuro de las ideas humanistas y demócrata cristianas'.
7   Cited by Soledad Loaeza, *El Partido Acción Nacional: la larga marcha, 1939–1994. Oposición leal y partido de protesta*, pp. 271–2.

Chapter 4: The Left – in danger of extinction?

1   A Mexican cracid bird. The term also means chatterbox.
2   After these words Taibo adds: 'This logic of his which has destroyed a part of Mexican intellectuality seems perverse to me. Corrupt. To get near to those in power to obtain benefits. And with that twopenny speech about intellectual autonomy. Every time the Prince allowed it, Paz came near. And he managed the funds, scholarships and cultural attaché offices and made phone calls "give this thing to that guy". He paid. He bought favours. He sold his soul. The soul and the ass should only be put on the table once; if you made a mistake, you were screwed – only once, but you'd better protect the virginity of both.' Ignacio Limon's interview with Paco Ignacio Taibo II.
3   'Nobody has to be vile', p. 10.
4   Slavoj Žižek, *Did Somebody Say Totalitarianism?*, p. 131.
5   Paul Berman, *Terror and Liberalism*. A detailed description of the repression against professors can be read in Vitali Shentalinski's book, *Denuncia contra Socrates. Nuevos descubrimientos en los archivos literarios del KGB*; see especially the chapter 'Fragmentos de la Edad de Plata'.

Chapter 5: The burdens of the Right

1   'Vuelve el humanismo político', in *Gobierno, derecha moderna y democracia en México.*
2   'Tres poetas católicos', in *Ensayos sobre poesía.*
3   'Muerte y resurrección de la cultura católica', in *Ensayos sobre poesía.*
4   Ideas fuerza. Mística de Acción Nacional, p. 39.
5   'La Iglesia católica y la educación en México', in *Identidad en el imaginario nacional.*

6   *Mis recuerdos. Sinarquismo y Colonia María Auxiliadora (1935–1944),* prologue by Salvador Borrego, p. 530.

7   *El porvenir posible,* p. 583.

8   Lorenzo Gómez Morín Escalante, '¿Hacia una sociedad de pieles rojas? El distanciamiento entre la ciudadanía y la Iglesia Católica en México', pp. 37–42.

9   Agustín Basave Fernández del Valle, *Vocación y estilo de México. Fundamentos de la mexicanidad.*

10 See footnote 92 in chapter 10, 'Ethnographic sonata in Nay-flat'.

11 'Vuelve el humanismo político'.

12 'Políticos católicos en México: coyunturas críticas y afinidades electivas en el siglo XX', in *Gobierno, derecha moderna y democracia en México.*

13 Agustín Basave Fernández del Valle, *Vocación y estilo de México,* pp. 736–7.

14 Carlos María Abascal and Salvador Abascal, 'Más allá de la izquierda y la derecha: recuperar el sentido de la política al servicio de la persona', in *Gobierno, derecha moderna y democracia en México.*

15 The reader can find a detailed development of my ideas on relativism and fundamentalism in the following articles: 'Ensayo lúgubre sobre la fama póstuma, los agujeros negros, el fundamentalismo moral y los jardines multiculturales' (*La sangre y la tinta: ensayos sobre la condición postmexicana*); 'Las redes imaginarias del terror político' (*Territorios del terror y la otredad*).

Chapter 6: Populism and democracy in Latin America

1   'Democracia representativa y clases populares' (1965), reproduced in G. Germani, Torcuato S. di Tella and Octavio Ianni, *Populismo y contradicciones de clase en Latinoamérica,* p. 29. Octavio Ianni's book, *La formación del Estado populista en América Latina,* is a good summary of the preoccupations of the Left about the phenomenon.

2   'Populismo y reformismo' (1965), in the book cited in footnote 49, pp. 38ff.

3   Ibid., p. 43.

4   *Política e ideología en la teoría marxista. Capitalismo, fascismo y populismo,* p. 231f.

5   Ibid., p. 205.

6   *La razón populista,* p. 130.

7   *L'autre cap,* p.16.

8   See the important recompilation of essays prepared by Ghita Ionescu and Ernest Gellner, *Populism: Its Meaning and National Characteristics.* About Europe, see Michel Wieviorka, *La démocratie à l'épreuve. Nationalisme, populisme, ethnicité.*

Chapter 7: The Mexican hydra:
the return of the authoritarian party

1 Joy Langston, 'PRI: evolución del dinosaurio' and especially her article
   'La competencia electoral y la descentralización partidista en México'.
   See also by Rogelio Hernández Rodríguez, *El centro dividido. La nueva
   autonomía de los gobernadores.*
2 'Territorios violentos'. Rubén Aguilar and Jorge Castañeda coincide with
   this interpretation in their book *El narco: la guerra fallida.*
3 'La muerte tiene permiso. Homicidios 2008–2009'.
4 'El día después', in *El México que nos duele: crónica de un país sin rumbo,*
   by Alejandro Rosas and Ricardo Cayuela Gally, Planeta, México, 2011,
   p. 194.
5 *Reforma,* 29 November 2011.
6 Jesús Silva-Herzog Márquez, 'Debajo del copete'.

Chapter 8: Intellectuals and scholars facing democracy

1 'The Bridge, The Border and the Cage: Cultural Crisis and Identity'
   (conference at the meeting of the American Sociological Association, 9
   August 1997), in *Blood, Ink, and Culture: Miseries and Splendors of the Post-
   Mexican Condition.*
2 Raúl Benítez Zenteno (ed.), *El perfil de México en 1980.* See volume 3
   especially.
3 *New Rules of Sociological Method,* p. 31.

Chapter 9: The labyrinth and its map

1 This article came into being in a conference dedicated to commemorating
   the fiftieth anniversary of *El laberinto de la soledad,* delivered 25 March
   2000 in the Palacio de Minería, Mexico City. A first version was published
   in *Claves de Razón Práctica* 112, 2001.
2 In 1959 Paz gave Elisa and André Breton a copy of the French edition
   of *Laberinto.* In the dedication he defines it as '*ce livre déjà ancien et que
   je n'aime plus,* a book of circumstances and that I dare to offer only as a
   weak testimony of my great friendship and admiration'.
3 Letter to E. M. Santí dated 12 May 1995.
4 Letter to R. Bartra dated 10 June 1995.
5 *De la démocratie en Amérique,* 1835, vol. 2, book 2, chapter XIII.
6 Letter to R. Bartra dated 5 April 2000.

7   Letter to E. M. Santí dated 7 April 2000. Curiously, *La jaula de la melancolía* was received with scorn by the same dogmatic Leftist critic who many years before had denounced *Laberinto* as a 'noxious' book. Emmanuel Carballo stated that my book was 'pretentious and failed', to refute Christopher Dominguez who had described it as one of the best Mexican works (*La Jornada*, 2 January 1988, p. 21).

8   I have explained this theme in more detail in the chapter 'El *spleen* del capitalismo: Weber y la ética pagana' in my book *El duelo de los ángeles*.

9   *The Cage of Melancholy, Oficio mexicano: miserias y esplendores de la cultura.*

10   The references are from the critical edition prepared by Enrico Mario Santí for the publisher Cátedra de Madrid, 1993, pp. 257f.

11   Octavio Paz, *Sor Juana Inés de la Cruz o las trampas de la fe*, pp. 505–6. See the reflections I develop respectively in my book *Melancholy and Culture: Diseases of the Soul in Golden Age Spain*.

12   After the expression of José Carlos Mainer.

13   *Cartas marruecas*, 27:154.

14   Antonio Machado, 'Proverbios y cantares'.

15   Rosalía de Castro, *En las orillas del Sar*, pp. 13–18.

16   Maurice Cranston, *The Romantic Movement*, p. 134.

17   *Madrid, guía sentimental*, 1918, a collection of articles published in *Blanco y negro* in 1913–14.

18   Ángel Gavinet, *Idearium español*, p.129

19   Manuel Durán, 'Existential Baroque: Francisco de Quevedo's Sonnet "Miré los muros de la patria mía"'.

20   Bolívar Echeverría, 'El ethos barroco', in *Modernidad, mestizaje cultural y ethos barroco*, pp. 20ff.

Chapter 10: Ethnographic sonata in Nay-flat

1   Guillermo Bonfil, author of the book *México profundo. Una civilización negada*, was the leader of the expedition.

2   'The Indigenous Peasant and Indigenist Ideology', in *Agrarian Structure and Political Power in Mexico*, p. 93. These funereal images were transferred to a documentary film *Ethnocide* for which I wrote the script (directed by Paul Leduc, Office national du film du Canada, 1976).

3   It is risky to try to pigeonhole those who could represent the different viewpoints, but I can suggest that each tendency will find inspiration in the following authors: the paternalists in Manuel Gamio, *Forjando patria*, 1916; the functionalists in Julio de la Fuente, *Educación, antropología y desarrollo de la comunidad*, 1964; the technocrats in Lucio Mendieta y Núñez, *Valor económico y social de las razas indígenas de México*, 1938; the

populists in Alfonso Caso, 'Definición del indio y de lo indio', 1948: the liberals in Gonzalo Aguirre Beltrán, *Formas de gobierno indígena*, 1953; the fundamentalists in Guillermo Bonfil, *México profundo*, 1987; the Marxists in Ricardo and Isabel Pozas, *Los indios en las clases sociales de México*, 1971; the relativists in Rodolfo Stavenhagen, *Las clases sociales en las sociedades agrarias*, 1969; and the guerrillas in the letters of Subcommander Marcos.

4 This declaration may be referred to in *La quiebra política de la antropología social en México*, pp. 519–25).

5 Guillermo Bonfil, the Mexican anthropologist who signed the Barbados declaration in 1971, was appointed director of the National Institute of Anthropology and History by the government the following year, institutionalizing the 'radical rupture'.

6 See the essay about the neo-Zapatistas, 'Tropical Kitsch in Blood and Ink', in my book *Blood, Ink, and Culture: Miseries and Splendors of the Post-Mexican Condition*.

7 This is the peculiar integration of the first three words of the hymn's verse: 'Mas si osare un extraño enemigo/profanar con su planta tu suelo' ('What is more, if a foreign enemy dare/desecrate your native soil with his sole') into a person's name. The foreign enemy appears to be named Masiosare.

8 Symptomatically, in an official account of the National Indigenist Institute, the section on the biographies of the intellectuals who have devoted themselves to this subject is entitled 'indigenist workers' (*Instituto Nacional Indigenista, 40 años*).

9 See my books *The Cage of Melancholy* and *Blood, Ink, and Culture: Miseries and Splendors of the Post-Mexican Condition*.

10 Carlos Basauri, *La población indígena de México*.

11 *Etnografía contemporánea de México*.

12 Stated by the lawyer of Mixe origin, ex-advisor of the EZLN, Adelfo Regino Montes in 'Diversidad y autonomía', p.23.

13 This 'sonata' was requested of me by the director of the National Institute of Anthropology and History, Sergio Raúl Arroyo, as part of the commemorations for the fortieth anniversary of the new museum's construction: *Museo Nacional de Antropología, México. Libro conmemorativo del cuarenta aniversario*.

Chapter 12: Memories of the counter-culture

1 There is a new edition of Bonnie Bremser's book with an introduction by Ann Charters. The page numbers cited here correspond to this new edition.

Chapter 13: Street life and politics

1   *The Idea of Europe*, p. 17.
2   'Introduction à la psycho-sociologie de la vie quotidienne', in *Encyclopédie de la psychologie*, pp. 102ff.

Chapter 14: The shadow of the future

1   'El destino del hombre era . . . «1984»'.
2   *In the shadow of tomorrow; a diagnosis of the spiritual distemper of our time,* translated from the Dutch by J. H. Huizinga.
3   Las sombras del mañana/La dimensión subjetiva de la política.
4   *Futures Past: On the Semantics of Historical Time.*
5   'Las sombras del mañana', p. 27.
6   *Familles, je vous aime/Politique et vie priveé à l'âge de la mondialisation.*
7   See my book *Las redes imaginarias del poder político.*
8   '¿Una nueva izquierda cosmopólita?'
9   *Autonauts of the cosmoroute, a timeless voyage from Paris to Marseilles,* translated by Anne McLean.
10 *Die gesellschaft der gesellschaft.*

Bibliography

Abascal Carranza, Carlos María, 'El futuro de las ideas humanistas y demócrata cristianas', *Bien Común:* 152 (August 2007).

Abascal, Carlos María and Salvador Abascal, 'Más allá de la izquierda y la derecha: recuperar el sentido de la política al servicio de la persona', in *Gobierno, derecha moderna y democracia en México,* Roger Bartra (ed.) (México: Herder, 2009).

Abascal, Salvador, *Mis recuerdos. Sinarquismo y Colonia María Auxiliadora (1935–1944),* prologue by Salvador Borrego (México: Tradición, 1980).

Aguilar, Rubén and Jorge Castañeda, *El narco: la guerra fallida* (México: Punto de Lectura, 2009).

Aguilar Rivera, José Antonio (ed.), *México: Crónicas de un país posible* (México: Fondo de la Cultura Económica, 2005).

Aguirre Beltrán, Gonzalo, *Formas de gobierno indígena* (Mexico: Imprenta Universitaria, 1953).

Alcántara, Rogelio, 'La Iglesia católica y la educación en México', in *Identidad en el imaginario nacional,* Javier Pérez Siller and Verena Radkau García (eds) (Puebla: Instituto de Ciencias Sociales y Humanidades, BUAP, 1998).

Azorín, *Madrid, guía sentimental* (Madrid: Biblioteca Estrella, 1918).

Bartra, Roger, *El poder despótico burgués. Las raíces campesinas de las estructuras políticas de mediación* (Barcelona: Península, 1977).

Bartra, Roger, 'Clases sociales y crisis política en México', in *Clases sociales y crisis política en América Latina,* published by Raúl Benítez Zenteno (México: Instituto de Investigaciones Sociales de la UNAM/Siglo XXI Editores, 1977).

Bartra, Roger, *La jaula de la melancolía* (Mexico: Grijalbo, 1987).

Bartra, Roger, 'Una discusión con Octavio Paz' (1980), *La Jornada Semanal* 71 (October 1990).

Bartra, Roger, *The Cage of Melancholy* (New Brunswick: Rutgers University Press, 1992).

Bartra, Roger, 'The Indigenous Peasant and Indigenist Ideology', in *Agrarian Structure and Political Power in Mexico* (Baltimore: Johns Hopkins University Press, 1992).

Bartra, Roger, *Agrarian Structure and Political Power in Mexico* (Baltimore: Johns Hopkins University Press, 1993).

Bartra, Roger, *Oficio mexicano: miserias y esplendores de la cultura* (Mexico: Grijalbo, 1993).

Bartra, Roger, 'Ensayo lúgubre sobre la fama póstuma, los agujeros negros, el fundamentalismo moral y los jardines multiculturales', in *La sangre y la tinta: ensayos sobre la condición postmexicana* (México: Oceano, 1999).

Bartra, Roger, Jorge G. Castañeda and Claudio Lomnitz, 'La transición: esa metáfora calva', *Fractal*, 12 (1999).

Bartra, Roger, *La democracia ausente*, first edition (México: Grijalbo, 1986); corrected edition (México: Océano, 2000).

Bartra, Roger, 'El laberinto y su mapa', *Claves de Razón Práctica* 112 (2001).

Bartra, Roger, 'Derechos indígenas: imaginería política e ingeniería legislativa', *Letras Libres* 29 (May 2001).

Bartra, Roger, *Blood, Ink, and Culture: Miseries and Splendors of the Post-Mexican Condition* (Durham: Duke University Press, 2002).

Bartra, Roger, 'Tropical Kitsch in Blood and Ink', in *Blood, Ink, and Culture: Miseries and Splendors of the Post-Mexican Condition* (Durham: Duke University Press, 2002).

Bartra, Roger, 'The Bridge, The Border and the Cage: Cultural Crises and Identity' (conference at the meeting of the American Sociological Association, 9 August 1997), in *Blood, Ink, and Culture: Miseries and Splendors of the Post-Mexican Condition* (Durham: Duke University Press, 2002).

Bartra, Roger, 'El *spleen* del capitalismo: Weber y la ética pagana' in *El duelo de los ángeles* (Valencia: Pre-Textos, 2004).

Bartra, Roger, 'Las redes imaginarias del terror político', in *Territorios del terror y la otredad* (Valencia: Pre-Textos, 2007).

Bartra, Roger, *Melancholy and Culture: Diseases of the Soul in Golden Age Spain* (translated by Christopher Follett), Iberian and Latin American Studies series (Cardiff: University of Wales Press, 2008).

Bartra, Roger, *Las redes imaginarias del poder político*, corrected, revised and augmented edition (Valencia: Pre-Textos, 2010).

Bartra, Roger, *The Imaginary Networks of Political Power. A New Revised and Expanded Edition* (La Jaula Abierta editores/Fondo de Cultura Económica, 2012).

Basauri, Carlos, *La población indígena de México*, 3 volumes (Mexico: Secretaría de Educación Pública, 1940).

Basave Fernández del Valle, Agustín, *Vocación y estilo de México. Fundamentos de la mexicanidad* (México: Noriega/Limusa, 1990).

Beck, Ulrich, '¿Una nueva izquierda cosmopólita?', *El País* (17 November 2006).

Benítez Zenteno, Raúl (ed.), *El perfil de México en 1980*, 3 volumes (Mexico: Siglo XXI, 1972).

Berman, Paul, *Terror and Liberalism* (New York: W. W. Norton, 2003).

Bonfil, Guillermo, *México profundo. Una civilización negada* (Mexico: CIESAS, 1987).

Bremser, Bonnie, *Troia: Mexican Memoirs* (Champaign: Dalkey Archive Press, 2007).

Cadalso, José, *Cartas marruecas* (Madrid: Cátedra, 1995).

Cárdenas, Lázaro, *Obras I: Apuntes, 1913–1940* (México: UNAM, 1972).

Cardoso, Fernando Henrique, 'Las clases sociales y la crisis política en América Latina', in *Clases sociales y crisis política en América Latina*, published by Raúl Benítez Zenteno (México: Siglo XXI Editores, 1977).

Caso, Alfonso, 'Definición del indio y de lo indio', *América Indígena* VII, 5 (1948), 145–81.

Castillo Peraza, Salvador, *El porvenir posible* (México: Fondo de Cultura Económica, 2006).

Castro, Rosalía de, *En las orillas del Sar* (Madrid: Cátedra, 1997).

Cayuela Gally, Ricardo, 'El día después', in *El México que nos duele: crónica de un país sin rumbo*, by Alejandro Rosas and Ricardo Cayuela Gally (Mexico: México, 2011).

Cortázar, Julio, 'El destino del hombre era . . .«1984»', *El País* (9 October 1983).

Cortázar, Julio, *Autonauts of the Cosmoroute, a Timeless Voyage from Paris to Marseilles*, translated by Anne McLean (New York: Archipelago Books, 2007).

Cranston, Maurice, *The Romantic Movement* (Oxford: Blackwell, 1994).

Derrida, Jacques, *L'autre cap* (Paris: Minuit, 1991).

Durán, Manuel, 'Existential Baroque: Francisco de Quevedo's Sonnet "Miré los muros de la patria mía"', *Calíope*, I (1995).

Echeverría, Bolívar, 'El ethos barroco', in *Modernidad, mestizaje cultural y ethos barroco* (Mexico: UNAM/El Equilibrista, 1994).

Escalante Gonzalbo, Fernando, 'Territorios violentos', *Nexos*, 384 (December 2009).

Escalante Gonzalbo, Fernando, 'La muerte tiene permiso. Homicidios 2008–2009', *Nexos*, 397 (January 2011).

Etnografía contemporánea de México (Mexico: Instituto Nacional Indigenista, 1995).

Ferry, Luc, *Familles, je vous aime/Politique et vie privée à l'âge de la mondialisation* (Paris: XO Éditions, 2007).

Gamio, Manuel, *Forjando patria* (Mexico: Porrúa, 1916).

García Mora, C. and A. Medina (eds), *La quiebra política de la antropología social en México* (y publishers) (Mexico: UNAM, 1986).

Gavinet, Ángel, *Idearium español* (Madrid: Espasa Calpe, 1940).

Germani, Gino, 'Democracia representativa y clases populares' (1965), reproduced in G. Germani, Torcuato S. di Tella and Octavio Ianni, *Populismo y contradicciones de clase en Latinoamérica* (Mexico: Ediciones Era).

Giddens, Anthony, *New Rules of Sociological Method* (London: Hutchinson, 1976).

Gómez Morín Escalante, Lorenzo, '¿Hacia una sociedad de pieles rojas? El distanciamiento entre la ciudadanía y la Iglesia Católica en México', *Bien Común* 156: 37–42 (2007).

González Guajardo, Claudio X, 'De Presidente de México a presidente del PAN', *Reforma* (14 July 2010).

Guerra López, Rodrigo, *Como un gran movimiento* (México: Fundación Rafael Preciado, 2006).

Guerra López, Rodrigo, 'Vuelve el humanismo político', in *Gobierno, derecha moderna y democracia en México*, Roger Bartra (ed.) (México: Herder, 2009).

Hernández Rodríguez, Rogelio, *El centro dividido. La nueva autonomía de los gobernadores* (Mexico: El Colegio de México, 2008).

Huizinga, Johan, *In the Shadow of Tomorrow: A Diagnosis of the Spiritual Distemper of Our Time*, translated from the Dutch by J. H. Huizinga (London, Toronto: W. Heinemann, 1936).

Ianni, Octavio, *La formación del Estado populista en América Latina* (Mexico: Ediciones Era, 1975).

Ibáñez, Luis Eduardo, 'Políticos católicos en México: coyunturas críticas y afinidades electivas en el siglo XX', in *Gobierno, derecha moderna y democracia en México*, Roger Bartra (ed.) (México: Herder, 2009).

Instituto Nacional Indigenista, 40 años (Mexico: INI, 1988).

Ionescu, Ghita and Ernest Gellner, *Populism: Its Meaning and National Characteristics* (London: Weidenfeld & Nicolson, 1969).

Koselleck, Reinhart, *Futures Past: On the Semantics of Historical Time* (New York: Columbia University Press, 2004).

Laclau, Ernesto, *Política e ideología en la teoría marxista. Capitalismo, fascismo y populismo* (Mexico: Siglo XXI Editores, 1978).

Laclau, Ernesto, *La razón populista* (Buenos Aires: Fondo de Cultura Económica, 2005).

Langston, Joy, 'PRI: evolución del dinosaurio', *Enfoque* (12 June 2011).

Langston, Joy, 'La competencia electoral y la descentralización partidista en México', *Revista Mexicana de Sociología*, 70, no. 3 (2008).

Lechner, Norbert, *Las sombras del mañana/La dimension subjetiva de la política* (Santiago de Chile: Iom, 2002).

Lefebvre, Henri, 'Introduction à la psycho-sociologie de la vie quotidienne', in *Encyclopédie de la psychologie* (París: Nathan, 1963).

Loaeza, Soledad, *El Partido Acción Nacional: la larga marcha, 1939–1994. Oposición leal y partido de protesta* (Mexico: Fondo de Cultura Económica, 1999).

Luhmann, Niklas, *Die gesellschaft der gesellschaft* (Frankfurt am Main: Suhrkamp, 1997).

Lujambio, Alonso, *¿Democratización vía federalismo? El Partido Acción Nacional, 1939–2000: la historia de una estrategia difícil* (México: Fundación Rafael Preciado, 2006).

Machado, Antonio, 'Proverbios y cantares', *Campos de Castilla* (Madrid: Cátedra, 2006).

Mendieta y Núñez, Lucio, *Valor económico y social de las razas indígenas de México* (Mexico: Dapp, 1938).

Merino, José, 'Los operativos conjuntos y la tasa de homicidios: una medición', *Nexos*, 402 (June 2011).

Museo Nacional de Antropología, México. Libro conmemorativo del cuarenta aniversario (Madrid-Mexico: Conaculta-INAH, Equilibrista-Turner, 2004).

Paz, Octavio, *Sor Juana Inés de la Cruz o las trampas de la fe* (México: Fondo de Cultura Económica, 1982).

Paz, Octavio, *El laberinto de la soledad*, critical edition prepared by Enrico Mario Santí (Madrid: Cátedra, 1993).

Pozas, Ricardo and Isabel, *Los indios en las clases sociales de México* (Mexico: Siglo XXI Editores,1971).

Preciado Hernández, Rafael, *Ideas fuerza. Mística de Acción Nacional* (México: PAN, 2008).

Regino Montes, Adelfo, 'Diversidad y autonomía', *Renglones*, 56 (2004).

Shentalinski, Vitali, *Denuncia contra Socrates. Nuevos descubrimientos en los archivos literarios del KGB* (Barcelona: Círculo de Lectores).

Silva-Herzog Márquez, Jesús, 'Debajo del copete', *Reforma* (5 December 2011).

Silva-Herzog Márquez, Jesús and Roger Bartra, *'Reparar o sembrar: una conversación sobre política mexicana'*, *Letras Libres* 54: 18–22 (2003).

Silva-Herzog Márquez, Jesús, 'El artilugio mayoritario', *Reforma* (29 March 2010).

Stavenhagen, Rodolfo, *Las clases sociales en las sociedades agrarias* (Mexico: Siglo XXI Editores, 1969).

Steiner, George, *The Idea of Europe* (Tilburg: Nexus Institute, 2004).

Taibo II, Paco Ignacio, 'Interview', *Emeequis* (9 April 2007).

Tella, Torcuato di, 'Populismo y reformismo' (1965) in *Populismo y contradicciones de clase en Latinoamérica* (Mexico: Ediciones Era).

Tocqueville, Alexis de, *De la démocratie en Amérique* (1835; reprinted in Paris: Bibliothèque de la Pléiade, Gallimard, 1992).

Villoro, Luis, 'Roger Bartra: Estado y sociedad civil' (1980), in *México, entre libros* (México: El Colegio Nacional/Fondo de Cultura Económica, 1995).

Wieviorka, Michel, *La démocratie à l'épreuve. Nationalisme, populisme, ethnicité* (Paris: La Découverte, 1993).

Zaid, Gabriel, 'Muerte y resurrección de la cultura católica', in *Ensayos sobre poesía* (México: El Colegio Nacional, 1993).

Zaid, Gabriel, 'Tres poetas católicos', in *Ensayos sobre poesía* (México: El Colegio Nacional, 1993).

Žižek, Slavoj, 'Nobody has to be vile', *London Review of Books* (6 April 2006).

Žižek, Slavoj, *Did Somebody Say Totalitarianism?* (London: Verso Books, 2001).

Index

Cadalso, José 111–12
Cage of Melancholy, The (Bartra) 11, 62, 107–8, 109, 159
Calderón, Felipe xiii, xiv, xv, 27, 29, 31, 34–5, 38–9, 40–1, 45–6, 48, 54, 84, 88, 90
Camacho, Manuel 37
campesino economy *see* traditional economy
campesino organizations 6, 9, 142, 144
Canada 54, 164
capitalism 5, 8, 9, 16–17, 44, 45, 53, 54, 55, 56, 58, 64–5, 71–2, 79, 94, 120, 131, 162, 165, 168; *see also* market economy; neoliberalism
Cárdenas, Cuauhtémoc 5, 6, 30, 32, 50, 54, 86, 136
Cárdenas, Lázaro 5, 14, 55, 77, 128
Cardenism 50, 56, 69, 76
Cardoso, Fernando Henrique xiv, 7–8
Castillo Peraza, Carlos 55, 60
Castro, Fidel 141, 160
Castro, Rosalía de 112–13
Castroism 55
Catholicism 5, 15, 17, 19, 20, 21, 30, 34, 35, 42–5, 46, 54–5, 58, 59–63, 64, 65, 67, 68, 87, 122, 130, 160
Cayuela, Ricardo 89–90
Centre, the 5, 34, 39, 47, 54, 66, 77
Centre-Right, the 5–6, 34, 44
Chávez, Hugo 54, 69, 73, 78, 130, 160
Chesterton, G. K. 64
Chiapas 22, 51, 123, 128, 129
Chile 47, 65, 77, 79, 164
China 76, 79, 120
Christianity 43–5, 47, 67, 133; *see also* Catholicism; Protestantism
civil resistance *see* social resistance
Coahuila 93
Coalition for the Welfare of All 37, 40, 49
coalitions xii–xiii, xiv–xv, 35, 47, 51, 85–7; *see also* alliances

Cocopa proposal 19–22
Colombia 69, 88
colonialism 22, 64, 70, 131; *see also* decolonization
common good 44, 45
communism 43, 53, 55, 56, 76, 144; *see also* Castroism; Leninism; Maoism; Marxism
Congress 19, 21, 22, 35, 85, 86, 98
conservatism x, xii, 4–5, 16–17, 21, 29–30, 35, 42, 45–6, 47, 54–5, 56, 64–5, 68, 91, 130–2, 158–9, 160–1
conspiracy 7–8, 9, 11, 33, 34, 38
constitutional patriotism 25, 26
contraception 35, 45, 55, 60, 65, 160
corporate interests *see* business interests
Corral, Javier 85
Correa, Rafael 69
corruption 6, 16, 18, 25, 26, 32, 34, 58, 65, 85, 88, 92–3, 126, 161, 163
Cortázar, Julio 156–7, 169
cosmopolitanism 167–9
counter-culture 134, 137–8, 139–46, 165
Cranston, Maurice 113
Creel, Santiago 85
Cuba 47, 55, 66, 77, 78–9, 120, 130, 141, 144, 156, 157, 160
cultural impoverishment 17, 127
cultural networks 15, 31–2, 124
cultural patrimony 126–7
cultural symbols 17, 102
Czechoslovakia 134

Day of the Dead celebrations 117–18
decentralization 14, 15, 17, 128
decolonization 121–2; *see also* colonialism
Democracia ausente, La (Bartra) 11
Democratic Revolution Party *see* Partido de la Revolución Democrática (PRD)